Faith Working Through Love

Contents

Abbreviations | vii
Preface | ix
Introduction | 1

On Fake News and Real News (vv. 1:1–9) | 19
On Credentials and Resumes (vv. 1:10—2:10) | 26
The Trouble in Antioch (vv. 2:11–21) | 35
On Samantha Stephens and Salvation (vv. 3:1–6) | 68
On Bad Checks, "Mirror Reading," and the Mosaic Law (vv. 3:7–14) | 74
On Lady Tremaine and God's Promise (vv. 3:15–22) | 89
Who Are God's True Children? (vv. 3:23—4:7) | 97
On Going Back to Prison (vv. 4:8–20) | 113
The Two Ladies and Their Two Jerusalems (vv. 4:21—5:12) | 120
On Freedom and Paul's "Third Way" (vv. 5:13–26) | 133
On Brotherly Love and Reaping the Whirlwind (vv. 6:1–10) | 149
The "New Creation" or Bust (vv. 6:12–18) | 157

Bibliography | 169
Subject and Name Index | 175
Scripture Index | 179

Abbreviations

Abbott-Smith	Abbott-Smith, *A Manual Greek Lexicon of the New Testament*
BDAG	Arndt, Bauer, Danker, and Gingrich, *Greek-English Lexicon of the New Testament and Other Early Christian Literature*
CEB	Common English Bible
CSB	Christian Standard Bible
ESV	English Standard Version
Friberg	Friberg et al., *Analytical Lexicon of the Greek New Testament*
GGBB	Wallace, *Greek Grammar Beyond the Basics*
KJV	King James Version
L&N	Louw and Nida, *Greek-English Lexicon of the New Testament: Based on Semantic Domains*
LSJ	Liddell, Scott, and Jones, *A Greek-English Lexicon*
LXX	Septuagint
OED	*Oxford English Dictionary*
NEB	New English Bible
NIV	New International Version
NIrV	New International Reader's Version
NLT	New Living Translation
NRSV	New Revised Standard Version
RSV	Revised Standard Version
TDNT	Kittel et al., *Theological Dictionary of the New Testament*
TLNT	Spicq and Ernest, *Theological Lexicon of the New Testament*

Preface

I submit this little commentary to the world after over two years of work stolen in spare moments in between a day job as an investigator for a Washington state agency, and the normal duties that occupy a bi-vocational pastor. My model for commentary writing is the Presbyterian pastor Albert Barnes, whose expositions of the Old and New Testaments have been my faithful companions for many years.

There is little "original" or "new" in these pages. My audience is the ordinary Christian who wants to understand the Scriptures, and so I made every effort to explain what the text says in a simple, ordinary way. This is not a "scholarly" commentary that explores important academic questions. Nor is it a "devotional" commentary that forsakes deep thought for practicality. If this work helps everyday Christians to better understand Paul's letter to the churches in Galatia, then it achieved its goal. The reader must judge whether it succeeds.

Just as a telescope is a tool which allows us to see the stars, Scripture is the vehicle the Holy Spirit uses to speak to his people. I hope this volume will help God's people to hear his voice in the letter to the churches in Galatia.

Introduction

ONCE UPON A TIME, in a far away land, there lived two doting husbands: Peter and George. From the outside, they were similar in every way. Peter was a successful businessman in the city, and George an executive at a large bank. Both were still younger men, around forty years of age. Both had been married about fifteen years. Both had two children. Each was blissfully unaware of the other's existence.

They lived and worked in the same city, commuted to the same suburb, and, quite unwittingly, frequented the same café every Tuesday morning (at nine sharp). They moved in the same circles, in overlapping orbits, but their lives never touched . . . until yesterday.

On that day, after a particularly hard day at the office, Peter and George each found their way to a upscale florist in the city. It was an expensive place, with scandalous prices. Peter and George didn't care—they were on a mission. Flowers and chocolates were the order of the day, and then a quick trip home to the wife. Fences needed to be mended, sores patched up, an armistice signed.

You see, Peter and George had each treated their wives in a beastly fashion lately, and it was time to make amends. Battles had been fought, blood had been shed; unforgivable things had been spoken. Now, both men were prepared to surrender, and flowers and chocolates were the first tentative steps toward a cease-fire.

Home they went, fighting the same traffic, the same commuters, even (ironically) each other at one point. Finally, they arrived home, steeled themselves for marital combat, and plunged into the arena, ready to set things right so peace could reign in their households once more . . .

What happened, you ask?

Faith Working Through Love

Peter's wife forgave him for his sins. George's wife hissed a few choice words at him, stuffed the flowers in the trash, and raced away to her mother's house for the night, bringing the children with her.

Why the different reactions?

Peter was genuinely sorry for his sins. He told his wife he was sorry and outlined what, exactly, he was going to do to fix things—starting now. He didn't just talk; he acted. He proved his sincerity by his actions, and together, they built their marriage stronger and forged ahead.

George wasn't sorry. The flowers and chocolates (hazelnut chocolate, of course) were a bribe, a holding action. He didn't want to change at all. But, he figured he could buy some time and perhaps some affection with his peace offering. It didn't work, of course. His wife saw through it all; he'd pulled this trick one too many times. George sat alone, in the dark, and thought pitiful thoughts while his wife seethed at her mother's.

Why the parable?

Because it illustrates two completely different approaches to a relationship with God: one Christian and the other pagan.

- Peter is the man who truly loves God. He admits when he does wrong (i.e., "confesses his sins"). When he says he's sorry, he means it. Not only that, he proves his sincerity by concrete action (i.e., "repents"). He serves God because he loves him, and when he makes mistakes (which are often), he is genuinely sorry.

- George is the man who doesn't love God. He claims he's sorry, but he lies. He doesn't mean it, because nothing ever changes. He's an empty suit, a man who lies out of habit. He's never sorry. He's just anxious to bribe his way out of trouble with false promises and false assurances.

Any wife can tell the difference between these two men. And, to extend the analogy of the parable, God can tell the difference between them, too.

The divide here is about *motivation*.

- Why do we serve God?

- What is our aim, our motivation, the self-conscious outcome we're looking for?

- Do we seek cheap favor with God by bribery, or do we seek to serve him because we love him?

Introduction

There is a great chasm between these two positions. Two very different motivations result in two very different reactions from people *who know* what those motivations are. God reacts much the same way—but the stakes are infinitely higher.

OUR PROBLEM

The Bible says there's something wrong with us. We're cracked. Broken. We're like some old, warped vinyl record that always knocks the needle off track and will never play true again. Jesus came to fix us. The fact that Jesus himself—"the one and only Son, who is himself God and is in closest relationship with the Father" (John 1:18)—has come to *personally* intervene and set things right tells us that the situation is pretty serious.

How to fix this? Here are a few false (but common) solutions on offer in this world:

- The Roman Catholic tradition in some respects resembles what Paul criticizes in the book of Galatians. It says that we *cannot* have certainty that we've obtained God's grace.[1] Sure, God gives us the initial grace that *begins* the process of salvation, but this grace must move us to do good works and merit eternal life—thus finishing the process.[2] In other words, God's grace *inspires* the good works that gain us eternal life. This is a framework that offers no final peace (Rom 5:1). The Roman Catholic Church says that there are so-called mortal sins we may commit that "causes exclusion from God's kingdom and the eternal death of hell."[3] Justification, conferred at baptism,[4] can therefore be lost if

---

1. The Roman Catholic Church, at the Council of Trent, declared: "For even as no pious person ought to doubt of the mercy of God, of the merit of Christ, and of the virtue and efficacy of the sacraments, even so each one, when he regards himself, and his own weakness and indisposition, may have fear and apprehension touching his own grace; seeing that no one can know with a certainty of faith, which can not be subject to error, that he has obtained the grace of God" (Schaff, "Council of Trent," Session 6, ch. 9, 2.99). For a discussion of the Tridentine debates on how the council struggled to handle the "assurance of salvation" issue, see McGrath, *Iustitia Dei*, 316–19.

2. Schaff, "Council of Trent," Session 6, ch. 11, 2.100; *Catechism of the Catholic Church*, art. 2010. The Roman Catholic perspective is that justification is a process. The Protestant framework sees the Bible as teaching that justification is an *event*, and sanctification the *result* on the other side of salvation.

3. *Catechism of the Catholic Church*, art. 1861.

4. *Catechism of the Catholic Church*, art. 1992, cf. art. 1266.

you don't repent of mortal sins via the sacrament of penance. This is the only way to convert afresh and recover the grace of justification.[5]

- Other (non-Christian) solutions focus on various forms of "resume-ism"[6]—if you do *this* then you get *that*. As long as you're better than the other guy, you'll probably be okay. Eternity is a merit system, and God grades on a curve. To be sure, grading on a curve saved me in high school algebra (thanks, Mr. Cook!), but it won't save you with God. The blunt word for this is "legalism."[7] The apostle Paul says this path rejects the righteousness God offers and seeks to establish *its own* righteousness (Rom 10:2–3).

- Still more alleged solutions ignore the problem altogether; there is no God, so there is no eternal judge, so there is no problem. One late British philosopher charged that religion was based mainly upon fear. "It is partly the terror of the unknown and partly, as I have said, the wish to feel that you have a kind of elder brother who will stand by you in all your troubles and disputes." We must face the world as it is, he argued, and not be afraid of it. The whole idea of God is "quite unworthy of free man."[8]

The Christian story—that is, the *true* version of the story—offers something different. Something infinitely better. As the apostle Paul sat in Corinth sometime in AD 51–52, he worried that the *real* version of the Christian story had become muddled among the churches he'd planted in southern Galatia (in what is now modern-day Turkey). So, he dictated a letter.

He likely wrote it sometime after the Jerusalem Council (Acts 15), to the churches in southern Galatia (e.g., Iconium, Lystra, Derbe). The date of writing and the exact recipients (to churches in southern or northern

---

5. If believers commit mortal sin (i.e., "grave sin," see art. 1874) they have "thus lost their baptismal grace." Through the sacrament of penance, they are offered "a new possibility to convert and to recover the grace of justification" (*Catechism of the Catholic Church*, art. 1446).

6. Throughout this book, I refer to self-righteousness as "resume-ism." I owe this analogy to the late pastor Tim Keller. He used it to explain justification by faith in a sermon series on the book of Romans. I can't for the life of me find the sermon again (I *think* it's somewhere around Rom 3), but it's out there somewhere.

7. "Attribution of great importance to law or formulated rule; strict adherence to the letter rather than the spirit of law" (*OED*, s.v. "legalism," sense 2, accessed July 2023).

8. Russell, *Not a Christian*, 22, 23.

Introduction

Galatia?) are disputed by scholars.[9] However, none of these issues matter much for understanding Paul's point or for grasping what God is doing with what he's saying to us in this letter.

And what Paul writes is "kind of a big deal." How *can* this *legal* problem between us and God be fixed? If it's serious enough for the Father to dispatch his only Son to handle it, then surely the problem is big.

It's as bad as it could be. There's a legal problem here—a *justice* problem. We commit crimes against God; "Indeed, there is no one on earth who is righteous, no one who does what is right and never sins" (Eccl 7:20). And the apostle John tells us that sin is "lawlessness" (1 John 3:4).

As a matter of justice, crime demands punishment to both (a) settle the legal issue, and (b) achieve personal reconciliation with the injured party. In the secular world, we understand this—an offender is first sentenced in a manner fitting to the crime committed (i.e., the legal issue), then serves a prison sentence to "pay his debt to society" (i.e., the reconciliation to the injured party).

So it is with Jesus. "But you know that he appeared so that he might take away our sins. And in him is no sin" (1 John 3:5). Jesus offers to remove our individual legal guilt, clearing the way for God to adopt us into his family—thus achieving personal reconciliation with God, who is the injured party in the divine courtroom. Pay attention to how the apostle John frames Jesus' mission in terms of "condemnation versus rescue." See what he says about God's wrath:

> For God so loved the world that he gave his one and only Son, that whoever believes in him shall not perish but have eternal life. *For God did not send his Son into the world to condemn the world, but to save the world through him.* Whoever believes in him is not condemned, but whoever does not believe stands condemned already because they have not believed in the name of God's one and only Son. . . . Whoever believes in the Son has eternal life, but *whoever rejects the Son will not see life, for God's wrath remains on them.* (John 3:16–17, 36)[10]

This legal issue (condemnation versus rescue) is behind the human quest to resolve the problem between us and God. If we're condemned by our sins, then *on what basis* does God rescue us? Legally, what *exactly*

---

9. See Wright and Bird, *New Testament in Its World*, 399–400; and Carson and Moo, *Introduction to the New Testament*, 457–60.

10. Emphasis to Scriptures added by the author throughout.

happens when we take the gift that Jesus offers? Are we fully pardoned[11] from our crimes? Or, are we placed into some sort of probationary status, where our legal pardon is conditioned on us *doing something*?

That's the question the Bible answers with "justification by faith." It's what the apostle Paul talks about in this letter. But this doctrine doesn't appear out of nowhere, without context. To really understand God's legal solution, we must first grasp the supernatural metamorphosis that happens when God rescues us.

THE SPIRITUAL TRANSFUSION THROUGH JESUS

God gave us the Mosaic law as a sort of mirror that reflects the awful truth of ourselves right back at us—"through the law we become conscious of our sin" (Rom 3:20).[12] This mirror follows us about, always there, always accusing, always whispering to us the terrible truth that *we cannot ever be good enough* to beat it.

This would be pretty depressing ... if God had left it that way. But he didn't do that. He offers us a solution—a delegate or proxy who (a) is truly human; (b) has been perfectly righteous for us; (c) has loved God for us with a depth, sincerity, and perseverance even the best of us cannot match in our warped state; (d) has suffered and died vicariously for our crimes in our place; and (e) has been raised from the dead to defeat Satan and the curse of death for us—to be proven innocent or *vindicated* as our representative. That solution is Jesus, God's one and only Son.

The Scriptures tell us that the issue is marrow deep—there's something fundamental about us at the cellular level that God must change. Jesus can change it. If you trust in him and his message, "there is now no condemnation for those who are in Christ Jesus" (Rom 8:1).

Why not?

Because the law—that is, the *spiritual law* which gives life—has set each of you free by means of Christ Jesus from the law which produces sin and death (Rom 8:2). You've been unshackled from "resume-ism," whereby

---

11. "The passing over of an offence without punishment; the overlooking or forgiveness of an offence or error and the treatment of the offender as if it had not been committed" (*OED*, s.v. "pardon," sense 3, accessed September 2023).

12. John Calvin writes: "Thus the Law is a kind of mirror. As in a mirror we discover any stains upon our face, so in the Law we behold, first, our impotence; then, in consequence of it, our iniquity; and, finally, the curse, as the consequence of both" (*Institutes* 2.7.7).

INTRODUCTION

we try to do our best (whatever that means) so God will let us in the door. Instead, we follow the *spiritual law* of the Holy Spirit:

1. We trust in Jesus and his message of substitutionary, vicarious grace ("I've done it all, because you can't"), and so,

2. God effects a divine ownership transfer in our souls, which gives us a new heart, a new mind, and his indwelling Spirit, which then

3. changes our hearts and minds so that we *respond in grateful love* to his commands and promptings ("We love Him because he first loved us," 1 John 4:19).

The *spiritual law* of "love me, because I first loved you!" sets us free from legalism and condemnation. It shatters the accusing mirror that has haunted us for far too long. God sent Jesus to be a sin offering for us (Rom 8:3, cf. Lev 4:1—6:7) "in order that the righteous requirement of the law might be fully met in us, who do not live according to the flesh but according to the Spirit" (Rom 8:4). Now, having been set free from resume-ism of all stripes, we fulfill the law to the extent that we let the Holy Spirit control our hearts and minds and lives.

Salvation is sort of like a mystic portal to a new dimension of existence. This is why Jesus speaks of being "born again" (John 3:3). The apostle Paul says: "Those who live according to the flesh *have their minds set on what the flesh desires*; but those who live in accordance with the Spirit *have their minds set on what the Spirit desires*" (Rom 8:5). Your mind is governed by some overriding power, an allegiance—the "flesh" (that is, your own desires) or the Holy Spirit (Rom 8:6).

These are two different realms, resulting from two very different *spiritual fusions*—flesh versus Spirit. "You, however, are not in *the realm of the flesh* but are in *the realm of the Spirit*, if indeed the Spirit of God lives in you" (Rom 8:9).[13] Salvation effects a divine transfer—you're rescued *from* the kingdom of darkness and *brought into* "the kingdom of the Son he loves" (Col 1:13).

This spiritual transfusion is necessary, because without it ain't nothing gonna happen:

---

13. The prepositions here (Ὑμεῖς δὲ οὐκ ἐστὲ ἐν σαρκὶ ἀλλ' ἐν πνεύματι . . .) express association or union; in this case, a spiritual fusion predicated on ultimate allegiance.

> The mind governed by the flesh is hostile to God; it does not submit to God's law, nor can it do so. Those who are in the realm of the flesh cannot please God. (Rom 8:7–8)

If all this is true, then *what exactly* happens to us when Jesus rescues us? How effective is this solution to the problem between us and God?

JUSTIFICATION—WHO CARES?

Most Christian traditions acknowledge that God's grace is necessary. Of course it is. But here's the issue—the difference between the true story and a perverted one is *the sufficiency of God's grace*.[14]

- What are the legal consequences for this problem between us and God?
- Does God solve the problem "once for all" or simply give us a divine boost?
- Many perspectives admit that divine assistance is necessary—but what is the *effect* of this intervention from on high?
- If salvation means a spiritual metamorphosis—a divine kingdom transfer from darkness to light—then what does that suggest about the *extent* of God's legal solution? A full pardon? A conditional pardon based on some form of resume-ism?

Circumstances in Galatia force the apostle Paul to address these issues in this letter. He later wrote to the church in Rome about the same subject:

> All have sinned and fall short of the glory of God, and all are justified freely by his grace through the redemption that came by Christ Jesus. God presented Christ as a sacrifice of atonement, through the shedding of his blood—to be received by faith. (Rom 3:23–25)

Throughout this letter, Paul grounds his explanation of "justification by faith" in the old covenant scriptures and shows us that this isn't a *new* thing, a *new* doctrine. It's the way it has always been. Teachers (then and now) who claim different are wrong. They preach "another gospel." We'll

---

14. I'm indebted for this insight to Dr. James White, from Alpha and Omega Ministries, who repeatedly makes this distinction in the context of ministry to Roman Catholics.

discuss "justification by faith" in some detail when Paul gets to it in his letter, but here is a summary statement:

JUSTIFICATION BY FAITH IN A NUTSHELL

In light of the New Testament revelation, "justification is God's declarative act by which, on the basis of the sufficiency of Christ's atoning death, he pronounces believers to have fulfilled all of the requirements of the law that pertain to them."[15] The person "has been restored to a state of righteousness on the basis of belief and trust in the work of Christ rather than on the basis of one's own accomplishment."[16]

God *reckons* or *imputes* Christ's righteousness to the believer as a judicial declaration—communicating his righteousness to us "by some wondrous way," transfusing its power into us.[17] For God to "justify" someone means "to acquit from the charge of guilt."[18] This he does "not as a creditor and a private person, but as a ruler and Judge giving sentence concerning us at his bar."[19]

One Baptist catechism explains that God "does freely endow me the righteousness of Christ, that I come not at any time into judgment."[20] Millard Erickson writes: "It is not an actual infusing of holiness into the individual. It is a matter of declaring the person righteous, as a judge does in acquitting the accused."[21] Union with Christ makes this possible in what Francis Turretin styled a "mystical . . . communion of grace by mediation. By this, having been made by God a surety for us and given to us for a head, Christ can communicate to us his righteousness and all his benefits."[22]

---

15. Erickson, *Christian Theology*, 884.
16. Erickson, *Concise Dictionary*, s.v. "justification by faith," 108.
17. Calvin, *Institutes* 3.11.23.
18. Calvin, *Institutes* 3.11.3.
19. Turretin, *Institutes* 2:16.3.2.
20. Collins, *Orthodox Catechism*, A55.
21. Erickson, *Christian Theology*, 884.
22. Turretin, *Institutes* 2:16.3.5.

> John Calvin explains that "being sanctified by his Spirit, we aspire to integrity and purity of life."[23] In other words, good works are the fruit of salvation. Thomas Oden summarizes: "Justification's nature is pardon, its condition is faith, its ground is the righteousness of God, and its fruits and evidences are good works."[24]

Now, we turn briefly to the circumstances that made Paul write the letter in the first place.

WHAT HAPPENED TO MAKE PAUL WRITE THIS LETTER?

Jewish agitators who believed themselves to be Christians were on the move among the churches in Galatia. Sure, they believed that Christians must trust in Jesus and his message, but they *also* believed we must observe Jewish boundary markers like the Sabbath, circumcision, old covenant feast days, and other culturally "Jewish" ways of life.

These agitators were likely right-wing, hardline Jews who had "converted" to Christ and had not shed their Pharisaic tendencies. David deSilva characterizes them as a sort of clean-up team that sought to "fix" Paul's "liberal" approach to the Mosaic law (cf. Acts 15:1–4; Phil 3:2–21). "They wanted to preserve fully the Jewishness of the new Christian movement and keep it firmly anchored within Judaism."[25]

In their eyes, Paul was a libertine who had tossed the Mosaic law aside. He couldn't be trusted. He wasn't teaching the truth, because he had forsaken the God-ordained cultural identity markers that made the Jews "God's people." So, the agitators attacked Paul's authority. Their perspective shared *some* kinship with the more "Jewish flavor" of the congregation in Jerusalem, which was never entirely comfortable with Paul's perspective on the Mosaic law's role in the life of a new covenant believer (Acts 21:21–22).

On the other side, Paul believed these agitators were not preaching the Christian message, but "another gospel" entirely. "I am astonished that you are so quickly deserting the one who called you to live in the grace of

---

23. Calvin, *Institutes* 3.11.1.
24. Oden, *Life in the Spirit*, 109.
25. deSilva, *Introduction to the New Testament*, 435.

Christ and are turning to a different gospel—which is really no gospel at all. Evidently some people are throwing you into confusion and are trying to pervert the gospel of Christ" (Gal 1:6–7).

Paul wrote this letter to warn the churches in southern Galatia against these false teachers. The letter is tinged throughout with a kind of hurt outrage—not bitterness, but wounded sorrow. "He writes to the Galatians in the agony of heart which comes of the feeling that his work in Christ is being undone by false teachers, factious rivalries, and a mixture of stupidity and vice."[26] He wonders if he's wasted his time on these believers (Gal 4:11). His relationship with them is particularly special because he first preached the gospel to them while ill, and the Galatians nonetheless welcomed him and listened to what he had to say (Gal 4:13).

But now so much has changed. They don't trust Paul—the agitators have poisoned their minds against him. He's forced to defend his credentials (Gal 1:11—2:10). He asks, "Have I now become your enemy by telling you the truth?" (Gal 4:16).

So, Paul writes to explain the truth of the gospel to them once again, to defend his own teaching, and to explain why "works of the law" can never be the vehicle for salvation. "This lively letter has become a classic expression of the meaning of justification by faith in Christ alone."[27]

HOW SHOULD CHRISTIANS UNDERSTAND THIS LETTER?

I like Nutella. A lot. My wife and I discovered it while we were stationed in Italy for six years, while I was in the military. Since we returned to the United States, we've made sure to always have some on hand. We often spread Nutella on toast, or maybe a croissant or a bagel. But, alas! some people don't like Nutella. They prefer jam, or butter, or even cream cheese. What you put on the bagel will affect how it tastes. It'll color everything about it. Sure, a bagel is a bagel—but it tastes very different with butter than with Nutella!

Bible interpretation is kind of like that. What you bring to the table will color how the scripture "tastes"—how you read and interpret it. Different Christian traditions have their preferred way to "eat" the bagel! The book of Galatians is particularly tricky, because there are at least five questions which any interpretation of Galatians must answer:

---

26. Nock, *St. Paul*, 14.
27. Carson and Moo, *Introduction to the New Testament*, 468.

1. What were the grounds of salvation under the old covenant (that is, the era from when God gave the law at Mt. Sinai in Exodus 19 until Jesus triggered the new and better covenant at Pentecost in Acts 2)?
2. How did these grounds of salvation relate to the "works of the law" about which Paul wrote in Galatians?
3. What were the Galatian agitators' opinions on "works of the law"?
4. What was Paul's position on the "works of the law"?
5. What was Paul's main burden in the letter to the Galatian churches?

Depending on the flavor of your Christian tradition, you'll answer each of these questions differently. This may surprise you. But the book of Galatians is a prism that refracts many assumptions about "what the Bible clearly says" and exposes them to the light of day. When that happens, we find that many Bible-believing Christians do not see eye to eye on "obvious" things.

We'll highlight three different theological frameworks below. Each framework answers those five questions differently. In faithful, Bible-believing churches in twenty-first-century America, it's likely you will find one of these three perspectives on offer.

Answer 1—Dispensationalism[28]

What were the grounds of salvation under the old covenant?	"The basis of salvation in every age is the death of Christ; the *requirement* for salvation in every age is faith; the *object* of faith in every age is God; the *content* of faith changes in the various dispensations."[29]

---

28. I'm describing a traditional flavor of dispensationalism that sees a more marked discontinuity between the old and new covenants.

29. Ryrie, *Dispensationalism*, 134; emphasis original.

Introduction

How did these grounds of salvation relate to the "works of the law" about which Paul wrote in Galatians?	The Dispensation of Law (i.e., the old covenant) was a condemnatory rule of life designed to show us our guilt and make us afraid of God.[30] This doesn't mean that "works of the law" were a merit system for salvation.[31] But it did mean that the shape of a believer's relationship to God was incessantly condemnatory under the Dispensation of Law, because the law as a "rule of life" placed the believer "under the law of God—the entire mosaic legal system in its indivisible totality—subject to its commands and liable to its penalties."[32] This meant a responsibility to show "perfect obedience to the entire Law; all of the time and with perfect motives."[33]
The Galatian agitators' opinion on "works of the law"	They are meritorious and necessary for salvation.
Paul's opinion on the "works of the law"	To rely on "works of the law" as a means for salvation is legalistic works righteousness that misunderstands our new freedom in Christ.
Paul's main burden in the letter to the Galatian churches	He writes to explain that the Dispensation of Law and its "condemnatory rule of life" is now over. It has been superseded by the Dispensation of Grace, which now "motivates believers to obedience by love."[34]

This perspective emphasizes a *very* strong difference between the old and new covenants. When explaining the letter to the Galatians, it sometimes presents life under the old covenant as a slog—a grind in which the divine mandate to "obey all the law" lurked like a splinter in your soul. Dispensationalists might describe the motivation for obedience under the Mosaic law as fear-based, whereas now (in Christ) love is the motivation. Relationship with God under the Mosaic law *was* condemnatory, *but now* grace reigns. When you hear some dispensationalists preach or explain Galatians, you may be forgiven for getting the mistaken impression that they believe

---

30. Houghton, *Law and Grace*, 12–18 ("Discovering Grace as a Rule of Life").

31. "Our salvation, from start to finish, is based upon God's promise and not upon our performance" (Houghton, *Law and Grace*, 14). However, Lewis S. Chafer believed that the apostle Paul, in Rom 7, described the law "as the representation of the merit system" that was the exact opposite of grace. Chafer said that man's failure to keep the law obligated God to "adopt another and more efficacious plan than that which the merit system represents" (*Systematic Theology*, 3:343, 344).

32. McClain, *Law and Grace*, 43.

33. McCune, *Systematic Theology*, 1:129.

34. Houghton, *Law and Grace*, 121.

the way of salvation was quite different in the old covenant. This perspective takes Paul very seriously and very literally when he criticizes the law. I believe this view seriously misunderstands what Paul is saying in this letter.

Answer 2—A New Perspective on Paul[35]

What were the grounds of salvation under the old covenant?	The grounds of salvation have always been by faith in Jesus and God's single-plan-through-Israel-for-the-world.
How did these grounds of salvation relate to the "works of the law" about which Paul wrote in Galatians?	God's people's continuation within this covenant relationship depended in large part on their obedience to the covenant law.[36] The law taught that "works of the law" are badges of religious identity that are required responses to God's covenant faithfulness.
The Galatian agitators' opinion on "works of the law"	The Galatian agitators believed these "boundary markers" were still in force and were a condition of their covenant faithfulness.
Paul's opinion on the "works of the law"	Paul believed the agitators' perspective *used* to be correct but was now obsolete.
Paul's main burden in the letter to the Galatian churches	Paul's burden was to explain that the boundary markers were indeed obsolete because God now declared people to be righteous based on his covenant faithfulness—what Christ had now done to bring along God's single plan through Israel for the world. Specifically, the new creation had dawned, God's covenant with Abraham was being fulfilled, and Christ had been vindicated by his death and resurrection.

This view *really* emphasizes the historical background of the New Testament era. It does this so much that some critics claim it majors on sociology and cultural analysis and values non-biblical documents over what the Bible says. You can spot this view because it keeps on emphasizing something like this over and over: "We can't read the debates between Martin Luther and the Roman Catholic church *back into* Galatians. We must understand Paul on *his own* terms, in *his own* context, as a *Jewish man* with a real *Jewish understanding* of the Torah! If we do this, we'll see that Paul isn't talking about legalism at all! Judaism wasn't legalistic!"

---

35. There are many New Perspectives on Paul. My summary here largely follows N. T. Wright, with a pinch of James D. G. Dunn. For a summary of the New Perspective on Paul, see Robbins, "What Is the New Perspective(s) on Paul?"

36. Dunn, "New Perspective View," 199–200.

Introduction

This view will ask you to recalibrate your entire understanding of the New Testament, and reframe your understanding of every discussion Jesus has with scribes, Pharisees, and the Sanhedrin. It disagrees with the traditional view of "justification by faith" from all the major Protestant creeds and confessions from the past five hundred years.

Answer 3—The Reformed View

What were the grounds of salvation under the old covenant?	Salvation has always been by faith in Jesus,[37] which is the only requirement of the Covenant of Grace which God has offered under various dispensations.[38]
How did these grounds of salvation relate to the "works of the law" about which Paul wrote in Galatians?	True works of the law must be "done in obedience to God's commandments" and "are the fruits and evidences of a true and lively faith."[39]
The Galatian agitators' opinion on "works of the law"	They are meritorious and necessary for salvation.
Paul's opinion on the "works of the law"	To rely on "works of the law" as a means for salvation is legalistic and misunderstands the gospel.
Paul's main burden in the letter to the Galatian churches	Paul's burden was to explain that we are only justified by faith in Christ Jesus, and it has always been that way.

This is the view with which most evangelical Christians will be familiar—even if they're only aware of it in a diluted form.

This commentary largely follows the Reformed perspective, with a few sprinkles from the other frameworks. Support for my perspective will follow in the commentary. For now, I'll just state my positions up front. I believe this is the best framework for understanding what Paul is saying:

---

37. "The condition, or terms of salvation, was the same then as now. It was not mere faith or trust in God, or simply piety, which was required, but faith in the promised Redeemer, or faith in the promise of redemption through the Messiah" (Hodge, *Systematic Theology*, 2:372).

38. See the Westminster Standard, "1647 Westminster Confession of Faith," art. 7.3; and Hodge, *Systematic Theology*, 2:373–77.

39. Westminster Standard, "1647 Westminster Confession of Faith," art. 16.2.

Answer 4—My View

What were the grounds of salvation under the old covenant?	Salvation has always been by faith in Jesus. The specific content of this faith has grown progressively as God has introduced new covenants.[40]
How did these grounds of salvation relate to the "works of the law" about which Paul wrote in Galatians?	The basis of relationship with God, in any age, is love (Deut 6:5, 10:12–16; Mark 12:28–32). This means we do what God says because we love him. It's always been this way. So, true works of the law must be "done in obedience to God's commandments" and "are the fruits and evidences of a true and lively faith."[41]
The Galatian agitators' opinion on "works of the law"	They are meritorious and necessary for salvation. The agitators believe this because of a misplaced Jewish nationalism that arose from the trauma of the exile. They believed "works of the law" were covenant boundary markers that identified them as God's people.
Paul's opinion on the "works of the law"	To rely on "works of the law" as a means for salvation is legalistic and misunderstands the gospel. The agitators believe the way they do because cultural tradition had perverted the true intent and purpose of the Mosaic law.[42]
Paul's main burden in the letter to the Galatian churches	Paul's burden was to explain that we are only justified by faith in Christ Jesus, and it has always been that way.

The apostle Paul's point in this letter is simple: "in Christ Jesus neither circumcision nor uncircumcision has any value. The only thing that counts is faith expressing itself through love" (Gal 5:6). We bring nothing to the table. We have nothing to offer God in exchange for salvation, rescue, reconciliation, and forgiveness. This is not a business transaction.

God loves us and rescues us through Jesus. In response, we trust in him and his message. Our faith *expresses itself* and *operates* by means of love. We don't do what God says to earn his love. Instead, we do what God says *because we already love him*, because he first loved us.

---

40. "Scripture presents a *plurality* of covenants (Gal 4:24; Eph 2:12; Heb 8:7–13) that *progressively* reveal our triune God's *one* redemptive plan for his *one* people, which reaches its fulfillment, telos, and terminus in Christ and the new covenant" (Wellum, Systematic Theology, 431; emphasis original).

41. Westminster Standard, "1647 Westminster Confession of Faith," art. 16.2.

42. I. Howard Marshall has an excellent summary of the problems of interpreting Paul and the law in *New Testament Theology*, 226–32.

Introduction

There are three possible motives that drive professing Christians. Each is "good" in and of itself, but only one of them belongs in the driver's seat. The other two are supporting players.

1. The first is *right doctrine.* This means understanding the gospel, the Trinity, Jesus' mission, atonement, resurrection, ascension—all the good stuff about Christian doctrine. The stuff you find in a systematic theology textbook. Knowing God and his story in the Scriptures is good! But you can over-emphasize cold, intellectual knowledge so much that you forget "faith without works is dead, being alone" (Jas 2:17). You also forget to have a heart. There might be a little warmth but a lot of ice. Your "faith" can become a brain, severed from a body or a heart. This means it's not "faith" at all.

2. The second is *right actions.* A tree bears fruit according to its nature. So, you want to do what God says. You'll work to "put off" the old you and "put on" the new person you are in union with Christ. Your church works to make brotherly love real in its ranks and be advocates for God's principles of justice as a witness for Christ's coming kingdom—where real justice will reign! But your church might emphasize community and social transformation so much that you forget who you are. You become social activists, divorced from the gospel. Individually, you can become a legalists. In short, you can unwittingly practice "another gospel."

3. The third possibility is *right heart.* We're talking about right affections, which works itself out as motive, here. You love God with everything you have (Deut 6:5). You don't forget who you are, and you don't work to earn salvation. You love God, so you want to do what he says!

This last option is the one the apostle Paul chose—"faith working through love" (Gal 5:6). God wants our hearts, because *motivation* comes from inside us. We do the right things because we love God. We want to know more about God because we love him. When King Josiah of Judah discovered the book of the covenant, he renewed the covenant by pledging "to follow the LORD and keep his commands, statutes and decrees *with all his heart and all his soul*" (2 Kgs 23:3). This wasn't a new concept—the Lord warned Moses to teach the people that "to love the LORD your God and to serve him *with all your heart and with all your soul*" was the way to faithfully obey his commands (Deut 11:13).

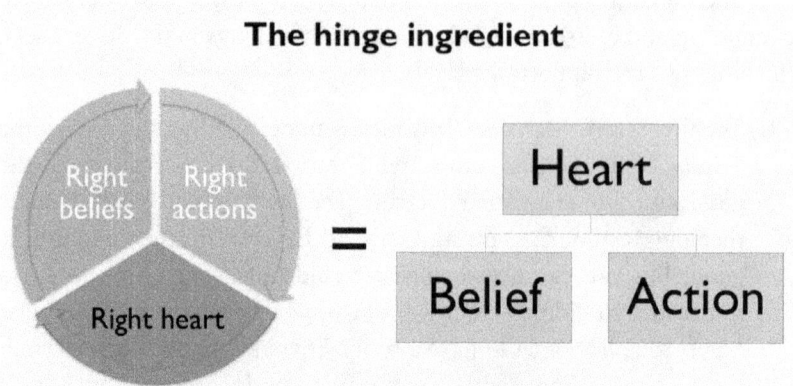

All three are necessary for a healthy relationship with God. Love for God drives them all. If you miss or distort one, you're missing it.

To suggest another way is to miss the boat. This letter is largely Paul's attempt to explain this error to them and to us.

On Fake News and Real News
(vv. 1:1–9)

NOBODY LIKES TO BE misrepresented. In some cases, it's a crime to do so. In my other life, as a fraud investigator for a state agency, we often investigated when we suspected insurance agents misrepresented key things on insurance applications to make sales. In one case, the agent wrote forty-eight "course of construction" policies for homes that were allegedly being built in a sub-division. He made twenty-five thousand dollars for these sales.

Just one problem. The homes didn't exist. They were fake.

Our investigator learned that most of these forty-eight fake policies were written *for the same address.* It's kinda hard to fit a bunch of homes on the same parcel! Even worse, the address itself was fake. It wasn't on some huge, vacant lot. It went to a site zoned for commercial use that was maybe two acres in size. It's true that they're building homes closer together these days, but you can't fit forty-eight homes on a two-acre parcel! The investigator visited the site and saw it was populated by what looked like a meth lab in a broken-down doublewide trailer.

The lot was fake. The homes were fake. The address was fake. The policies were fake. The agent misrepresented all of this to the insurance company and made himself twenty-five thousand dollars.

Not good.

That's misrepresentation—you lie to someone, they believe you, and then they act on this bad information because they've been tricked. This happened to an insurance company, which makes it kind of impersonal. Sure, it's bad—but what's twenty-five thousand dollars to this company? Not much.

Misrepresentation is worse when it happens to a *person.* The stakes are higher because it's *personal.* It's frustrating to be misrepresented. There's an urge to set the record straight, to protect folks who are being confused by the lies. It's even more frustrating if you're far away and text messages, phone calls, or video chats aren't an option. That's what's happening with the apostle Paul (and ultimately to God and his message), and this frustration prompts perhaps the most sharply worded letter in the New Testament. Even in his greeting "to the churches," he sounds distant and frigid.[1]

> Paul, an apostle—sent not from men nor by a man, but by Jesus Christ and God the Father, who raised him from the dead—and all the brothers and sisters with me, to the churches in Galatia. (Gal 1:1-2)

Throughout this letter Paul argues against certain false teachers. This conflict colors the way he writes and how he structures the letter.[2] We catch a glimpse of their tactics in the opening line. Paul stresses that he was sent by Jesus and God the Father. He's an "apostle," which means a messenger, an envoy—an ambassador. Every Christian is an envoy of sorts, but Paul means that he's a *special* ambassador because Jesus sent him.[3] Specifically, Paul was sent and trained by Jesus *after* his resurrection (see Gal 1:12). His authority as an apostle isn't self-appointed or directed by others ("sent not from men nor by a man"). The Christians in Galatia need to understand that! They should trust Paul more than the folks who are spreading lies. He is rhetorically "beating down the false apostles."[4]

More than that, Paul reminds the readers that this is the same God who raised Jesus from the dead—*this* is the God who appointed Paul and sent him out with the gospel message. This means his opponents are suggesting the opposite. They're spreading "fake news" about Paul and his message. "Paul isn't *really* an apostle. He isn't *really* sent by God . . ."

We don't know how they framed their slander. It's possible they acknowledge that Paul *used to be* a leader at the church in Antioch and so in that sense was an "apostle." But, the argument goes, he didn't have any

---

1. Chrysostom writes: "The flame of error had spread over not one or two cities merely, but the whole Galatian people" ("Commentary on Galatians," 4).

2. "Appearing at the very outset of the epistle, and read in the light of the great stress which Paul subsequently places on his independence of the Jerusalem church (1:18—2:10), his assertion reflects a polemical situation in which the dignity, indeed the validity, of his apostolic status is being challenged" (Fung, *Galatians*, loc. 669-70). See also Luther, *Galatians*, 29-30; and Longenecker, *Galatians*, 4.

3. "Paul clearly regards himself as completely equal in apostolic status to the first apostles" (Fung, *Galatians*, loc. 662). See also Longenecker, *Galatians*, 2.

4. Luther, *Galatians*, 28.

"special" status. He's just a guy. A teacher, sure, but just a guy.[5] We can imagine how this probably went.

"Paul is a good guy, of course. He loves the Lord."

Now would come a sad shake of the head.

"But . . . Paul can get carried away. We all get carried away, sometimes. Nobody's perfect! The truth is that he isn't some 'super teacher' with special insight. And, he's said some things that need clarification . . ."

It's this issue—the misrepresentation of Paul and the gospel—that prompts Paul to write this letter and send it along to the churches in Galatia. This last bit is important, because it isn't a letter to a single church. It's addressed "to the churches in Galatia," which is roughly equivalent to a portion of modern-day Turkey. It was evidently meant to be physically passed along from one church community to the other.[6] Paul didn't have the option to "cc" his letter, so this was the next best thing.

The following lines are the last kind words Paul will write for some time. In fact, "this is the sole instance where St. Paul omits to express his thankfulness in addressing any church."[7] Instead, he abridges the greeting and adds a description of Christ's work because *this* is the issue—what has Jesus done for us? This is the question this letter is all about.

> Grace and peace to you from God our Father and the Lord Jesus Christ, who gave himself for our sins to rescue us from the present evil age, according to the will of our God and Father, to whom be glory for ever and ever. Amen. (Gal 1:3–5)

This is a marvelous summary of the Good News. Grace and peace are the gifts that both God the Father and God the Son are offering to us. *Grace* because the gift of righteousness from God isn't earned, deserved, or

---

5. See Dunn, *Galatians*, 25–26. "In other words, we have a strong hint already that the authority of Paul's original preaching to the Galatians was being subtly undermined—not by means of an outright denial of his claim to be an 'apostle,' but by the argument that his commissioning and its consequent authority were less weighty than Paul claimed. If he was simply an 'apostle' of the church at Antioch, then his message and its authority were subject to the higher authority of those commissioned by Jesus himself (at Jerusalem), just as the church at Antioch itself was subject to the authority of the church in Jerusalem." See also Lightfoot, *Galatians*, 72.

6. "That is, the churches located somewhere in the province of Galatia. It may be inferred that they were not all in one city, but were independent bodies found in different places. None of them can be positively assigned to particular cities, as Ancyra, Pessinus, or Tavium" (Hovey, *Galatians*, 14).

7. Lightfoot, *Galatians*, 75.

merited. *Peace* because the reconciliation, forgiveness, and adoption into God's family (all due to grace) brings "peace with God through our Lord Jesus Christ" (Rom 5:1). Martin Luther explains:

> Grace releases sin, and peace makes the conscience quiet. The two fiends that torment us are sin and conscience. But Christ has vanquished these two monsters and has trodden them underfoot, both in this life and the life to come.... Only Christians have this kind of teaching and are armed with it in order to gain the victory against sin, despair, and everlasting death.[8]

This gift is available because Jesus "gave himself for our sins"—his sacrifice was knowing, willing, and voluntary. The NIV renders this in a substitutionary way ("gave himself *for* our sins" Gal 1:3), but the force is probably more causal—Jesus gave himself *because of* our sins.[9] He did it to rescue us from this evil age. The idea is a transfer from one *realm*, *sphere* of influence, or *kingdom* to another (cf. Col 1:13–14)[10]—from Babylon to the new Jerusalem!

To effect this rescue, God must first deal with sin. Justice isn't served unless and until the offender serves her sentence—whatever that might be. When Jesus "gave himself" because of our sins, he served our sentence for us and made rescue and reconciliation available for anyone who wants it. There are two aspects here: legal and personal. Jesus offers to *first* absolve us of the legal sanction and *then* to reconcile us to God on a personal basis.

If we need this "rescue," it means we can't get ourselves out of it. We need to phone a friend. We need a savior, a rescuer—Christianity is a "rescue religion."[11] We need help from without. This help isn't something we

---

8. Luther, *Galatians*, 32.

9. There are two other possible uses for the preposition in this phrase (τοῦ δόντος ἑαυτὸν ὑπὲρ τῶν ἁμαρτιῶν ἡμῶν). The first is benefaction, which would mean Jesus gave himself "for the benefit of" our sins, which makes no sense. The other usage is substitutionary, which would have Jesus giving himself "in place of" our sins, which also makes no sense (contra Longenecker, *Galatians*, 8). Jesus didn't die in the place of our sins—he died in the place of us! So, the better way is to see the preposition as expressing reason—Jesus gave himself "because of" our sins, as a substitute. See also Fung, *Galatians*, loc. 706; deSilva, *Galatians*, 4; and Hovey, *Galatians*, 14.

10. Johann Bengel writes, "The whole economy of sin under the authority of Satan is denoted" (*Gnomen*, 4:2). See also Luther, *Galatians*, 43–44.

11. Stott, *Galatians*, 18.

earn, but a plan devised "according to the will of our God and Father." If we have Jesus, we now need *nothing else*. Christ is enough.[12]

1. We sin.
2. So, Jesus sacrifices himself because of our sins.
3. He does this to rescue us from this present evil age,
4. because God the Father planned the rescue mission and wanted him to do it.
5. So, we give glory to God forever and ever.
6. And that means Jesus and what he's done is enough—it's all we'll ever need.

Now comes Paul's complaint. Pay particular attention to the exasperation, the frustration, the "I can't *believe* this!" attitude that leaps from the page.

> I am astonished that you are so quickly deserting the one who called you to live in the grace of Christ and are turning to a different gospel—which is really no gospel at all. (Gal 1:6–7)

The Christians in the Galatian churches are being fooled. Tricked. They've deserted God and have embraced a different kind of Good News. They've switched sides.[13] They've turned away from God (cf. CEB, NLT). They've defected. In fact, their new opinions are so different that they really don't believe in the Good News at all anymore. It's not that they've deliberately rejected Jesus—they think they still have him. It's that their emphases and understanding of Jesus' message are now *so* backward that it no longer qualifies as the Christian message. Jesus came to offer a specific message. That message has content, shape, form. There's a point at which it changes so much that it becomes something completely different.

Whatever the sinister work is that Paul's opponents are doing in Galatia (we haven't gotten there yet, but we will)—that's what has happened. Jesus' message has been perverted. Switched. Changed. Perhaps worse—and

---

12. "Paul has in fact touched on the chief argument of the letter, and succinctly announced in anticipatory fashion the main contents of its doctrinal section, inasmuch as the point of the controversy between Paul and his Galatian opponents lies precisely in the significance of Christ and his redemptive work and more specifically in the bearing of this work on the law" (Fung, *Galatians*, loc. 740–42).

13. See LSJ, s.v. "μετατίθημι," sense 4, 1117.

Faith Working Through Love

this is what irritates Paul so much—the new believers in Galatia are falling for it. They're falling for it "so quickly," too. This is just what the Israelites did after the exodus from Egypt![14] God told Moses, "They have been *quick* to turn away from what I commanded them" (Exod 32:8). Now, in the spiritual new covenant exodus which that first one foreshadowed, the same thing has happened in miniature! How can this be?

> It may take ten years' labor before a little church is properly ordered; then some lunatic gets in who can do nothing but speak slanderously and spitefully against sincere preachers of the Word, and in one moment upsets everything . . . one person with mad ideas may destroy in a short time all that has been built up over many years by many true ministers laboring night and day.[15]

This betrayal isn't just about a message. It's about "the one who called you." To betray the Christian story is to betray God himself. It's a very *personal* betrayal, a sort of spiritual adultery. The Christian story is about relationship—the whole Bible is about God making a family community through Jesus.[16]

> Evidently some people are throwing you into confusion and are trying to pervert the gospel of Christ. But even if we or an angel from heaven should preach a gospel other than the one we preached to you, let them be under God's curse! As we have already said, so now I say again: If anybody is preaching to you a gospel other than what you accepted, let them be under God's curse! (Gal 1:7–9)

Whoever these people are, Paul says they're doing this all on purpose. He doesn't elaborate on this point until the end of the letter (Gal 6:11–12), but he's certain it's deliberate. Their aim is to "pervert the gospel of Christ." How serious is this? What does Paul think about people who would do such a thing? He wishes for them to be cursed by God. The New English Translation translates this as "let him be condemned to hell." Paul doesn't explicitly

---

14. Schreiner, *Galatians*, 84–85.
15. Luther, *Galatians*, 47.
16. A fuller statement of the Christian story is this: "God's plan through Israel (i.e., King Jesus) to fix the world, to fix us, and to create a family he can love and which loves him back." The covenants are the skeleton for the story—like episodes in a divine miniseries that move the plot along.

say that, but it seems to be what he's *hinting* at. He's almost penning a wish, a plea—these people need to be cursed.¹⁷

Intent matters, and it's difficult to imagine God moving Paul to write such a harsh thing if the conduct weren't deliberate. This underscores how serious the issue is. Whatever the details of the misrepresentation are, whatever the motives of Paul's opponents might be—the issue is as serious as it gets. And it all begins by criticizing Paul, who brought them the gospel in the first place.

---

17. "Excommunication by the church is not in view here but eschatological punishment meted out by God. It is evident from the strong language used that Paul does not consider the Galatian opponents to be believers, for they preach a different gospel" (Schreiner, *Galatians*, 87–88).

On Credentials and Resumes
(vv. 1:10—2:10)

THE DOCTRINAL HEART OF this letter doesn't begin until chapter 3. But first Paul has some personal business to address—his credentials. The Christians in Galatia know Paul. He's the one who brought them the Good News, who taught them, mentored them. Sure, other teachers have done their part, but Paul is undeniably the dominating human force in their spiritual lives.

The false teachers are trying to trash all that. Spreading rumors. Spreading lies. Denying that he's an apostle sent by God and his Son. "Sure," they say, "Paul is a great teacher and a spiritual giant. But he doesn't have any 'special' authority. In fact, he's gotten some things wrong—important things..."

Well, in this section Paul aims to set the record straight. He didn't get his training from Peter, James, John, or anyone else. He was personally trained by Christ. He isn't a second-hand apostle (e.g., "I was trained by John, who was trained by Jesus"). He's a first-hand apostle, and *that* means Paul has special authority, and *that* means the Christians in Galatia ought to listen when he says these other folks are false teachers.

> Am I now trying to win the approval of human beings, or of God? Or am I trying to please people? If I were still trying to please people, I would not be a servant of Christ. (Gal 1:10)

Most people prefer to avoid conflict. To go with the flow. In any controversy there are three groups: one that agrees, another that disagrees, and the majority in the middle who just don't want to deal with the fighting. But sometimes, you just gotta stand for something. That's where Paul is. He isn't

On Credentials and Resumes

trying to get along. He doesn't want conflict, but if it comes he's ready. He won't trim his sails to curry favor.[1] He serves Christ.

That's pious. It sounds nice. We all know people who use piety and religion as a cloak. We also know honest people who *don't* do that. Paul is one of those. He *means* this. It'd be easy for him to curb his message to accommodate the right-wing hardliners (that's who these false teachers are—but we'll get to that in a later section). But he can't do that. The gospel is at stake.

This isn't melodrama. It's real. If it comes to a decision between (a) going along to get along, and (b) following Christ, then (c) Paul is gonna choose option (b). "If I were still trying to please people, I would not be a servant of Christ."

> I want you to know, brothers and sisters, that the gospel I preached is not of human origin. I did not receive it from any man, nor was I taught it; rather, I received it by revelation from Jesus Christ. (Gal 1:11–12)

This is as clear as it gets. Paul didn't go to seminary, nor was he trained by any man or woman—"rather, I received it by revelation from Jesus Christ." You could say that Jesus gave Paul the same personal training and attention that the *other* twelve apostles received during his ministry.[2] To be sure, Paul knew *lots of facts* about the Christian story—he witnessed Stephen's explanation of how the Jewish scriptures pointed to Christ (Acts 7), and he was well-trained in theology. But he didn't *feel, trust, believe,* or *pledge himself* to Jesus. The "light bulb" hadn't yet come on, but it did on that road outside Damascus and in the revelations that followed.[3]

People wonder when this happened. Some people believe Paul was sojourning in the Arabian wilderness for three years (cf. Gal 1:17–18). As

---

1. Hendriksen, *Galatians*, 44.

2. "Paul's claim, then, is this. His gospel, which was being called in question by the Agitators and deserted by the Galatians, was neither an invention (as if his own brain had fabricated it), nor a tradition (as if the church had handed it down to him), but a revelation (for God had made it known to him)" (Stott, *Galatians*, 30).

Schreiner hedges and claims that Paul is not emphasizing a "radical independence" at all. Instead, he believes Paul is simply saying he received the "fundamental truths" of the gospel from Jesus, while leaving the door open to the possibility Paul received other details by tradition, citing 1 Cor 15:3 (*Galatians*, 96). This is incorrect.

3. Hendriksen is particularly helpful here (*Galatians*, 48–50). "Paul is 'not saying that all that he has to say concerning Jesus was imparted to him by direct, ecstatic revelation'; only, the conviction, through revelation, of the resurrection of the crucified 'altered at a stroke his whole attitude to what he already knew of Jesus,'" (Fung, *Galatians*, loc. 860–62).

we'll see, this is unlikely.[4] We really don't know the *how* or *when* regarding Christ's instruction of Paul. We just know it happened. Perhaps it was a "living presence" sort of thing accompanied by periodic visions and instruction from on high (cf. Acts 22:17).[5] Unbelievers may scoff at this suggestion, but Christians should not.

Now Paul defends this statement.

> For you have heard of my previous way of life in Judaism, how intensely I persecuted the church of God and tried to destroy it. I was advancing in Judaism beyond many of my own age among my people and was extremely zealous for the traditions of my fathers. (Gal 1:13–14)

Paul had been a notorious zealot with impeccable Pharisaic credentials (see Phil 3:4–6), "a very scrupulous as well as zealous Pharisee, a pronounced ritualist, and a conspicuous adversary of the new sect that was rising in Jerusalem."[6] He wasn't the only man commissioned by the Sanhedrin to hunt down Jewish Christians in communities abroad and bring them to a heresy trial in Jerusalem (Acts 8:3; 9:1–2; 22:2–5). But he might have been the most *zealous* man. Like too many religious fanatics, he believed so passionately that God was "on his side" that he resorted to the arrest, imprisonment, and execution of those who disagreed (Acts 26:9–11). To Paul and the Sanhedrin, Jews who embraced Jesus as Messiah were traitors. Turncoats. They deserved the same kind of death that renegades got under the old covenant (e.g., Num 15:29–31; 25:6–13). After all, the Maccabean revolt was sparked when one righteous Jewish man decided he was "mad as hell and wasn't gonna take it anymore,"[7] then killed an apostate (1 Macc 2:19–24).

> But when God, who set me apart from my mother's womb and called me by his grace, was pleased to reveal his Son in me so that I might preach him among the Gentiles, my immediate response was not to consult any human being. I did not go up to Jerusalem to see those who were apostles before I was, but I went into Arabia. Later I returned to Damascus. (Gal 1:15–17)

4. Contra Stott, *Galatians*, 33.

5. Barnes, "Galatians," 294. Fung believes the entire revelation and training from Jesus occurred on the Damascus road (*Galatians*, loc. 858). I disagree.

6. Hovey, *Galatians*, 19.

7. This is a reference to the mad news anchor Howard Beale from the classic film *Network* (1976).

On Credentials and Resumes

Only God could change the heart and mind of so dedicated a fanatic![8] The important bit here is Paul's insistence on his "apostle status." Once he became a believer (Acts 9:1–17), Paul *did not* go to Jerusalem to consult with the Christian community.[9] He doesn't derive his authority from them; "my immediate response was not to consult any human being." Instead, he spends a bit of time in Damascus (where his conversion occurred and he was welcomed in by the Christian community), then goes to Arabia to preach the gospel, and then returns to Damascus for some time.

Comparing Paul's summary here with Luke's account in the book of Acts, we have something like this:

1	Paul is converted.	Acts 9:1–17
2	Paul spends a short time in Damascus.	Acts 9:18–21
3	Paul goes to Arabia[10]—likely to preach the gospel. This creates animosity between him and the Nabataean king,[11] who has his governor in Damascus orchestrate an assassination plot against Paul (2 Cor 11:32–33) once he leaves Arabia and returns to Damascus.[12]	Gal 1:17
4	Paul returns to Damascus for an extended period and survives an assassination attempt, which prompts him to flee for Jerusalem (Gal 1:18).	Gal 1:17–18; Acts 9:22–25 (cf. 2 Cor 11:32–33)

He continues:

> Then after three years, I went up to Jerusalem to get acquainted with Cephas and stayed with him fifteen days. I saw none of the

---

8. "Now a man in that mental and emotional state is in no mood to change his mind, or even to have it changed for him by men. No conditioned reflex or other psychological device could convert a man in that state. Only God could reach him—and God did!" (Stott, *Galatians*, 32).

9. "He did not need or desire an apostolic imprimatur on the gospel he proclaimed. Since he received his gospel by a revelation of Jesus Christ, he did not need anyone else to confirm its truth" (Schreiner, *Galatians*, 102).

10. This is a general term for a large area now occupied by roughly modern-day Jordan, Syria, Iraq, Kuwait, and the entire Arabian Peninsula. See R. L. Drouhard, "Arabia," in Barry et al., *Lexham Bible Dictionary*.

11. This is Aretas IV, who ruled over Nabataea, which was a desert kingdom in what is now southwestern Jordan—within the broad area of what Paul terms "Arabia." Its best-known feature is Petra, which was also the infamous site where the noted archaeologist Dr. Henry Jones drank from the Holy Grail, gained eternal life, and rescued his father from certain death at the hands of Nazis (see *Indiana Jones and the Last Crusade*).

12. I'm following F. F. Bruce here (*Acts*, loc. 6994). See also Schreiner, *Galatians*, 102; and Barnes, "Galatians," 297–98.

> other apostles—only James, the Lord's brother. I assure you before God that what I am writing you is no lie. (Gal 1:18–20)

This is very likely the account Luke relates in Acts 9:26–28, wherein Paul receives a cold and fearful reception from the church in Jerusalem. It has been about three years since his conversion ("after three years"), and Paul has been preaching and teaching in Damascus and in broader Arabia, but the Christian community in Jerusalem knows none of this. They last saw him as the bloodthirsty Jewish fanatic, and so they're not keen on having this "changed" guy over for supper. Barnabas saved the day and vouched for him (Acts 9:27), gaining him limited entrée to speak to Cephas (the Aramaic rendering for "Peter") and James.

John Stott explains, "To sum up, Paul's first visit to Jerusalem was only after three years, it lasted only two weeks, and he saw only two apostles. It was, therefore, ludicrous to suggest that he obtained his gospel from the Jerusalem apostles."[13]

> Then I went to Syria and Cilicia. (Gal 1:21)

This is when Paul flees Jerusalem ahead of yet another assassination plot and heads for Tarsus (Acts 9:29–30), a city in the province of Cilicia and adjacent to Syria.

> I was personally unknown to the churches of Judea that are in Christ. They only heard the report: "The man who formerly persecuted us is now preaching the faiths he once tried to destroy." And they praised God because of me. (Gal 1:22–24)

The Jerusalem church didn't know him. All they (eventually!) knew was that his conversion was genuine, and so they rejoiced. He only consulted with Peter and James, and that very briefly. His ministry in Jerusalem was apparently more or less a solo affair, and it was likely Peter and James (or others acting on their orders) who spirited Paul away when he'd worn out his welcome.

Aside from this brief sojourn, Paul had no contact with the Jerusalem church for quite some time.

> Then after fourteen years, I went up again to Jerusalem, this time with Barnabas. I took Titus along also. I went in response to a revelation and, meeting privately with those esteemed as leaders, I presented to them the gospel that I preach among the Gentiles. I

---

13. Stott, *Galatians*, 35.

wanted to be sure I was not running and had not been running my race in vain. Yet not even Titus, who was with me, was compelled to be circumcised, even though he was a Greek. (Gal 2:1–3)

This "fourteen years" is likely reckoned from the time of Paul's conversion, though it could be from the time he fled Jerusalem for Tarsus. In the interim, Paul had become a pastor of the church in Antioch along with Barnabas (Acts 11:25–26) and together they had journeyed to Macedonia and back to preach the gospel (Acts 13:1—14:28). The congregation in Antioch was a community of gentile converts and diaspora Jews (Acts 11:19–26; 13:1–3). It was infinitely more cosmopolitan regarding gentile inclusion than the stiff conservatives in Jerusalem. Picture Jerusalem as a very traditional Southern Baptist church in Rhea County and Antioch as a hip urban church in New York City: they may share the same faith, the same Lord, and the same baptism—but they ain't the same!

This second visit to Jerusalem "after fourteen years" is probably the visit they undertook to settle the problem of the false teachers described in Acts 15.[14] Paul and Barnabas met with the leaders of the Jerusalem church, explained their understanding of the gospel, and found they agreed. Paul notes that even Titus, a non-Jewish man, was not obligated to be circumcised during this visit. If old covenant rituals were still binding on the new covenant believers as an adjunct to Jesus (as, we'll soon see, the false "brothers" claim), then surely the Jerusalem church *would have* pressured Titus to submit, right? But that didn't happen, Paul declares—how do you like them apples?[15]

This visit was not a teaching session, but more a "we're all on the same page, right?" kind of meeting. His quest to ensure he hadn't been "running my race in vain" (Gal 2:2) seems less a genuine anxiety about the content of his message and more a request for an endorsement—though Paul would

14. Some believe this second visit is actually the famine relief visit both Paul and Barnabas made in Acts 11:27–29, in which case the "revelation" that prompted Paul to head for Jerusalem might be that of Agabus (Acts 11:28). But that visit had nothing to do with consultation about false teaching. The Acts 15 visit did, and it generally fits with the situation Paul describes here in Gal 2:1–5. See also Hovey, *Galatians*, 24; Ridderbos, *Epistle to Galatia*, 78–80; Barnes, "Galatians," 303; and Hendriksen, *Galatians*, 70–74.

15. Later Paul would persuade a different apprentice, Timothy, to accept circumcision "because of the Jews who lived in that area, for they all knew that his father was a Greek" (Acts 16:3). However, that situation was entirely different. It is a damnable error to make old covenant rituals a factor in salvation. It's quite another thing to get it done to avoid being a stumbling-block to folks you're trying to reach with the gospel (see Schreiner, *Galatians*, 122–23). Timothy was also half-Jewish (Acts 16:1–2).

surely bristle at that characterization. In Paul's eyes it was a tactical move to outflank the Jewish agitators by cementing *partnership* with Peter, James, and John.[16] It succeeded—they gave him "the right hand of fellowship" (Gal 2:9).[17] Without this sanction, his mission to craft a more inclusive "one people" framework within the broader Christian movement (à la Gal 3:28) likely would have sputtered.[18]

> This matter arose because some false believers had infiltrated our ranks to spy one the freedom we have in Christ Jesus and to make us slaves. We did not give in to them for a moment, so that the truth of the gospel might be preserved for you. (Gal 2:4–5)

Paul now labels his opponents for the first time—they're false brothers who have "infiltrated" the church to "spy" on them all and "make us slaves." This is dark language, but Paul is not known for his subtlety. Some people like to handle sensitive matters with velvet gloves. Paul prefers a sledgehammer—the "truth of the gospel" is at stake. The nature of this "gospel issue" isn't yet before us, but it's coming.

Of course, much more happened at this meeting (see Acts 15:4–30), but Paul is emphasizing his credentials and his independence here. The

---

16. Stott is surely correct to observe, "It was to overthrow their influence, not to strengthen his own conviction, that he laid his gospel before the Jerusalem apostles" (*Galatians*, 41). Schreiner suggests Paul sought "ratification" from the Jerusalem church as a bulwark against the agitators (*Galatians*, 121). This is likely correct, but surely Paul would have objected to the characterization. In this letter he would have never acknowledged this because it would betray a subordinate status. Nonetheless, it was true. Paul wanted the equivalent of a "grip and grin" photo-op to strengthen his own position.

17. This is, of course, the opposite of that phenomenon well-known to some Christians: the "right *boot* of fellowship."

18. "Unless he could gain the support of James, Peter, and John, with most of the church at Jerusalem, there was no human prospect of maintaining the liberty of the Gentile churches, without breaking wholly with the converts from Judaism" (Hovey, *Galatians*, 26). See also Longenecker, *Galatians*, 49; and Fung, *Galatians*, loc. 1297.

Paul's vision was at odds with the more conservative perspective of the Jerusalem church, demonstrated by among other things (a) their hostile questioning of Peter about his gentile evangelism (Acts 11:1–18) and (b) James's plea with Paul shortly before his arrest to help him placate the hardline faction within the Jerusalem congregation (Acts 21:20–26). Michael Grant is correct to note that Paul is of a very different mind: "Paul's innovation, however, in seeking Gentile adherents to Christianity was to shift the emphasis altogether away from this half-way type of conversion. Agitators and even Jewish converts (especially if un-circumcised) had alike tended to be second-class Jews. Paul's Gentile converts, on the other hand, were to be first-class Christians, every bit as Christian as any Christian of Jewish origin" (*Saint Paul*, 150).

On Credentials and Resumes

point is that he was appointed and trained by Jesus, and so *he is* an apostle, *he has* authority, and therefore the false teachers skulking around Galatia *are not* to be trusted.

> As for those who were held in high esteem—whatever they were makes no difference to me; God does not show favoritism—they added nothing to my message. (Gal 2:6)

Peter, James, and John didn't correct him, rebuke him, or pat him on the head. They acknowledged him as a fellow believer and an evangelist.

> On the contrary, they recognized that I had been entrusted with the task of preaching the gospel to the uncircumcised, just as Peter had been to the circumcised. For God, who was at work in Peter as an apostle to the circumcised, was also at work in me as an apostle to the Gentiles. James, Cephas and John, those esteemed as pillars, gave me and Barnabas the right hand of fellowship when they recognized the grace given to me. They agreed that we should go to the Gentiles, and they to the circumcised. All they asked was that we should continue to remember the poor, the very thing I had been eager to do all along. (Gal 2:7-10)

And so, Paul's long defense of his independence, of his apostleship, of his "I didn't learn this from someone else—I learned it all from Jesus!" claim is now complete. Paul is defensive about this. Although in other contexts he can be diplomatic (Acts 23:5) and cunning (Acts 23:6-10), in this matter Paul flatly refuses to defer to Peter, James, and John ("whatever they were makes no difference to me; God does not show favoritism," Gal 2:6). This doesn't indicate hostility per se, but more an understandable touchiness about his status.[19]

Luke has no skin in this game and so matter-of-factly reports that Paul and Barnabas carried the decision (the Greek is "dogma," Acts 16:4) *of the Jerusalem church* at this meeting to Christian communities abroad—a move that suggests (but does not prove) a more subordinate status than what Paul is willing to acknowledge here. Paul was never a part of the Jerusalem establishment and was always very conscious of this fact. He acted outside its orbit, not quite as an independent agent but certainly more freelance than his friends in Jerusalem would have liked (see Acts 21:17-26).

---

19. Longenecker observes that Paul has a dismissive tone, not about Peter, James, and John themselves, but regarding the exalted status the false brothers seem to assign them (*Galatians*, 48). It's no accident that these false brothers align with the Jerusalem church's leaders—it was always very tentative about full gentile inclusion in the Jesus community.

Faith Working Through Love

In fact, Paul argues in the next section, his independence is proven by the fact that he once *publicly* rebuked the apostle Peter himself for caving to peer pressure and hedging on the gospel. This example is Paul's segue into the very heart of the letter and the specific issue Paul has with the Christians and false teachers in Galatia.

The Trouble in Antioch

(vv. 2:11–21)

IT HAPPENED IN ANTIOCH, which is Paul's home base. This is where Barnabas summoned him from Tarsus (Acts 11:25). If any congregation could qualify as Paul's "home church," then Antioch was it. This was a cosmopolitan place. It was the Roman capital of the province of Syria. It was a major crossroads for trade between Egypt, Asia Minor, Greece, Italy, and Mesopotamia. Like all the great cities of the world, it was a bustling place full of all sorts of characters from everywhere. All sorts of *very different* people found their way there—including Christians.

This was the city where people first called Christ followers "Christians" (Acts 11:26). After the deacon Stephen's death (Acts 7), believers fled Jerusalem for safety abroad. Some fled to Jewish communities, taking their prejudices with them, and would only tell the Good News to fellow Jews (Acts 11:19). But others were less inhibited and told *gentiles* about Jesus—especially in Antioch (Acts 11:20). It's telling that these believers were possibly gentiles themselves ("men from Cyprus and Cyrene") and so had less cultural prejudice baked into their personalities. "The Lord's hand was with them, and a great number of people believed and turned to the Lord" (Acts 11:21).

The church community in Antioch was what we today might call multi-ethnic (Acts 13:1).

- There was a prophet and teacher named Simeon (called "Niger") who was dark-complexioned and likely hailed from Africa[1]—possibly sub-Saharan Africa.

---

1. Bruce, *Acts*, loc. 8792; Schnabel, *Acts*, 554; Hays, *Every People and Nation*, 175–78.

- Another, named Lucius, was from Cyrene in North Africa, on what is now the Libyan coast.
- There was a man named Manaen who was likely from a wealthy Jewish family, who had "been brought up" with Herod Antipas (Acts 13:1).

Again, it would be helpful to mentally compare (a) an urban church in New York City to (b) a very traditional Baptist congregation in Rhea County, Tennessee. It was to this multicultural place that the apostle Peter came one day, and it was here that Paul had his confrontation with the man.

> When Cephas came to Antioch, I opposed him to his face, because he stood condemned. (Gal 2:11)

Paul's words are very certain. Peter was "very wrong" (NLT). He "stood condemned" (NIV). He "was to be blamed" (KJV). Paul confronted Peter directly "to his face." Whatever happened, it was serious.

> For before certain men came from James, he used to eat with the Gentiles. But when they arrived, he began to draw back and separate himself from the Gentiles because he was afraid of those who belonged to the circumcision group. The other Jews joined him in his hypocrisy, so that by their hypocrisy even Barnabas was led astray. (Gal 2:12–13).

The question was whether tradition would trump the gospel—the old conundrum of "legalism versus truth." The issue was specific Jewish dietary traditions, and *that* issue lurks behind much of the Gospels and the book of Acts.

There were plenty of faithful Israelites throughout the ages who loved God and followed his laws for the right reason. One thinks of Simeon and Anna from the Gospel of Luke. But, Jesus, Peter, and Paul ministered in a place and context where too many of the teachers, leaders, and people had a religion of legalism and externalism.

Peter had lots of trouble ditching this after his salvation. Even after multiple divine revelations from God to the contrary (Acts 10:9–23), Peter could still tell Cornelius and his household: "You are well aware that it is against our law for a Jew to associate with or visit a Gentile" (Acts 10:28). This is wrong. No such law exists. Moses' first wife was a Midianite (Exod 2:21), and his second a black woman ("a Cushite," Num 12:1). Judah married a Canaanite woman (Gen 38:2), and Jesus himself is descended from Judah's adulterous liaison with Tamar (Gen 38:13–30; cf. Matt 1:3, 16), who was likely a Canaanite woman. When Peter said that to Cornelius, he was speaking from *tradition* and not the Bible.

How did this happen?

RABBIT TRAIL NO. 1: WHY DID SO MANY JEWS NOT LIKE THE GENTILES, ANYWAY?

The Assyrians conquered the northern kingdom of Israel in about 721 BC, and these Israelites vanished from the stage as a community group.[2] The southern kingdom of Judah held on a bit longer. The Babylonians formally conquered them in 586 BC, though the kingdom had been on life support for some time prior. It is these Israelites from the southern kingdom of Judah who figure in the Bible's story from that point forward.

The Persians conquered the Babylonians not long after. The Persians allowed Israelites in exile to return to the promised land if they wished (see Ezra and Nehemiah). Some took them up on the offer and returned in successive waves, over a long period of time. Others, like Esther, decided to stay in the old Babylonian Empire (now Persia).

Once back in Israel, the leaders wanted to guard against idolatry and unfaithfulness—they didn't want to make the same mistakes again (see Neh 10:28–39). There was no longer a "king" over Israel. So, the priests were the de facto leaders of the community. They placed a strong emphasis on doing what God said. Ezra was descended from Aaron (Ezra 7:1–5) and represented a priest at his best: "For Ezra had devoted himself to the study and observance of the Law of the LORD, and to teaching its decrees and laws in Israel" (Ezra 7:10).

Even so, the quest for doing what God says began to shade into legalism. In Ezra 9, we read that the leaders (and Ezra himself) are distressed because the people began to marry foreign women and had "mingled the holy race with the peoples around them" (Ezra 9:2). Actually, the problem was not pollution of a so-called holy race—or else we must write off both Ruth and Tamar! The problem was that marrying *non-believers* was wrong. The people in Ezra's day had already begun to distance themselves from gentiles—they'd overcorrected from externalism to legalism.

But the real division wasn't about blood. It was about belief.

---

2. See esp. Schurer, *History of the Jewish People*, 2.1:25, 2.2:26, 28; and Cohen, *Maccabees to the Mishnah*, chapter 2.

This confusion had reached a fever pitch by the time Jesus came of age as a boy and in the early years of the church. Why?

In Israel, the centuries that followed witnessed (a) the spectacular rise and fall of the Greeks under Alexander the Great (333–323 BC), (b) the civil war among Alexander's successors—a struggle upon which hinged the fate of the promised land—(c) the rise of the Seleucid and Ptolemaic Empires in the eastern Mediterranean, (d) the fundamentalist resistance movement of the Maccabees and the rise of Hasmonean dynasty, and (e) the advent of Roman influence in the eastern Mediterranean.[3]

Herod the Great was the last quasi-representative of the old Hasmonean dynasty (which derived from the Maccabean rebellion).[4] Rome allowed him to rule Judah, Samaria, and Galilee as a semi-independent rump state. Soon after Herod's death in AD 4, the Romans installed their own civil servants to govern what remained of Herod's realm. This is why an official like Pilate (and not a descendent of Herod the Great) was the magistrate who dealt with Jesus.

This is a lot of water under the bridge. A lot of change. A lot of uncertainty. If you're an Israelite, what does "being faithful to God" *look like* when (a) you have no king ruling in Jerusalem, (b) you have no political independence, (c) you have very weak or non-existent social and political infrastructure to "keep the world out," and (d) your sacred scriptures come from a perspective which largely assumes the opposite is true?

Three options are immediately clear:

1. First, the progressives and the pragmatists will champion accommodation. This will often mean a reinterpretation of religious texts in a liberal or pragmatic direction, which will always alienate the conservatives. There will be talk of "facing the hard reality" or of "adapting to challenging circumstances."

2. Second, the militant conservatives will become an angry minority and perhaps eventually withdraw. They will be outraged, indignant, accuse the first group of "selling out." They will work to establish their own

---

3. It is impossible to adequately sum up about six hundred years of history in a single paragraph, and it's certainly beyond the scope of this commentary. Try to sum up American history from the early seventeenth century to the present, and you'll see what I mean! For a good overview of this period, see Cohen, *Maccabees to Mishnah*, chapter 1; and Athas, *Bridging the Testaments*, 16–22.

4. On Herod, see Grant, *Herod the Great*.

alternative ecosystems where they can plant "true religion" that's safe from "liberal" contamination.

3. Third, the moderate conservatives and more conservative liberals will try to forge a "third way" that captures good aspects from the first two groups. The conservatives will often despise this group as "weak" and use them as a punching bag, while the progressives will challenge them to have "more courage" and use them as tools to attract moderate converts.

Of course, these perspectives are on a spectrum, and each group had different reasons for its emphases. They're generic descriptions of how people often respond to cultural pressures. The options are the same today. In every arena we face the same dilemma, even in twenty-first century America.

The same three options—accommodation, militant withdrawal, or a moderate reply—play out over and over again when cultural and political circumstances challenge our religious convictions. Different words, but the same notes. And so, the song was much the same in Judea and Galilee in the time leading up to the New Testament era.

Gradually, in response to cultural and religious pressure, a division emerged between (a) the priestly aristocracy in Jerusalem, and (b) the Pharisees and scribes. Jewish society in Judea and Galilee was dominated by these two groups:[5]

1. First, the high priest aristocracy in Jerusalem. Their focus was often the temple and the high priestly families, and they seemed to be largely Sadducees. These people often collaborated with the Romans to maintain control. Think of Caiaphas and Annas. Read John 11:45–57. This group was often more interested in maintaining power and position and less interested in remaining "pure" from secular culture. These were the machine politicians.

2. Second, there were the scribes and Pharisees who taught the people in the synagogues and schools. They were more legalistic, more exclusivist, more insular. They were the more hardline conservatives. These

---

5. Perhaps it's helpful to think of the various Jewish groups (there were more than the two I'm highlighting here) as different "denominations." Each represented different responses to the political, social, and cultural pressures of being a minority community in a religiously pagan environment. See Athas, *Bridging the Testaments*, 517–22; and Cohen, *Maccabees to Mishnah*, chapter 5.

folks were in Galilee, in Judea—anywhere a Jewish community and a synagogue existed. This is "Pastor Jeb" from Rhea County who, as it were, distrusts "the politicians in Washington."

As you can imagine, these two groups didn't always mix well. In twenty-first-century America, one can compare (a) the executive committee of the Southern Baptist Convention (the so-called machine politicians) with (b) the more hardline denominational conservatives represented by "humble pastors" in the trenches. In the pre-exile years, everything had centered on the temple. And, sure—the relative few who returned constructed a new temple in Jerusalem. But, in the meantime, Jews were scattered hither and thither, at home and abroad. There was a great democratization and leveling—a shift of power from Jerusalem to a more local setting in the synagogue. That meant a de facto power shift from the priests at the temple in Jerusalem to the local teachers like Pharisees and scribes.[6]

And so, in this New Testament environment, the Pharisees and many of the scribes had become very influential spiritual leaders. They had synagogues and the schools, and they conducted the religious instruction. On the other hand, the Sadducees worried about Jerusalem's relationship with Rome (the Sanhedrin was the Roman governor's conduit to the Jewish people), and the priests busied themselves with the sacrificial system in the temple. This was a bifurcation of spheres, and the Pharisees had the upper hand.

The scribes and Pharisees were anxious to "fence" the law and protect people from breaking it.[7] This was a good motivation that eventually ossified into dead ritual and formalism. It made relationship with God less about love (see 1 John 4:10; cf. Deut 6:5; Mark 12:28–32) and more about *doing the right things the right way*. It flipped things upside down. Their understandable fear of failing God yet again produced a very literal, hardline, and "puritanical interpretation of the Torah"[8] in reaction to the aristocracy's perceived compromise. This led them to codify nearly every aspect of civil, public, and private life with the Hebrew scriptures as the springboard. The thinking went like this:

1. If you love God, you'll want to follow his law.
2. If you want to follow his law, you must know what it says.

---

6. Cohen, *Maccabees to Mishnah*, 73–75; Scott, *Jewish Backgrounds*, 152–58.
7. Neusner, *Mishnah*, Aboth 1:1; 3:14.
8. Athas, *Bridging the Testaments*, 519.

The Trouble in Antioch

3. Everyone can read what it says, but you need someone to tell you *what it means* in concrete terms, in real life—that's why you need teachers.
4. But the Hebrew scriptures don't cover every situation, so you need help filling in the blanks for real life.

The result was an endless probing, studying, and teaching about the Hebrew Bible on virtually every aspect of life. This studying and teaching on the Jewish scriptures eventually became an avalanche of tradition that functioned almost like an inspired commentary.

This tradition was oral (until the *Mishnah*, ca. AD 200) and memorized and passed on by way of elaborate recitation drills.[9] The scribes and Pharisees believed you couldn't understand the law without a guide, and those guides were (a) the rabbis and the scribes and (b) the tradition (i.e., commentary) they held in their heads. This tradition eventually became functionally more important than the scriptures themselves:

1. They believed a person went to hell if he disagreed with oral tradition about some aspect of the Mosaic law.[10]
2. They believed God's wrath came upon the world if you disagreed with and taught differently than oral tradition.[11]
3. They believed violating tradition was more serious than violating the Hebrew scriptures themselves.[12]

They didn't believe this because they were *trying* to be legalistic; they believed it because they thought their tradition was the authentic and right interpretation of the Bible. They weren't trying to be wrong, but the results of their ideology *were* terrible. They thought it made God happy the more they tried to follow the law. "Judaism became a religious system that sanctified the life of each individual through the constant observance of the commandments of God . . . [it believes] humanity is capable of finding favor in God's eyes. The means to this end are repentance, prayer, Torah study, and good deeds."[13]

---

9. "He that forgets one word of his study, the Scripture reckons it to him as though he was guilty against his own soul" (Neusner, *Mishnah*, Aboth 3:9).
10. Neusner, *Mishnah*, Aboth 3:12.
11. Neusner, *Mishnah*, Aboth 5:8.
12. Neusner, *Mishnah*, Sanhedrin 11:3.
13. Cohen, *Maccabees to Mishnah*, 75, 96.

Faith Working Through Love

They believed this because they didn't understand God and they didn't understand grace. The *Mishnah* records one Jewish rabbi as saying, "[The rules about] bird-offerings and the onset of menstruation—these are essentials of the Halakoth."[14] They taught that God gave so many laws in the Bible because that would give the Jews more opportunity to gain favor by following them.[15]

What developed was a Judaism of pure externalism—one centered on law, not creed.[16]

1. Follow the law,

2. which means following the tradition that explains how to follow the law,

3. and you must follow it in every area and aspect of your life,

4. and *then* God will be happy with you,

5. and *then* you'll have a place in the world to come.[17]

This is why Jesus had such harsh words for the scribes and Pharisees:

> They tie up heavy burdens, hard to bear, and lay them on people's shoulders, but they themselves are not willing to move them with their finger. (Matt 23:4)

> Woe to you, scribes and Pharisees, hypocrites! For you are like whitewashed tombs, which outwardly appear beautiful, but within are full of dead people's bones and all uncleanness. So you also

---

14. Neusner, *Mishnah*, Aboth 3:19.

15. Neusner, *Mishnah*, Makkoth 3:16. "R. Hananiah b. Akashya says: The Holy One, blessed is he, was minded to grant merit to Israel; therefore hath he multiplied for them the Law and commandments, as it is written, 'It pleased the Lord for his righteousness' sake to magnify the Law and make it honourable.'"

16. Cohen, *Maccabees to Mishnah*, 128–31.

17. Cohen represents this perspective. In the preface to his excellent *Maccabees to Mishnah*, he wrote: "According to Rabbinic lore, when a person comes before the heavenly tribunal after his death he is asked, 'Did you conduct your trade honestly? Did you set aside time for study of the Torah? Did you raise a family?' My father lived his life in such a way that he could answer all those questions in the affirmative. In business he had a reputation as a man whose word could be trusted. Every morning before going to work and every night before going to sleep, he would sit in his favorite chair and study a Jewish book. I miss him, and I dedicate this book to his memory" (*Maccabees to Mishnah*, 12). The anecdote is both touching and tragic. There is no sin, so salvation, no mercy, no grace, no adoption, no forgiveness, no legal pardon, no love from God, no Messiah—let alone one who saves and rescues. There is only "did you do this list of things?"

outwardly appear righteous to others, but within you are full of hypocrisy and lawlessness. (Matt 23:27-28)

This externalism produced a nasty elitism, a holier-than-thou attitude and major arrogance among some. In the decades after the destruction of the temple by the Romans in AD 70, an unknown Jewish author consumed with bitterness wrote to God: "it was *for us* that you created this world. As for the other nations that have descended from Adam, you have said that *they are nothing*, and that *they are like spittle*, and you have compared their abundance to a drop from a bucket" (2 Esdras 6:55–56 NRSV).[18] However, the Lord says that non-Jewish people are precious and he would gather them to himself (Isa 56:3, 6–8), Ezekiel says that God will provide a shepherd for his people (Ezek 34), and Jesus promised that he would gather other sheep from outside to make *one* flock with *one* shepherd (John 10:16). And yet we have 2 Esdras saying that gentiles are *nothing*, that they're *spittle*. Somebody has gone off the deep end—and it isn't God. In 2 Esdras, we see the popular Jewish hostility against gentiles curdling into hateful disgust only a generation after Paul and Peter had their confrontation. In the days of Jesus and the apostles, the process was well underway.

This attitude filtered down into casual, everyday prejudice:

1. There was a belief that gentiles defiled you and made you ritualistically unclean and unfit to stand before God or perform religious duties. So, you couldn't have contact with gentiles—which is what Peter told Cornelius.
2. If you held a copy of scripture that was not in Hebrew, you would become defiled and unclean.[19]
3. People should fear their rabbis just as much as they feared God in heaven.[20]

---

18. David deSilva explains: "Fourth Ezra represents one serious attempt to wrestle with the difficulties of recovering the meaningfulness of traditional Jewish convictions about God, Torah, and covenant in the light of that devastation and, more especially, of Rome's continued prosperity. The close of the first century CE was an important time of reformulation of what it meant to be Jewish, to be faithful to the God of Israel, and to live out the covenant in a world with, once again, no temple" (*Introducing the Apocrypha*, 355).

19. Neusner, *Mishnah*, Yadaim 4:5.

20. Neusner, *Mishnah*, Aboth 4:12.

4. You should help rabbis recover lost property before you help your own parents do the same.[21]
5. Your rabbi was worth more honor than your own father.[22]

This is why Jesus warned:

> Beware of the scribes, who like to walk around in long robes and like greetings in the marketplaces and have the best seats in the synagogues and the places of honor at feasts, who devour widows' houses and for a pretense make long prayers. They will receive the greater condemnation. (Mark 12:38–40)

So, back to Peter eating with gentiles—who cares?

The issue is ceremonial uncleanness and the ritual "washing" an old covenant believer did to become "clean." By Jesus' day, tradition had evolved to include elaborate rituals for "purification" of hands, cups, platters, plates, and other food-related items. All this was about ceremonial purity and ritual "cleanness"—not about actual dirt. The Bible speaks of two kinds of impurity:

1. *Moral impurity* is about relationship with God and his legal charges against us. In our natural state, without Jesus' rescue, we're each sinful and so we're each spiritually dead. We have no relationship with God. We're morally "unclean." Jesus fixes this.

2. *Ceremonial impurity* is about access. It's about being fit (or unfit) to draw near to God (see Lev 11–15). Before Mary could present her newborn child at the temple, she made a purification offering (Luke 2:22–24). This was about *ceremonial* impurity. Mary didn't sin by having a baby. This wasn't about sin at all—it was about a circumstance totally apart from sin that made her "unclean" to approach God in the temple. It's probably best to see this as a grand object lesson.[23]

The ceremonial laws teach us that God is holy and you and I are sinful. They teach us that there are a million different things in this world (having nothing to do with sin) that *pollute* us, *defile* us, and make us *unfit* to approach God. That everything about this entire world has been ruined

---

21. Neusner, *Mishnah*, Baba Metzia 2:11.
22. Neusner, *Mishnah*, Kerithoth 6:9.
23. See Calvin, *Institutes* 2.7.1–2. "But the type shows that God did not enjoin sacrifice, in order that he might occupy his worshippers with earthly exercises, but rather that he might raise their minds to something higher" (2.7.1).

by the curse of sin, and that the simplest things make us unclean. And no matter how hard you try, the normal course of everyday life makes you polluted over and over again. It teaches us that, for God to have a *new*, *better* and *closer* relationship with his adopted children—to give us better and permanent access to him—something permanent must be done to fix this problem.

If you fix the *relationship*, then you fix the *access* problem, too. This is one of the things that Jesus Christ did. This is why every believer can now come boldly to the throne of grace to find mercy and help in time of need (Heb 4:16).

So, again, what about Peter and the food thing in Antioch? Here it is:

1. Tradition assumed your hands were *always* defiled, from deliberate or accidental contact with something that was unclean (like a gentile). Maybe you touched a dead animal. Maybe you touched mold. Maybe you touched blood. Maybe you were standing near a gentile like Cornelius?
2. So, tradition said you should *always* ritualistically wash your hands, to ceremonially cleanse you and anything you touch.
3. If you touch your food with defiled hands, your food is now unclean, and now you're unclean.

Now come the gentiles. They were *always* unclean. They ate unclean food. They lived in unclean ways. They didn't do purification offerings. They didn't do ceremonial washings. They were like walking petri dishes of pollution. Like COVID-19, they infect everything they touch and every space they enter. They make everything "unclean." Or so the oral tradition taught. Both they and allegedly "worldly" Jews were not good people. This is why the scribes and Pharisees were constantly angry about Jesus *eating* with tax collectors and "sinners" (Mark 2:16-17). No true rabbi would associate with these "unclean" people.

So, what should a pious Jew do? According to many of the scribes and Pharisees, the answer was easy—stay away from them!

An entire culture and ethos had developed which said that gentiles were unclean and ought to be avoided. That's why Peter told Cornelius what he did. It's also why, in Antioch, Peter reacts the way he does when hardliners from Jerusalem show up in town with their legalistic ways.

BACK TO GALATIANS—
THE CONFRONTATION IN ANTIOCH

We don't know when this event occurred. One good guess is that it happened after the great meeting in Acts 15, when Paul and Barnabas arrived back in Antioch with news of the decree from Jerusalem.[24] Peter likely arrived at that time. Paul is reaching back for the penultimate example that shows he isn't beholden to the apostles.[25] Paul writes:

> For before certain men came from James, he [Peter] used to eat with the Gentiles. (Gal 2:12)

Peter had changed since that day in Cornelius's home. He'd gotten rid of his cultural prejudice and embraced the true gospel. He now had no problem eating with gentiles. He wasn't concerned about ritual washings or uncleanness because Jesus has permanently washed us from all uncleanness—moral and ceremonial. Peter had stopped observing the traditions based on old covenant purity laws.

Some scholars believe the issue wasn't about unwritten traditions based on supposed gentile "impurity," but about the actual, biblical laws concerning clean and unclean food.[26] This is incorrect. Both issues are at play at the same time.

Paul never mentions *what* Peter was eating, but *with whom* he shared a meal. He was "eating *with* the Gentiles." He then "began to draw back and *separate himself from* the Gentiles" (Gal 2:12). The problem was his *contact with* the gentiles, not necessarily what they ate. Yes, there were differences of opinion about how the old covenant laws ported over into the new covenant (see Acts 15). Food laws were part of that controversy.

But all that was back of a more fundamental objection—in the eyes of the "circumcision party" gentiles would always be second-class *because they were gentiles*. That is the issue. They would always be "other." They would always be at the back of the bus, not because of racial animosity per se, but because they weren't Jewish. They weren't members of "the holy race" (Ezra 9:2).

---

24. Lightfoot, *Galatians*, 111.

25. "Paul is not interested here in relating the biography of his relationship with Peter, nor is he trumpeting himself as superior to Peter. Rather, he refers to his rebuke of Peter because it proves the independence and authority of his gospel" (Schreiner, *Galatians*, 139).

26. See Schreiner, *Galatians*, 140; Brown, *Galatians*, 84–85.

The Trouble in Antioch

Earlier, hardliners from Jerusalem ("the circumcised believers," Acts 11:2) had heavily criticized Peter as soon as they heard that gentiles were joining Christian communities (see Acts 11:1–2; cf. Acts 10:9–23). Peter explained about the incident with Cornelius and his wonder that God would send the Holy Spirit to *people like them*. "So if God gave them the same gift he gave us who believed in the Lord Jesus Christ, who was I to think that I could stand in God's way?" (Acts 11:17). The hardliners in Jerusalem were astonished: "So then, even to Gentiles God has granted repentance that leads to life!" (Acts 11:18). The idea that God *cares about gentiles* blew them away. God cared about *those* people, too? Amazing!

Why would they think that? Had they not read God's promise that "my house will be a house of prayer for *all nations*" (Isa 56:7)? God told foreigners to never think they had no place in his family (Isa 56:3). He promised to bring foreigners "to my holy mountain and give them joy in my house of prayer" (Isa 56:7). The God who swore to gather the exiles of Israel from the four corners of the earth also promised, "I will gather still others to them besides those already gathered" (Isa 56:8). This is what Jesus meant when he declared, "I have other sheep that are not of this sheep pen. I must bring them also. They too will listen to my voice, and there shall be one flock and one shepherd" (John 10:16).

One family. One flock. One shepherd. Jews and gentiles as equal partners. Anyone who believes in God and his promise is a true child of Abraham (see Gal 3). But culture intrudes. Old prejudices die hard. And so, in Antioch, it's the fact that *gentiles* are in the mix that's the real problem. Food laws, sure—but it's really about gentiles being gentiles.

There are three issues at play:

1. *Works righteousness baggage.* The former scribes and Pharisees who have allegedly become Christians want to retain a works-righteousness framework for understanding relationship with God. "It is popular because it is flattering. It tells a man that if he will only pull his socks up a bit higher and try a bit harder, he will succeed in winning his own salvation."[27]

2. *Prejudice against gentiles.* Some of these same people retain a distaste for gentiles.

3. These then combine with *a militant, conservative mindset*. Remember that the mindset of the militant conservatives (in any age) is to

---
27. Stott, *Galatians*, 62.

withdraw, to create alternative ecosystems, to build cultural, social, and religious walls to keep "them" away. This is what I call "the Alamo mindset." You hunker down, you conserve ammunition, you wait for backup, you endure—you open the gates at midnight just wide enough to let a few pilgrims in, then quickly shut and bar the doors. This mindset clashes with a more cosmopolitan and missionary mindset like the one in the church at Antioch.

Each of these issues are at play at the same time. They can't be untangled. You can't understand this letter without getting that straight. Paul is against all of this, especially the first two—(a) works righteousness isn't what Christ (or Moses) taught, and (b) gentiles can be full, equal brothers and sisters in God's family. They can be children of Abraham too.

But then "certain men came from James." They were former Pharisees who now claimed Christ (cf. Acts 15:5). James later clarified by letter that hadn't sent out these folks or others like them (Acts 15:24). But at the time Paul wrote to the Galatians he seemed to believe James *had* sent them. James wouldn't have sent them with malicious intent, but people with agendas always have a way of going beyond their orders. That's probably what's happening here.[28] Men arrived from Jerusalem. James had sent them for some unknown purpose.[29] Perhaps the best guess is that, in the wake of the Jerusalem Council (Acts 15), James sent them to caution Peter to be more tactful about gentile inclusion in deference to the conservatives in Jerusalem—something James would later ask of Paul, too (Acts 21:17-25).[30] Full of themselves, fueled by righteous fervor, they used James's imprimatur as cover to be legalists.[31] In that sense, James didn't send them. They had exceeded their orders and gone off the rails.

---

28. "It is not improbable however, that they came invested with some powers from James which they abused" (Lightfoot, *Galatians*, 112).

29. "We must finally confess uncertainty about what James told the couriers to say" (Schreiner, *Galatians*, 140).

30. Bruce, *Paul*, 176-78. Henry Alford writes, "The candid reader will I think at once recognize in the words a mission from James: and will find no difficulty in believing that that Apostle, even after the decision of the council regarding the Gentile converts, may have retained (characteristically, see his recommendation to St. Paul, in Acts 21:18 ff.) his strict view of the duties of Jewish converts,—for that is perhaps all that the present passage requires" (*New Testament*, 2:330).

31. "They posed as apostolic delegates" (Stott, *Galatians*, 50).

The Trouble in Antioch

> But when they arrived, he began to draw back and separate himself from the Gentiles because he was afraid of those who belonged to the circumcision group. (Gal 2:12)

What happened? Peer pressure happened. Peter "was afraid" of the hardliners.[32] They were Christians, but they were legalists. It's as if stuffy Brother Jeff from Rhea County had visited his cousin Jamie at River of Life in urban New York City and began judging the pastor with his skinny jeans, spiked hair, and missing pulpit. Peter "began to draw back" and push the gentiles away. The worst thing is that Peter is only doing this because he's self-conscious about the hardline conservatives from Jerusalem[33] who are watching him, judging him, eyes narrowed. This is why Paul says Peter is clearly wrong.

> The other Jews joined him in his hypocrisy, so that by their hypocrisy even Barnabas was led astray. (Gal 2:12–13)

Other Jews jump on the bandwagon, picking up the old prejudices just as easy as you please. Soon this multicultural community is dividing along racial lines—Jew versus gentile. And it's *the teachers* who are forcing the division—even Barnabas! This is all happening because some folks from Jerusalem are in town. It's "hypocrisy" because Barnabas, Peter, and the other Jews know that truth has nothing to do with this pulling back.[34]

> When I saw that they were not acting in line with the truth of the gospel, I said to Cephas in front of them all, "You are a Jew, yet you live like a Gentile and not like a Jew. How is it, then, that you force Gentiles to follow Jewish customs?" (Gal 2:14)

---

32. Some scholars believe Peter was afraid for the Christian communities in Judea, that they faced imminent persecution from non-Christian Jews. So, Peter withdrew from the gentiles because he feared non-Christian Jews who, in this interpretation, would be "the circumcision party" that Paul mentions (Fung, *Galatians*, loc. 1499; Longenecker, *Galatians*, 74–75).

33. Schreiner doesn't believe the "circumcision party" is the folks from Jerusalem, but his reasons are unconvincing (*Galatians*, 143).

34. "Their withdrawal from table fellowship with Gentile believers was not prompted by any theological principle, but by craven fear of a small pressure group" (Stott, *Galatians*, 52). Alvah Hovey remarks, "For a brief period it seemed as if a great wave of Jewish ritualism were about to sweep away the old landmarks of the church, as if the form of godliness were to take the place of its power, and pretense get the upper hand of sincerity" (*Galatians*, 31).

Paul says they're living as though the gospel isn't true—as if Jesus hadn't made the two groups one, hadn't destroyed the dividing wall and its hostility, hadn't *set aside* those ceremonial purity laws (Eph 2:14–15) and the tradition that had encrusted over top of them. It's as if Jesus had not created "in himself one new humanity out of the two, thus making peace" (Eph 2:15). As if he had not in one body reconciled both of them to God through the cross (Eph 2:16).[35]

No—Peter, Barnabas, and the rest of the Jews were reverting to the old, prejudiced ways because of peer pressure. Paul won't have it. He accuses Peter to his face. He's making the gentiles believe in the false equation: "Jesus + following the law the right way = salvation." He is, in effect, forcing gentiles to follow Jewish customs as a condition of membership in God's family. This is wrong. It isn't the gospel. It's the old, perverted form of religion to which Judaism had degenerated. It's what Jesus protested (see Mark 7). Paul says, "Peter, you're acting like a hypocrite!"

He continues this conversation with Peter.[36]

> We who are Jews by birth and not sinful Gentiles know that a person is not justified by the works of the law, but by faith in Jesus Christ. So we, too, have put our faith in Christ Jesus that we may be justified by faith in Christ and not by the works of the law, because by the works of the law no one will be justified. (Gal 2:15–16)

RABBIT TRAIL NO. 2: JUSTIFICATION BY FAITH—WHAT DOES IT MEAN?

Paul mentions "justification" for the first time. The concept is similar to "righteousness." This character trait is part of God's nature. When we say that God is "righteous," we mean that he is good and just. He *personifies* rightness and goodness. He *is* these things.

---

35. Brown believes Peter and Paul are really of the same mind, but that Peter is being too deferential to the visitors from Jerusalem and is dissembling. "I apprehend that Peter and Barnabas acted with perfect integrity, i.e., they acted according to their views of present duty, though these views were mistaken ones. They did not think that their conduct compromised any truth, and they conceived that it was necessary to prevent 'the offence'—in the Scripture sense of the term, the 'stumbling'—of their brethren from Jerusalem" (*Galatians*, 87). This is a very charitable reading of the situation.

36. Some scholars believe Paul's remarks to Peter stop at 2:14. I agree with Schreiner that it continues until 2:21 (*Galatians*, 150). See also Barnes, "Galatians," 315–16.

So, it makes sense that when God warns the Israelites on the east bank of the Jordan River that "it is not because of *your righteousness* or your integrity that you are going in to take possession of their land" (Deut 9:5), he means, "You *are not* good and right and just. You *didn't* earn this gift. I'm just deciding to give it to you."

When David wrote that God "rules the world *in righteousness* and judges the peoples with equity" (Ps 9:8), he meant that God judges *rightly, appropriately,* and *fairly,* and according to *right standards.* Because "God is a righteous judge" (Ps 7:11), he is *fair* and sees *justice* done.

> Let all creation rejoice before the LORD, for he comes,
> he comes to judge the earth.
> He will judge the world in righteousness,
> and the peoples in his faithfulness. (Ps 96:13)

When Paul speaks of being "justified by faith," he's talking about a status, a state of being. We're perhaps most familiar with the concept in a negative sense as *self-righteousness*. We're each inclined to believe we're righteous, right, and good. This is why someone who is "self-righteous" is smug, intolerant, and arrogant—he is convinced he's right, good, and better than you. It's *self*-righteousness because he has assigned this status to himself. So, the writer Luke tells us that the question which prompted the parable of the good Samaritan came from a scribe who "wanted to *justify himself,* so he asked Jesus, 'And who is my neighbor?'" (Luke 10:29). Jesus criticized the Pharisees and charged, "You are the ones who *justify yourselves* in the eyes of others, but God knows your hearts" (Luke 16:15).

When we move "righteousness" from this sphere to the eternal tribunal, we confess that God *sets, weighs,* and *evaluates* his own standards. That means this "righteousness" or "justification" is a legal status God grants.[37] It says you've met the "righteous requirement of the law" (Rom 8:4) through Jesus' substitutionary atonement. God says his standard of rightness, goodness, is met in you. The Good News is that, because you cannot meet this standard, God's eternal Son has met it for you, in your place, as your substitute. It means God has declared you to be righteous and treats you that way.[38] The 1833 New Hampshire Confession explains:

---

37. The General Baptist "Orthodox Creed" (1679) states justification is "a declarative, or judicial sentence of God the father" (art. 24, quoted in Lumpkins, *Baptist Confessions*, 314).

38. See LSJ, s.v. "δικαιόω," sense 3.3, 429; Abbott-Smith, s.v., "δικαιόω," sense 2.2, 116.

1. Justification includes the pardon of sin and the promise of eternal life on principles of righteousness.
2. God bestows this righteousness, not in consideration of any works of righteousness which *we* have done, but solely through faith in Jesus' life and death in our place, as our delegate and substitute.
3. By virtue of our faith and trust in what Jesus has done, God freely imputes or credits to us Jesus' perfect righteousness.
4. This imputation of Christ's righteousness brings us into a state of most blessed peace and favor with God and secures every other blessing needful for time and eternity.[39]

This means we don't "grade our own work," but we'd like to. Tim Keller has likened "righteousness" to a resume. We always want to come to God with a nicely formatted paper listing our knowledge, skills, and abilities. We want to show how we meet the required and desired qualifications. We want to submit our application and wait for the job interview. We want to solve this great problem like we do everything else in life—by hard work and diligent effort. But that isn't the way.

So, the question follows: "What then must we do *to obtain* this righteous status from God?"

This is the greatest question. Paul wrote in another letter, "in the gospel the righteousness of God is revealed—a righteousness that is by faith from first to last, just as it is written: 'The righteous will live by faith'" (Rom 1:17; quoting Hab 2:4).

What does this mean?

If you read this through a works-righteousness lens, it sounds like a scary thing! If (a) "righteousness" is God's standard, his yardstick, a measurement he defines, and (b) if God is infinitely great and powerful, then (c) his "righteousness" is an impossible standard. If God's righteousness is revealed in the gospel, then you could read this as a message of condemnation, of guilt—one that has God saying: "My expectations are way *up here*, and you are way *down there*, and good luck trying to close that gap. I'll be waiting."

That's how Martin Luther, the great Protestant Reformer, interpreted those same words.[40] In 1505, when he was twenty-two years old, Luther

---

39. I've added a word or two of commentary and changed some language from passive to active voice, but this is substantially what art. 5 of the 1833 New Hampshire Confession reads (Schaff, *Creeds of Christendom*, 3:743–44).

40. See Hillerbrand, *Reformation*, chapter 1; and Bainton, *Here I Stand*, chapter 3. "I

entered a Roman Catholic monastic order after pledging his life to God during a terrifying lightning storm. As the years went by, he was given to severe introspection about his conscience, his heart, and his own sin.[41] His religious training taught him that sins were only forgiven through confession and that God's grace depended on doing your very best to obey the commandments—but can one ever *really* say he's done his *very* best?[42]

For an introspective person this is not reassuring, and so Luther ransacked heart and mind for every sin. His confessions wearied even the priests—at least one confession lasted six hours![43] He found no peace, because he perceived that "sin" went deeper than individual transgressions—the whole person seemed to be corrupt. "These words 'righteous' and 'righteousness of God' struck my conscience as flashes of lightening, frightening me each time I heard them: if God is righteous, he punishes."[44]

Luther was appointed to be a Bible teacher at the new university at Wittenberg, where his woes continued. He began to almost hate God,[45] seeing him as a tyrant who kept dangling an impossible standard far out of reach—the "righteousness of God" was a taunt, a tease, a curse. How could anyone meet this standard? The gap was too much.

Between 1513 and 1517, Luther lectured on the Psalms, Romans, and Galatians—at which point the Holy Spirit began to shine gospel light into his heart. Coming to Ps 22:1 ("My God, my God, why have you forsaken me? Why are you so far from saving me, so far from my cries of anguish?"), Luther was puzzled. He saw his own sorrow, struggles, and pain in Christ's words. But Christ *didn't deserve* to be forsaken, tortured, and assassinated—why did it happen? Christ must have been acting as stand-in, a substitute, a delegate—but for whom? Luther concluded it must have been for us.

---

hated that word 'righteousness of God,' because in accordance with the usage and custom of the doctors I had been taught to understand it philosophically as meaning, as they put it, the formal or active righteousness according to which God is righteous and punishes sinners and the unjust" (Hillerbrand, *Reformation*, 27).

41. "I was indeed a pious monk and kept the rules of my order so strictly that I can say: If ever a monk gained heaven through monkery, it should have been I. All my monastic brethren who knew me will testify to this. I would have martyred myself to death with fasting, praying, reading, and other good works had I remained a monk much longer" (quoted in Hillerbrand, *Reformation*, 24).

42. On the theological context, see especially Lindberg, *European Reformations*, 56–70. See also Calvin, *Institutes* 3.4.2.

43. Bainton, *Here I Stand*, 54–55.

44. Hillerbrand, *Reformation*, 28.

45. Hillerbrand, *Reformation*, 27.

However, Jesus' love is all fine and good, but what about justice? What about the "righteousness of God"—the severity, the justice, the righteous moral standards that the gospel sets as the divine expectation? This is when Paul's quotation from Habakkuk clicked into place: "in the gospel the righteousness of God is revealed—a righteousness that is by faith from first to last, *just as it is written: 'The righteous will live by faith'*" (Rom 1:17; quoting Hab 2:4).

How is righteousness from God[46] being unveiled or revealed? By means of the gospel. How do we get this righteousness? It comes by means of faith, so that others would believe.[47] Now Paul quotes Habakkuk, who says "the one who is righteous by means of faith will live" (cf. RSV, NEB, REB).[48]

Gradually, Luther saw that he'd been reading the passage backward. He was correct that God's righteousness was the highest standard. He was wrong to believe the gospel was a mirror showing us how badly we fail to meet it. The gospel wasn't an accusatory mirror—it was Good News of hope. It is revealed *by faith*. There is no "work" involved.

I can't meet God's righteous standards. I'm scared, I'm angry, I fear God. I see Jesus was forsaken for my sake, which is well and good, but that doesn't solve the justice gap. God's righteousness is still revealed, still on the

---

46. Gk: δικαιοσύνη γὰρ θεοῦ is a genitive of source ("righteousness *from* God").

47. Gk: ἐκ πίστεως εἰς πίστιν. Woodenly, this reads "from faith for faith." It's likely the phrase is epexegetical, explaining more about this righteousness that is revealed by means of the gospel. It's a righteousness that is *by means of* faith (ἐκ πίστεως), *for the purpose of* faith (εἰς πίστιν); i.e., so that others would also believe.

48. Gk: ὁ δὲ δίκαιος ἐκ πίστεως ζήσεται. You can translate the sentence in two different ways, and each hinges on what to do with the phrase ἐκ πίστεως. The *first way* is to see ἐκ πίστεως as modifying ζήσεται, explaining what a believer's life should look like: "the one who is righteous will live by means of faith." The *second way* is to see ἐκ πίστεως as going with ὁ ... δίκαιος, explaining how righteousness comes: "the one who is righteous by means of faith will live." This second view is the best option. The objection is that this makes Paul use the Habakkuk quotation out of context because Habakkuk wasn't referring to salvation at all. Instead, Habakkuk was telling the citizens of Judah how they ought to live while they waited for the Babylonians to arrive and destroy their nation—they should trust God (Hab 2:4a). But this is not an obstacle. Paul simply borrows the basic principle (trust in God!) and deploys it here in a different context. Habakkuk's context was temporal ("trust God and you'll get through this"), while Paul's context is eternal ("have faith in Jesus, and you'll be righteous"). Moses Stuart remarked, "If it be viewed as a simple illustration of a general principle, all difficulty about the quotation vanishes. As the Israelite, in the time of Habakkuk, was to be saved from evil by means of faith, so Jews and Gentiles are now to be saved by means of faith. What real difficulty can there be, in such a comparison as this?" (*Romans*, 69). That Paul interprets Hab 2:4 in this manner is clear from his quotation at Gal 3:11 (Bruce, *Galatians*, loc. 4494).

table as a yardstick I can never meet, no matter how hard I try. But then, I realize righteousness from God is revealed *by means of faith*.

This suggests *our faith* is the instrument for receiving this righteousness,[49] but how is that justice? Who pays for our sins? This reminds us of Jesus (Ps 22:1) being forsaken, bring despised, being abandoned in our place—but why?

Now we can see why Luther had been reading Rom 1:17 backward. God isn't holding righteousness out as a standard we must meet. Instead, it's a gift he gives us that comes by means of faith—it's a righteousness *from* God. It's "the power of God that brings salvation to everyone who believes" (Rom 1:16). Jesus paid for our sins. Jesus was perfect. Jesus was righteous for us. God gives us Christ's righteousness ("righteousness *from* God," Rom 1:17) as a gift. This divine life comes by means of faith and trust in Jesus—that's why God's righteousness is revealed "in the Gospel" (Rom 1:17).

That's why, when Paul quoted Hab 2:4, he meant that "the one who is righteous by means of faith will live." Luther explained: "Then, finally, God had mercy on me, and I began to understand that the righteousness of God is that gift of God by which a righteous man lives, namely, faith."[50]

BACK TO GALATIANS—
AGAINST WORKS RIGHTEOUSNESS

> We who are Jews by birth and not sinful Gentiles know that a person is not justified by the works of the law, but by faith in Jesus Christ. So we, too, have put our faith in Christ Jesus that we may be justified by faith in Christ and not by the works of the law, because by the works of the law no one will be justified. (Gal 2:15–16)

Paul's comparison between "we who are Jews by birth and not sinful Gentiles" (Gal 2:15) is sarcasm.[51] *Everyone* is sinful—gentiles are not in a category of their own. We should picture Paul writing "sinful gentiles" in scare quotes here. He's referring negatively to the Jewish cultural prejudice against gentiles.[52]

49. Calvin, *Institutes*, 3.11.7.
50. Hillerbrand, *Reformation*, 27.
51. "Not without a shade of irony, as better enforcing St Paul's argument" (Lightfoot, *Galatians*, 115).
52. This is contra Schreiner, who writes: "Paul does not deny that they were sinners. His point is that they were not sinners in the same way as Gentiles, for the Gentiles were

By showing gentiles that inclusion into God's family is predicated on "following rules," Peter is teaching salvation by works.[53] Paul focuses very specifically on the *means* of obtaining righteousness from God. We are not justified *by means of* the works of the law, but *by means of* faith in Jesus Christ.[54] We believe in Jesus and what he's done for us, and so God rescues us. He saves us. He adopts us. There is no "Jesus + something = salvation." There is only "Jesus = salvation."

In his letters, Paul consistently takes a sledgehammer to works righteousness. If you're counting on *anything other* than Jesus' righteousness to you as a gift, Paul wants to smash to it to bits. "For in the gospel the righteousness of God is revealed—a righteousness that is by faith from first to last, just as it is written: 'The righteous will live by faith'" (Rom 1:17).

Peter knows this, but like many of us the crucible of real life has made him skittish. Paul isn't speaking in the calm, confidential notes of a friend, but indignantly. Angrily. He's condemning Peter because he's clearly in the wrong (Gal 2:11).

> So we, too, have put our faith in Christ Jesus that we may be justified by faith in Christ and not by the works of the law, because by the works of the law no one will be justified. (Gal 2:16)

We have put our faith in Christ Jesus—but why? So that we would be declared righteous (or justified) *by means of* faith in Christ and not *by means of* works of the law.[55] This is passive—we don't declare ourselves righteous, but instead we receive this status from God.

---

not part of God's covenant people (see Eph 2:11–12), and hence they did not receive God's saving promises. Paul focuses on the great privileges he and Peter enjoyed as part of Israel" (*Galatians*, 154).

53. Schreiner does not believe the "works of the law" refers to legalism per se, but to all the deeds demanded by the entire Mosaic code (*Galatians*, 159). I see this as a distinction without a difference. Yes, "works of the law" specifically refers to the Mosaic law in this context, but the point is that his opponents see the Mosaic law *as the means* to obtain justification—which is legalism. He writes, "Human beings do not stand in the right before God by observing the law, but only through faith in Jesus Christ" (*Galatians*, 162). I agree with this.

54. Gk Gal 2:16a: εἰδότες [δὲ] ὅτι οὐ δικαιοῦται ἄνθρωπος ἐξ ἔργων νόμου ἐὰν μὴ διὰ πίστεως Ἰησοῦ Χριστοῦ. The title "Jesus Christ" is an objective genitive. He is the object of faith, which is the means by which we obtain righteousness from God. This is quite clear in the last part of the verse where Paul writes, "so we too have put our faith in Christ Jesus" (Gal 2:16b).

55. The prepositions both express the means by which we obtain righteousness from God: by means of faith (ἐκ πίστεως Χριστοῦ) and not by means of the works of the law

The Trouble in Antioch

But why the focus on faith *in Christ*? What's wrong with works of the law? Is it wrong to follow the law of Moses? Well, it is wrong if you believe obedience to the law is *the means* to obtain righteousness from God. Why? Because nobody will be declared righteous *by means of* works of the law.[56] Martin Luther explains:

> There can be danger in tradition and ceremonies, and yet we cannot do without them. What is more necessary than the law and its works? Yet there is great danger in that it may lead people to deny Christ, for the law often brings with it a trust in works, and then there is no trust in Christ. Therefore Christ is soon denied and soon lost, as we see in Peter, who knew about justification better than we do.[57]

Another theologian explained:

> [Paul's] rebuff to works-righteousness—the illegitimate son of legalism—is not directed against the law, but against the sinful man who thinks himself good enough to obtain righteousness before God and who uses the law as a ladder. Israel did this when she began to look on the law as the way of salvation par excellence.[58]

Paul continued:

> But if, in seeking to be justified in Christ, we Jews find ourselves also among the sinners, doesn't that mean that Christ promotes sin? Absolutely not! (Gal 2:17)

Again, it's best to see two scare quotes here, so it would read: "we Jews find ourselves among the 'sinners' . . . Christ promotes 'sin.'"

Paul doesn't agree with this. That's why you should interpret him as using scare quotes. But, his opponents are saying that by pursing justification by Christ alone, they're committing sin against the Mosaic law. Paul is responding to two charges made by his supposedly "Christian" opponents:

(καὶ οὐκ ἐξ ἔργων νόμου).

56. Gk: ὅτι ἐξ ἔργων νόμου οὐ δικαιωθήσεται πᾶσα σάρξ.

57. Luther, *Galatians*, 81.

58. Berkouwer, *Faith and Justification*, 77.

What Paul says		What the Jewish agitators are saying that make Paul say this
"We Jews find ourselves among the 'sinners'"	=	Can you *believe* that Paul doesn't tell Jewish Christians to stay away from gentiles—who everyone knows are rotten "sinners"?
"Doesn't that mean that Christ promotes 'sin'"?	=	Paul is teaching sinful things, in that he's presenting a *different* path to God—one that isn't centered on doing what the law says! Paul doesn't care about the law! Blasphemy!

Both so-called errors, the accusation goes, make Paul and those who follow him "sinners." Yes, they would acknowledge, pursuing Christ is important—but to make gentiles full partners in his family *and* to forsake the law of Moses? Madness! Both these charges are false. These false teachers are "perverting everything!"[59] We'll consider the first charge here and the second at Gal 2:18–21.

First, the cultural wall against which Paul keeps hitting his head throughout the book of Acts was about whether gentiles could come into God's family and what this "coming in" looked like.

The Jewish agitators believed the "coming in" meant observing certain Jewish "boundary markers" like circumcision, the Sabbath, and the laws about cleanness and uncleanness—that is, becoming Jews. God gave these laws to keep his people separate from the world—he wants us to be different! These "works of the law" also broadened to include "the distinctively Jewish way of life"[60]—a sort of cultural identity to which the boundary markers pointed.

This "set-apartness" ethic is what motivated the agitators we read about in Galatians. It is this clash that is "evidently the theological rationale behind Peter's 'separation' from the Gentiles of Antioch."[61]

> Judaism was not missionary minded. Why should it? Judaism was primarily an ethnic religion, the religion of the residents of Judea, that is, Judeans. So it was natural for Second Temple Jews to think of Judaism as only for Jews, and for non-Jews who became Jews. This was where Christianity, initially a Jewish sect, broke the established mold. It became an evangelistic sect, a missionary movement, something untoward, unheard of within Judaism.[62]

59. Luther, *Galatians*, 92.
60. Dunn, "Whence, What and Whither?," 27–28.
61. Dunn, "Whence, What and Whither?," 30–31.
62. Dunn, "New Perspective View," 186–87.

The Trouble in Antioch

Being a "believer" meant "being Jewish." Paul and the Jerusalem church in Acts 15 said this was no longer true.[63]

In Paul's day, the conservatives in Jewish society are the Pharisees and the scribes. They've chosen isolation, which is why prejudice exists against gentiles in great swaths of Jewish popular culture. They believe part of being "God's people" is to be separate from the world, and their "Jewishness" acts as cultural boundary markers to highlight these differences. This is fine, so far as it goes, but they've taken it too far. They *actively dislike* gentile people. This is what Paul's talking about here. So, this is why seeing scare quotes at Gal 2:17 is best—this is how the CSB version renders it. He presents his opponent's arguments, then dismisses them:[64]

1. If, while trying to be declared righteous by means of Christ,
2. believers find themselves to be "sinners" because they ignore the tradition about gentile impurity,
3. then doesn't this mean that Christ is a messenger for "sin"—in that he encourages us to associate with gentiles and ignore the purity laws?
4. God forbid! That isn't true at all, because point 2 is wrong.

To bring back un-biblical traditions about the purity laws would be bad enough. To then apply them to gentile Christians—to brothers and sisters in Christ in his community in Antioch or anywhere else—is an abomination. It's evil. It's wrong. It's saying there are two tiers of Christian—Jewish and non-Jewish. How ridiculous!

> If I rebuild what I destroyed, then I really would be a lawbreaker.
> (Gal 2:18)

---

63. Chrysostom criticized "the undue maintenance of Jewish customs" and said "its unseasonable observance was injurious to the Gospel" ("Commentary on Galatians," 13, 8).

64. Gk: εἰ δὲ ζητοῦντες δικαιωθῆναι ἐν Χριστῷ εὑρέθημεν καὶ αὐτοὶ ἁμαρτωλοί, ἄρα Χριστὸς ἁμαρτίας διάκονος; μὴ γένοιτο. This means: "But if, while attempting to be justified by Christ, we Jews are then found to be 'sinners' [*predicate nominative; contra NIV*], is Christ therefore a messenger for 'sin'? God forbid!"

Lightfoot is excellent here: "We may regard Χριστὸς ἁμαρτίας διάκονος as an illogical conclusion deduced from premises in themselves correct; 'Seeing that in order to be justified in Christ it was necessary to abandon our old ground of legal righteousness and to become sinners (i.e., to put ourselves in the position of the heathen), may it not be argued that Christ is thus made a minister of sin?' This interpretation best develops the subtle irony of ἁμαρτωλοί; 'We Jews look down upon the Gentiles as sinners: yet we have no help for it but to become sinners like them'" (*Galatians*, 116–17). See also Hendriksen, *Galatians*, 100.

Faith Working Through Love

Now we've moved to the second objection—that Paul has forsaken Moses by not encouraging "works of the law" as a means to obtain righteousness from God. He explains why this idea is absurd, why he writes "God forbid!" at the very thought of it.[65] It isn't true that Christ is a messenger for "sin"—because salvation was never about doing the right things (i.e., the works of the law) in exchange for righteousness from God. Baptist theologian Alvah Hovey explains:

> We did not then break the law and commit sin by looking to Christ alone for acceptance with God, although in doing this we ceased to keep the law as a means of justification. Just the opposite of this is true.[66]

Now, freed from every form of the works-righteousness equation, we're free to live for God. There is no more legalism. No more alternative pathways to peace—in any form. There is only living for God, through Jesus, who has fulfilled the law for us. The law was never about salvation; it was a fence, a guardrail, a hedge to preserve us as his people and to show us our sin and the need for a permanent solution (Gal 3:19–25; Rom 7:7–13).[67] Hovey explains:

> The true purpose of the law was to convince men of sin and drive them away from itself to Christ. Hence those who turn back to legal works as a condition of forgiveness and life, transgress the very nature and purpose of the law.[68]

If this is true, it means (a) if Paul tries to "rebuild" the *very same* works-righteousness ethic ("the law") which he just destroyed by means of faith in Christ,[69] then (b) Paul would *truly* be a lawbreaker. That would be the greatest crime of all—to let Jesus set you free, then cheerfully return to captivity.

---

65. The conjunction γὰρ at the beginning of v. 18 is explanatory.

66. Hovey, *Galatians*, 33.

67. Emil Brunner writes, "The meaning of all the Commandments is not to destroy that which God has so wondrously bestowed upon you—this life which is holy because it is God's gift; God's commandments are given to protect life from gross infringement, like a wall thrown about a glorious garden. The commandments of God are gifts of God" (*Our Faith*, 60–61). This is Calvin's third use of the law (*Institutes* 2.7.12).

68. Hovey, *Galatians*, 33.

69. Schreiner is incorrect to state: "The things torn down or 'destroyed' refer to the OT law" (*Galatians*, 169). The problem isn't the Mosaic law per se. The problem is the perverted use of that law as a means to obtain righteousness from God.

The Trouble in Antioch

The "law" in this context doesn't mean the Mosaic law per se. In specific terms, it means the perverted form of the Mosaic law that taught salvation comes by good works[70]—which is what Paul is combatting in this entire letter. In general terms, "law" means *all attempts* to find peace and ultimate meaning in anything other than relationship with God through Jesus Christ, by the power of the Holy Spirit.[71]

> For through the law I died to the law so that I might live for God. (Gal 2:19)

Here, Paul explains why endorsing a "Jesus + works = salvation" equation is such a terrible idea. "Because, by means of the law, I died so far as the law is concerned, so that I would live a life fixed on God" (my translation of Gal 2:19; cf. NIrV, NLT).[72] The thought is that the law is now dead to Paul so that he can live for God—and the law itself was the means of this death. The law, in effect, *killed* or *canceled itself out* so that Paul could live for God. How did this happen? By way of Jesus, who "killed" the law by abolishing its righteous requirements by his perfect life, sacrificial and substitutionary death, and resurrection.[73] Paul said the same thing at Rom 7:4 (cf. Rom 10:1–4): "So, my brothers and sisters, you also died to the law through the body of Christ, that you might belong to another."

> I have been crucified with Christ and I no longer live, but Christ lives in me. The life I now live in the body, I live by faith in the Son of God, who loved me and gave himself for me. (Gal 2:20)

---

70. The phrase "works of the law" is "a catch phrase to signal the whole legalistic complex of ideas having to do with winning God's favor by a merit-amassing observance of the Torah" (Longenecker, *Galatians*, 86).

71. See Fung's comments along this line (*Galatians*, loc. 1537).

72. Gk: ἐγὼ γὰρ διὰ νόμου νόμῳ ἀπέθανον, ἵνα θεῷ ζήσω. The first prepositional phrase (διὰ νόμου) expresses means ("by means of the law"), and both datives indicate reference (νόμῳ ἀπέθανον ... θεῷ ζήσω).

73. "Since Jesus lived under the law, he could free those who lived under the dominion of sin and the law. The reign of the law ended, therefore, 'through the law.' Jesus in his death took the full penalty of the law upon himself, even though as the sinless one he did not deserve its curse (3:10, 13). By dying under the law he ended the era of the law, and those who have died with Christ share in his victory over the law" (Schreiner, *Galatians*, 171). See also Alford, *New Testament*, 2:332.

The other possibility is that Paul is referring to the believer's experience. His attempts to achieve righteousness by means of the law fail, and so he is driven to Jesus (see Lightfoot, *Galatians*, 118–19). I don't believe this fits best, but it is certainly defensible.

God somehow joins believer's souls and beings to Christ in an invisible union with his death and resurrection. Paul makes the same point at length in Rom 6:1–14. Our souls and identities are fused with Christ's. Paul is talking about why being "dead to the law" (that is, to all attempts to earn God's favor by any means other than faith in Christ) frees one to live for God—because *now* there has been a divine metamorphosis of soul, spirit, and identity. These are not metaphors, they're real. Salvation means we no longer live for ourselves, but for God whom we love because he first loved us. His Son "loved me and gave himself for me." This is sweet and simple and precious. It is truth. It kills all ideas of earning salvation by merit—or it ought to.

1. Christ was crucified and died—so has the "old you"
2. Christ has been raised from the dead and given new life—so has the "new you"

Jesus can do this for us because he is our new and better proxy or delegate. In Rom 5, Paul introduces this analogy of a delegate. This is a person who is appointed to act for and represent others.[74] For example, under the terms of the US Constitution the president is chosen by *electors* or *delegates* from each state who represent the will of their jurisdiction's choice as expressed by popular vote. So, the state of Washington sends *electors* to Congress who cast votes for the nominee which reflects the Washington state popular vote result for the ticket. Citizens do not directly elect a president—our *electors* or *delegates* act for us, on our behalf. Their actions become ours.

In the eternal sphere there are two great delegates: (a) we are each born belonging to Adam, but (b) a new and better delegate is on offer in the person of Jesus of Nazareth. We each belong to Adam, which is bad news for us. Adam is not a good delegate, because he and Eve chose to rebel against God. They acted for us. "Therefore, just as sin entered the world through one man, and death through sin, and in this way death came to all people, because all sinned" (Rom 5:12). This is the explanation for sin and evil:

1. Because our first delegate back in the garden in Gen 3 represented us so badly, he ruined us. He ruined our hearts, our minds, and severed our prospective relationships with God. Adam's failure as our delegate made us all God's enemies (cf. Rom 5:10).

---

74. *OED*, s.v. "delegate," sense 1.a, accessed July 2023.

The Trouble in Antioch

2. So, we're each born following that warped moral track our first parents laid. We are "by nature utterly void of that holiness required by the law of God, positively inclined to evil; and therefore under just condemnation to eternal ruin, without defense or excuse."[75]

3. and so we each sin,

4. and so we each die,

5. and so our only hope is a *new and better delegate* to take us along a better track.

Therefore, because he loves us (John 3:16), God has sent us this better delegate whom we can choose instead of Adam—his own beloved Son. Jesus never rebelled against God. Jesus loved his Father perfectly and obeyed his law cheerfully. Therefore, Satan has no legal charge against Jesus, and so the penalty of death doesn't apply to him. Our delegate determines our fate—so which delegate do we want to represent us?

Paul contrasts this choice of delegates—Adam or Christ?—throughout Rom 5:12–21. God's gracious gift of righteousness is not like that first trespass, because his *responses* to each are so startlingly different (Rom 5:15). Your delegate determines your fate:

The *results* of the two delegate's actions are also different. Adam gives his followers legal condemnation because of his one single sin, while Jesus offers the gift of righteousness from God despite our *many, repeated* sins (Rom 5:16):

---

75. Schaff, *Creeds of Christendom*, 3:743, "1833 New Hampshire Confession," art. 3.

Delegate No. 1: Adam	Delegate No. 2: Christ
Judgment followed one sin and brought condemnation.	The gift followed many trespasses and brought legal acquittal and pardon.

Why is this so? Because of the dueling "reigns" which each delegate offers. By means of Adam's sin, death reigns through him.[76] But those who "receive God's abundant provision of grace and of the gift of righteousness" will reign in life through Jesus Christ (Rom 5:17). Righteousness is a *gift*.

Delegate No. 1: Adam	Delegate No. 2: Christ
Adam's sin brings a reign of death through Adam.	God's gift of righteousness brings a reign of life through Jesus.

As a result, while on the one hand (a) Adam's one sin resulted in a legal conviction ("condemnation") for everyone, the other choice is that (b) Jesus' one righteous act (his death on the cross) results in justification—a gift and declaration of righteousness—for all people (Rom 5:18). "For just

---

76. Gk: εἰ γὰρ τῷ τοῦ ἑνὸς παραπτώματι ὁ θάνατος ἐβασίλευσεν διὰ τοῦ ἑνός. The dative in τῷ τοῦ ἑνὸς παραπτώματι likely expresses means, but it may denote reason ("because of the trespass of the one man"). The preposition at διὰ τοῦ ἑνός conveys personal agency ("through Adam").

as through the disobedience of the one man the many were made sinners, so also through the obedience of the one man the many will be made righteous" (Rom 5:19).

This "Jesus = our delegate or proxy" analogy involves both (a) the idea of a simple substitute (him for us, in our place) and (b) the concept of a representative—Jesus speaks and acts for us, in our name, as our legal proxy. We act in and through him and vice versa. God has punished us, via Jesus as proxy, because he is our legal representative. This is a substitutional representation, "an inclusionary place-taking."[77]

We return to Galatians:

> I have been crucified with Christ and I no longer live, but Christ lives in me. The life I now live in the body, I live by faith in the Son of God, who loved me and gave himself for me. (Gal 2:20)

If we choose Jesus as our delegate, then our souls and identities are fused with his. He died. We died. He rose to new life. So did we. Salvation is like a divine portal that transforms us—body, soul, and mind—and invokes a status shift. It's *righteousness from God*—the divine gift of Rom 5:17—that is the hinge: "You have been set free from sin and have become slaves to righteousness" (Rom 6:18). This salvation portal is a "before and after" passageway that shifts reality in a very real way. We're rescued from the evil kingdom and transferred to the kingdom of God's dear son (Col 1:13).

---

77. Craig, *Atonement and the Death of Christ*, 204. See esp. all of Craig's chapters 10–11.

Faith Working Through Love

Fusion of soul and identity with Jesus.

Paul explains elsewhere: "We know that our old self was crucified with him so that the body ruled by sin might be done away with, that we should no longer be slaves to sin" (Rom 6:6). The "old you" is now gone—crucified and "killed" in union with Jesus Christ—so that it could be tossed aside, be ended, be finished, be buried and forgotten. Because the "old you" is dead and buried (as it were), that means slavery's chain is broken. Now you're a *new person*, because you've been "born again" and given spiritual life from above (John 3:3, 16–17).

If this is true, then spiritual life has nothing to do with whether you follow old traditions about purity laws. It never did. Moses never taught that. David never taught that. Nothing in the Mosaic law taught that. Salvation is not a merit system, where your status as a child of God depends on how well you play the game. Instead, salvation is trusting that Jesus can rescue you from Satan, cleanse you from all unrighteousness, obtain legal satisfaction for your sins, and restore your relationship with God—and it is deciding to make him your King in response to this good news.

The result is to "live by faith in the Son of God, who loved me and gave himself for me." It is true joy and peace—freedom from all merit-based schemes to earn favor with God (i.e., freedom from "the law"). Paul sums the whole matter up in this beautiful statement:

> I do not set aside the grace of God, for if righteousness could be gained through the law, Christ died for nothing! (Gal 2:21)[78]

---

78. Gk: Οὐκ ἀθετῶ τὴν χάριν τοῦ θεοῦ· εἰ γὰρ διὰ νόμου δικαιοσύνη, ἄρα Χριστὸς δωρεὰν

If we could be good enough on our own, then Christ wouldn't have had to come and die for our sake. But, we can't. So, he did. It's really that simple.[79]

If anything we do *could be* good enough to become righteous in God's eyes, then why did Christ have to come here? To believe otherwise would be to *cancel, nullify, frustrate,* or *toss aside* God's grace. It would be treating it like a Christmas gift of socks with little reindeer on them—the kind where you say, "Oh . . . thanks!" before setting them aside and forgetting about them. You don't value the reindeer socks. You don't care about the reindeer socks. You smile politely and toss them. That's what Peter and Barnabas are doing to God's grace when they push gentile Christians away. It's what anybody does when they (a) claim to know, believe, trust in, and love Christ, but (b) believe our righteousness still depends on *what we do*.

Now that the stage is set and the issues are squarely on the table, Paul has arrived at the heart of this letter.

ἀπέθανεν. "I do not cancel God's grace. Because, if righteousness could come by means of the law, then Christ died for no reason."

79. "Evidently Paul assumes that a falling back upon legal works for justification or righteousness is radically inconsistent with justification through faith in Christ. It must be one thing or the other: a combination of the two is out of the question. If a man can be justified by the law, he needs no Saviour. If he needs Christ at all, it is because he is condemned by the law. Observe how closely the death of Christ and the grace of God are here connected" (Hovey, *Galatians*, 35).

On Samantha Stephens and Salvation
(vv. 3:1–6)

SAMANTHA STEPHENS IS A witch who fell in love with an advertising executive. Such was the depth of their love that Samantha is ready to cast aside spells, sorcery, and other dark arts to become a sweet suburban housewife. Her mother disapproved—how could her darling daughter marry a mortal man? The first episode of the series *Bewitched* shows the disappointed mother visiting Samantha on her wedding night. The anxious husband waits outside to consummate their union, while the mother tries in vain to convince her daughter to ditch the guy. But Samantha won't budge. So, the happy couple starts a life together.

The first installment of *Bewitched* also featured Samantha's magical revenge upon catty guests at a dinner party. The episode ends with the witch casting a spell upon the dinner dishes to clean themselves while she and her husband adjourn to the bedroom.

Samantha's bewitching powers were benign, silly. They make us laugh. The idea, of course, is that an otherworldly force is at work to trick, to deceive. Samantha deploys this mischievous force by twitching her nose. The apostle Paul uses the idea in the same way, but in an infinitely darker context—the word he uses in his language conjured up images of "the evil eye." Bad people have tricked the Christians in Galatia, to the point that Paul sarcastically suggests they're under a spell of some sort. It's the nature of this error that occupies Paul's time throughout chapters 3–4.

This is a tricky issue, and it's the heart of Paul's message in this letter. But, there is a key—a simple question one can ask that will unlock the whole thing. It's a question for which every reader of Galatians must have an opinion. How you answer this question will determine whether you

On Samantha Stephens and Salvation

rightly or wrongly understand this letter. Here is the question: *Did God intend the Mosaic law to be a means of salvation?*

That's it. That's the question. If you can answer it, then you've unlocked the key to this letter. No matter what happens, if you continually ask yourself *this question* and remind yourself of the answer, then you can understand this book. If you don't ask the question, then you'll likely go wrong. If you answer it wrongly, then you'll take a bad turn pretty quick. I'll explain by and by—let's dive into the heart of this letter.

> You foolish Galatians! Who has bewitched you? Before your very eyes Jesus Christ was clearly portrayed as crucified. (Gal 3:1)

They've been tricked. Fooled. Hoodwinked. They know the truth, but they've been convinced otherwise. Paul preached the truth to them—they saw him explain with their own eyes, heard with their own ears. Paul *clearly* and *vividly* described Christ as having been crucified. He died for a reason, didn't he? Remember this:

1. If righteousness from God *could have* come by means of the law (i.e., by means of works righteousness of any sort), then Christ died for no reason (Gal 2:21).
2. But we *cannot* gain righteousness from God by means of works of the law. This is why the Christian story centers on a divine intervention in our lives by the eternal Son of God—Jesus.
3. So, Christ *did* die for a reason.
4. That reason was to fulfill all righteousness for us, in our place, as our substitute: "Christ is the culmination of the law so that there may be righteousness for everyone who believes" (Rom 10:4).

The Christians in Galatia used to know this. Yet they're being bewitched, and by someone much more sinister than Samantha. They know better than this. As Paul asks his question in Gal 3:2, we should picture him holding up his hand to forestall any heated objection from his audience.

> I would like to learn just one thing from you: Did you receive the Spirit by the works of the law, or by believing what you heard? (Gal 3:2)

"No!" he says. "You listen! Lemme ask you one thing—did you receive the Spirit by *doing things to gain God's favor*, or by just believing what you heard? Which one!?"

The question is rhetorical. They know the answer. They know what Paul taught them. There's nothing to say. The Spirit is tied to salvation, and that has never been by works—by *doing things* from the Mosaic law.

Paul is always focused on the *means* of obtaining righteousness from God. How do we get it? What must we do? There are only two possible answers: (a) by *means of* works of the law (i.e., works righteousness of any sort), or (b) by *means of* faith and trust in Jesus Christ and his Good News for you.[1] Did you receive the Holy Spirit by means of the law or by means of believing what you heard?

> Are you so foolish? After beginning by means of the Spirit, are you now trying to finish by means of the flesh? (Gal 3:3)

Paul is deliberately provocative. To miss the gospel and wander off into Jewish legalism is a terrible mistake. He'll explain just how big a mistake it is later (Gal 4:8–10). But, for now, he presses the point home with another rhetorical question. If they admit they *did* receive the Holy Spirit by simply believing the truth about Jesus (not by working to curry favor), then do they *really suppose* they must now add "things" to Jesus, to seal the deal? Add works? Add rules as a vehicle for merit?

What about the psalmist who wrote, "I seek you *with all my heart*; do not let me stray from your commands. I have hidden your word *in my heart* that I might not sin against you" (Ps 119:10–11)? What about the prophet Samuel, who in his farewell address to the people told them, "be sure to fear the LORD and serve him faithfully *with all your heart*; consider what great things he has done for you" (1 Sam 12:24)? Loving obedience is the fruit of real relationship with God. This is the same principle the apostle John learned from Jesus: "This is love: not that we loved God, *but that he loved us* and sent his Son as an atoning sacrifice for our sins. . . . *We love because he first loved us*" (1 John 4:10, 19).

Rules are fine. Rules are good. God has standards of conduct. But these flow from a true love for God—not the other way around. This is the great tragedy of Judaism in Jesus' day and in Paul's. It's why Jesus was so unhappy with the religious establishment. It's why they were so angry at him. They spoke different languages, as it were—they had different faiths. They had a different God.

---

1. Paul continues his dueling prepositions that contrast the means of each option. "Did you receive the Spirit by the works of the law [ἐξ ἔργων νόμου], or by believing what you heard [ἢ ἐξ ἀκοῆς πίστεως]?"

On Samantha Stephens and Salvation

The Jewish establishment had a God of legalism, where relationship was predicated on *right conduct* (orthopraxy). To have a relationship with God, you gotta follow the rules. So, for example:[2]

1. A beggar who reaches inside a home on the Sabbath to receive a food gift has committed sin. The act of reaching *inside* the window makes it so.[3]
2. If you search your clothes for fleas on the Sabbath, you have sinned.[4]
3. On the Sabbath, you must only roast meat if there is time for a crust to form on the surface, during the daytime. If you fail in this, you have sinned.[5]
4. If you rise to extinguish a lamp because you're afraid of gentiles or thugs, don't worry—it isn't a sin![6]
5. God kills women in childbirth because they are insufficiently reverent when preparing the dough offering.[7]

I could go on. But it's clear there is little love in this kind of relationship. Where is the love? There can't be loving obedience under this kind of system. This is why Jesus said, "They tie up heavy, cumbersome loads and put them on other people's shoulders" (Matt 23:4). One writer summed up this "other gospel" pretty well:

> Nothing was left to free personality. Everything was placed under the bondage of the letter. The Israelite, zealous for the law, was obliged at every impulse and movement to ask himself, what is commanded.
> At every step, at the work of his calling, and prayer, at meals, at home and abroad, from early morning till late in the evening, from youth to old age, the dead, the deadening formula followed

---

2. The Mishnah dates from approximately AD 200. But it is a generally accurate compendium of tradition and rules that were around in Jesus' day. We see a strong resemblance of its Sabbath regulations in Mark 7. Even if one wishes to quibble about the precise applicability of a book compiled around 170 years after Jesus' death, it still captures the *flavor* and *ethos* of the relationship this system imagines God has with his people.

3. Neusner, *Mishnah*, Shabbat 1:1.
4. Neusner, *Mishnah*, Shabbat 1:3.
5. Neusner, *Mishnah*, Shabbat 1:10.
6. Neusner, *Mishnah*, Shabbat 2:5.
7. Neusner, *Mishnah*, Shabbat 2:6.

> him. A healthy moral life could not flourish under such a burden, action was nowhere the result of inward motive, all was, on the contrary, weighed and measured.
>
> Life was a continual tournament to the earnest man, who felt at every moment that he was in danger of transgressing the law; and where so much depended on the external form, he was often left in uncertainty whether he had really fulfilled its requirements.[8]

So, yes—it's foolish to fall for this. To believe *this* is a real relationship with God. To believe the false teachers who are peddling this nonsense. That's why Paul is upset.

> Have you experienced so much in vain—if it really was in vain? So again I ask, does God give you his Spirit and work miracles among you by the works of the law, or by your believing what you heard? (Gal 3:4–5)

Is everything they've suffered and experienced pointless?[9] The Jews in these churches had likely been alienated from family, from friends, from the diaspora society. They'd been shunned. They'd suffered. Was it all worthless? All for nothing? Paul repeats his question under a different cover—do we *work* to be rewarded with salvation's blessings, or do we simply *believe* what we hear about Christ? By what means do we obtain righteousness from God? By what means did God grant the Holy Spirit? By means of the works of the law, or by means of believing what they heard? Again, the answer is clear.

> So also Abraham "believed God, and it was credited to him as righteousness." (Gal 3:6)

The answer is "we believed what we heard about Christ." Good! They're in great company, then—because Abraham also believed God and was counted righteous. He received righteousness from God (cf. Rom 1:17). We should all follow Abraham's example! He had the right idea long before the post-exilic community twisted up the Mosaic law into knots and perverted the whole thing. The Bible is the story of what N. T. Wright calls God's "single-plan-through-Israel-for-the-world."

---

8. Schurer, *History of the Jewish People*, 2.2:125. See also all 2.2:28.

9. The word could mean *suffering*, or it could be a more general term meaning to *experience* something. Most modern English translations choose the latter, but it could be the former. See LSJ, s.v. "πάσχω," 1346; and L&N, s.v. "πάσχω," 33.66, 33.191.

God had a single plan all along through which he intended to rescue the world and the human race, and that this single plan was centered upon the call of Israel, a call which Paul saw coming to fruition in Israel's representative, the Messiah. Read Paul like this, and you can keep all the jigsaw pieces on the table.[10]

To believe in "salvation by resume-ism" is to ignore the Bible's story, to lose the plot. So, Paul suggests, let's *go back to Abraham* and see what he can teach us about real faith—what the Christian story has always been about.

---

10. Wright, *Justification*, loc. 326–29. To be sure, Wright would disagree with my traditional view of Paul's point in Galatians. But he's on the right track about the Bible's story.

On Bad Checks, "Mirror Reading," and the Mosaic Law

(vv. 3:7–14)

Have you ever listened to just one side of a conversation? You know the kind I mean—someone near you is talking on the phone, you can't hear the other person, so you try to figure out what's going on by listening closely to what the person next to you is saying. If you're able to ask the person about it afterward, you might discover you figured it out right, or you might have got it all wrong!

We do stuff like this all the time. Some time ago, I once ran an investigations team for a state agency. In one case, we had an insurance agent who we suspected had stolen lots of money from commercial clients. These companies would write the agent checks for property and general liability insurance for one-year terms. The agent would then alter the payee field to falsely say the consumer wrote the check out to his own personal, unrelated business account. He'd then deposit the checks and provide fake certificates of insurance to the companies. He never placed the insurance. Nobody knew a thing—until someone tried to file a claim. Oops.

But there was something weird. The agent also wrote a few checks out to his agency *from that same unrelated business account*, but he'd falsify the payor field to say it was from a commercial client. We had no idea why he did this—he refused an interview with our investigators. So, we had to do what theologians call "mirror reading." This means we have to guess at the context which prompted the action—we have to speculate, just like you did with that one half of a phone call you listened to.

In this case, we guessed the agent felt pressured to send at least *some* of the money he stole along to the agency, so people wouldn't grow too suspicious. There were smarter ways to do it, but that was our best guess. Nobody ever said this guy was a genius!

My point is that when we read chapters 3–4 from the book of Galatians, we also must do a bit of mirror reading. We must take what we know about God, the gospel, salvation, and relationship with God and bring it to bear to decipher what Paul is saying. Here, we'll see why the "key question" I mentioned before is so important.

I'll let Paul explain what I mean.

> Understand, then, that those who have faith are children of Abraham. (Gal 3:7)

Who is a child of Abraham? Well, it certainly isn't about biology. About genetics. About who your parents are. John the Baptist understood that (Matt 3:7–10). No, it isn't about race or ethnicity—it's about common faith in Jesus. It's about faith, not blood!

Your status as a child of Abraham springs *out of* or *from* faith—this faith is the fountainhead and source of your family status (contra NIV, which obscures the nuance of the Greek).[1] It has nothing to do with your genetics. If you have Abraham's faith, then you're one of his children.

This is a straightforward statement that has enormous implications for the Christian life and for understanding the Christian story aright. Abraham is the biological father of the Israelites. Being an "Israelite" had long been understood to be a genetic marker, not a spiritual one. The old covenant scriptures repeatedly refer to "Israel" as the *physical* descendants of Abraham (Isa 29:22; 41:8). Abraham is their father and Sarah is the mother "who gave you birth" (Isa 51:2). God said the Israelites were "my people . . . my nation" (Isa 51:4).

But Paul now upends this whole idea. The "child of God" concept isn't an ethnic thing at all. He says it's a *spiritual marker*, a status awarded by faith. So, when Paul writes, "we know, then, that the ones who derive from faith are Abraham's children" (Gal 3:7), he is, in effect, saying, "the ones who have been justified by means of faith in Christ Jesus (Gal 2:16)—*these* are the ones who are Abraham's children."

So far, Paul's argument beginning from Gal 3:5 onward goes like this:

---

1. Gk: οἱ ἐκ πίστεως. "The ones from faith . . ." The preposition expresses space or derivation (see Robertson, *Word Pictures*, on Gal 3:7; and Alford, *New Testament*, 2:335).

1	*Justification from God comes by means of faith.* God gives Christians his Spirit and works miracles by means of believing the gospel, and not by means of works of the law.	Galatians 3:5
2	*It was the same with Abraham.* In the same way, Abraham also believed God, who then credited him with righteousness.	Galatians 3:6
3	*Who, then, is a child of Abraham?* Everyone whose righteousness derives from faith is a child of Abraham.	Galatians 3:7

Paul continues:

> Scripture foresaw that God would justify the Gentiles by faith, and announced the gospel in advance to Abraham: "All nations will be blessed through you." (Gal 3:8)

God announced the gospel to Abraham *in advance* when he announced that "all nations will be blessed through you" (see Gen 12:3; 18:18; 22:18). God always intended the gospel to be for the gentiles *as well as* the physical descendants of Abraham. He'd planned to declare the gentiles to be righteous *by means of* their faith and trust in his promise.[2]

This tracks with Isaiah's prophecy of the Lord's special servant who would "bring justice to the nations" (Isa 42:1) and never rest "till he establishes justice on earth" (Isa 42:4). Isaiah declared, "In his teaching the islands will put their hope" (Isa 42:4). These "islands" are Cyprus, Rhodes, and smaller isles across the Aegean Sea and the eastern Mediterranean—they are clearly gentiles. The LXX (the Greek translation of the Old Testament from which Jesus and the apostles quoted) is even more specific about the Messianic implications. It reads, "And in His [the servant's] name the nations will hope!"[3] God declared that he would make his chosen servant "to be a covenant for the people and a light for the Gentiles" (Isa 42:6). God "watches over the foreigner" in the same way he sustains the fatherless and the widow (Ps 146:9)—*anyone* who loves him is a member of his family.

God will send out his law or instruction to the world, and "my justice will become a light *to the nations*" (Isa 51:4). The metaphors pile up! What is the content of this instruction? It must be related to God's *justice* and *decision* that follow on its heels. It also must be attractive, because this divine justice is a light that draws *the nations* to God. What can it be but the Good News of righteousness from God by faith in Jesus? After all, "Christ is the culmination of the law so that there may be righteousness for *everyone* who believes" (Rom 10:4). Returning to Isaiah, the prophet then declared:

2. Gk: ἐκ πίστεως.
3. Gk: καὶ ἐπὶ τῷ ὀνόματι αὐτοῦ ἔθνη ἐλπιοῦσιν.

> My salvation is on the way,
> and my arm will bring justice *to the nations.*
> *The islands* will look to me
> and *wait in hope* for my arm. (Isa 51:6)

Earlier, Isaiah had predicted the most powerful nations of his time (Assyria and Egypt) would one day worship the Lord along with Israel (Isa 19:23–25)—what one commentator called a "one world, one people, one God" reality.[4] There would even be a "highway" (Isa 19:23; cf. "Road of Holiness" at Isa 35:8) connecting Assyria and Egypt to Israel—a metaphor Isaiah often used to convey the idea of a mass exodus from "Babylon" to safety in Zion (see Isa 35:8–10).

It's safe to say gentiles have always been a part of God's plan. To be sure, things sometimes only seem "clear" *after* the fact. Paul acknowledged that full gentile participation in God's family had been a mystery not fully appreciated. "This mystery is that through the gospel the Gentiles are heirs together with Israel, members together of one body, and sharers together in the promise in Christ Jesus" (Eph 3:6).

But the Messiah has now come and gone. The Spirit provides spiritual illumination and communion with Father and Son. The mystery has been revealed—why the resistance?

Tradition is so powerful. In light of promises so explicit, how could the Jewish religious culture degenerate to the point where Peter could tell Cornelius, "It is against our law for a Jew to associate with or visit a Gentile" (Acts 10:28)? This is wrong, Paul says, because the "Scripture foresaw that God would justify the Gentiles by faith" (Gal 3:8).

Who is the conduit for this blessing to the nations? Is it (a) Abraham himself, (b) the Israelite nation as a geopolitical entity, (c) the Jewish people in general, or perhaps (d) a very special descendant from Abraham?

God told Abraham, "All nations will be blessed through you" (Gen 12:3; cf. 18:18; 22:18). On its face, this seems to be a promise that (a) Abraham or (b) the nation that will emerge from him will be the source of blessing to the nations. The apostle Peter tells us that Jesus' resurrection triggered the era of this blessing (Acts 3:25). Peter also said that *one singular offspring*[5] from Abraham would be the channel for this divine blessing (Acts 3:25), which is a point Paul will soon note (Gal 3:16–20).

---

4. Motyer, *Isaiah*, 154.

5. Gk: καὶ ἐν τῷ σπέρματί σου ἐνευλογηθήσονται πᾶσαι αἱ πατριαὶ τῆς γῆς. The "descendant" is singular.

This suggests the conduit for divine blessing (a) is not Abraham himself, (b) is not the geopolitical nation of Israel, and (c) is not the Jewish people in general. Instead, the mediator of the gospel blessing is one very special "son of Abraham" (Matt 1:1) who reveals "the power of God that brings salvation to *everyone* who believes" (Rom 1:16).

Who is he, then? Who in the Christian story is linked with Abraham and *directly blesses* gentile believers (actually, all believers)? Of course, it is Jesus. He (the ultimate Israelite) is the hinge of God's single plan through Israel for the world.

Paul's train of thought now looks like this:

1	*Justification from God comes by means of faith.* God gives Christians his Spirit and works miracles by means of believing the gospel, and not by means of works of the law.	Galatians 3:5
2	*It was the same with Abraham.* In the same way, Abraham also believed God, who then credited him with righteousness.	Galatians 3:6
3	*Who, then, is a child of Abraham?* Everyone whose righteousness derives from faith is a child of Abraham.	Galatians 3:7
4	*Gentiles were always part of the gospel plan.* God promised to justify the gentiles by faith and swore that a special descendant from Abraham would bless the nations with the gospel.	Galatians 3:8

> So those who rely on faith are blessed along with Abraham, the man of faith. (Gal 3:9)

You could translate this as something like, "this means, then, that those who derive from faith are blessed together with faithful Abraham."[6] If you want to be one of Abraham's children, then (just like him, cf. Gen 15:6) your status *derives from* or *finds its source* and fountainhead in faith. But, faith in what? In Jesus and the gift of righteousness from God which he offers *by means of* faith. These people are blessed in the same way as Abraham—that crediting of righteousness which God granted to Abraham is now ours, too. It's the *same* status change, the *same* declaration from God. And, it's all derived from faith and not biology.

---

6. The Greek reads: ὥστε οἱ ἐκ πίστεως εὐλογοῦνται σὺν τῷ πιστῷ Ἀβραάμ. The conjunction ὥστε is inferential and introduces a conclusion from what preceded, and once more the NIV elides the nuance of the Greek. The preposition at οἱ ἐκ πίστεως expresses source or derivation, as at Gal 3:7. It is not "those who rely on faith" but "those who derive from faith." The σὺν is a preposition linking two objects—it means those whose status derives from faith in Jesus are blessed *in the same way* as Abraham.

On Bad Checks, "Mirror Reading," and the Mosaic Law

This is extraordinary. The false teachers skulking around the area are pushing the rules-based legalism we noted earlier. The apogee of their "faith" is to be as Jewish as possible, which, in their warped understanding, means to follow the rules and traditions of the elders very strictly (see Phil 3:4–6). Thus, the Mishnah says you violate the Sabbath if you put spices into a pot, but all is well if you add spices to food served on a dish![7]

Not so, says Paul. Your pedigree before God has nothing to do with this. It only has to do with whether your status before God (righteous or unrighteous?) is derived from faith and trust in God's promise—just like Abraham's.

1	*Justification from God comes by means of faith.* God gives Christians his Spirit and works miracles by means of believing the gospel, and not by means of works of the law.	Galatians 3:5
2	*It was the same with Abraham.* In the same way, Abraham also believed God, who then credited him with righteousness.	Galatians 3:6
3	*Who, then, is a child of Abraham?* Everyone whose righteousness derives from faith is a child of Abraham.	Galatians 3:7
4	*Gentiles were always part of the gospel plan.* God promised to justify the gentiles by faith and swore that a special descendant from Abraham would bless the nations with the gospel.	Galatians 3:8
5	*People who derive from faith and trust in Jesus share the same blessing of righteousness that God gave Abraham.* These people can be Jews, gentile, or whoever—anyone who has the righteousness from God that comes by means of faith, not by means of works.	Galatians 3:9

Now, we get down to the hard part. Remember that question about which I said you must have an opinion? Let's ask ourselves again:

- *Question*: Did God ever intend the Mosaic law to be a way of salvation?
- *Answer*: Nope! It never happened.

This means that, however difficult Paul may be to follow from here on out, he *cannot be agreeing with the false teachers* that the Mosaic law was a vehicle for salvation. Never. It isn't an option. God doesn't change the terms of salvation. It's always been by means of faith and trust in Jesus. So, remember this question *and* the right answer, because Paul now shifts into high gear.

Why are the people whose status before God derives from faith blessed alongside Abraham, the man of faith (Gal 3:9)? Paul explains:

---

7. Neusner, *Mishnah*, Shabbat 3:5.

> For all who rely on the works of the law are under a curse, as it is written: "Cursed is everyone who does not continue to do everything written in the Book of the Law." (Gal 3:10, quoting Deut 27:26)

The NIV translation once again tries to help too much.[8] Paul writes: "those who *derive from* the works of the law are under a curse." These are folks whose status before God *comes from* the works of the law. The *source* of their identity, status, and being comes from merit. This is a contrast between Gal 3:9 and Gal 3:10—where is the source of your identity, status, and relationship with God? Is it faith or works?

Galatians 3:9		Galatians 3:10
Those who *derive from faith* (ἐκ πίστεως) are blessed with faithful Abraham	vs.	Those who *derive from works of the law* (ἐξ ἔργων νόμου) are under a curse

The "for" at the beginning of Gal 3:10 is explanatory.[9] It could be rendered as something like, "so, this is what I'm saying—everyone who derives from the works of the law is under a curse." What is this curse? Paul quotes Deut 27:26 and seems to suggest that everyone who doesn't follow the law perfectly is cursed.

Now, remember—because the Mosaic law (a) was never *about* salvation, and (b) was never a vehicle *for* salvation, then (c) Paul cannot seriously be suggesting the Mosaic law means this. He can't be.

I believe he means, "Look, if you want to go that route and try to earn your salvation, then have at it—here's a quote from Moses that you can chew on!" He accurately quotes *the text* of Deut 27:26 but must be deliberately subverting the *meaning* to make a point. Moses didn't preach salvation by works. When he asked the people to swear that promise in Deut 27:26 (along with a bunch of others), he *presupposed* that everyone understood that love was the driving force behind relationship with God (Deut 6:4–5; 10:12–16). Moses had already told them *why* they must obey God: "follow these decrees and laws; carefully observe them *with all your heart and with all your soul*" (Deut 26:16). I'm saying Paul misapplied Deut 27:26 the same way the Jewish agitators were doing. Paul is saying, "If you want to go that way, have fun trying to accomplish *this*." His point relies on you understanding everything he just wrote in Gal 3:7–9.

---

8. The preposition at Ὅσοι γὰρ ἐξ ἔργων νόμου εἰσίν, ὑπὸ κατάραν εἰσίν conveys *source* or *derivation*, just as at Gal 3:9.

9. The preposition is γὰρ, which is explanatory.

On Bad Checks, "Mirror Reading," and the Mosaic Law

1. Salvation is by faith—always has been.
2. Abraham had faith and was counted righteous.
3. That's how you become one of Abraham's children—righteousness by means of faith in the promise.

So, the "curse" Paul mentions isn't the Mosaic law as it really was. Instead, the "curse" is the impossible burden of trying to adopt the Judaizers' *wrong understanding* of the Mosaic law. Some Christians wrongly imagine old covenant life as an oppressive burden, a millstone dragging the believers to a watery grave until Christ came! They believe this because they take Paul literally in Gal 3:10–12—they believe he's describing the Mosaic law as it really was. They're mistaken.

1	*Justification from God comes by means of faith.* God gives Christians his Spirit and works miracles by means of believing the gospel, and not by means of works of the law.	Galatians 3:5
2	*It was the same with Abraham.* In the same way, Abraham also believed God, who then credited him with righteousness.	Galatians 3:6
3	*Who, then, is a child of Abraham?* Everyone whose righteousness derives from faith is a child of Abraham.	Galatians 3:7
4	*Gentiles were always part of the gospel plan.* God promised to justify the gentiles by faith and swore that a special descendant from Abraham would bless the nations with the gospel.	Galatians 3:8
5	*People who derive from faith and trust in Jesus share the same blessing of righteousness that God gave Abraham.* These people can be Jews, gentile, or whoever—anyone who has the righteousness from God that comes by means of faith, not by means of works.	Galatians 3:9
6	*On the other hand, people who derive from works of the law are under a curse.* If you want to misinterpret the Mosaic law as a means of salvation, then have fun trying to do everything it says. According to that wrong interpretation, you'll be cursed if you fail to follow the law perfectly.	Galatians 3:10

Instead, Paul *adopts the Judaizers' arguments* to show how bankrupt they are. Read Ps 119 and see if the writer is being crushed by the law! "Open my eyes that I may see wonderful things in your law" (Ps 119:18). He doesn't sound cursed! He loves God and loves his word (including the Mosaic law). The law is only a millstone if you think it's a means for salvation and righteousness. But, it ain't one, so it ain't a millstone.

Faith Working Through Love

I'm comfortable suggesting this, because Paul then sweeps aside this silly idea of "earning my salvation by merit."

> Clearly no one who relies on the law is justified before God, because "the righteous will live by faith." (Gal 3:11, quoting Hab 2:4)

Nobody will be declared righteous in God's eyes by means of the law.[10] Again, the law was never a means of salvation. The law can't make you righteous. Paul quotes Hab 2:4, which indeed says that "the righteous will live by faith." An alternative (and equally plausible translation) would be: "the one who is righteous *by means of faith* will live!" So, when he quotes Moses from Deut 27:26, he can't *really* be saying Moses meant it *that* way. Paul just adopts the arguments from the Jewish agitators or from similar sources floating about in the first century interwebs and suggests they have fun trying to do the impossible.

1	*Justification from God comes by means of faith.* God gives Christians his Spirit and works miracles by means of believing the gospel, and not by means of works of the law.	Galatians 3:5
2	*It was the same with Abraham.* In the same way, Abraham also believed God, who then credited him with righteousness.	Galatians 3:6
3	*Who, then, is a child of Abraham?* Everyone whose righteousness derives from faith is a child of Abraham.	Galatians 3:7
4	*Gentiles were always part of the gospel plan.* God promised to justify the gentiles by faith and swore that a special descendant from Abraham would bless the nations with the gospel.	Galatians 3:8
5	*People who derive from faith and trust in Jesus share the same blessing of righteousness that God gave Abraham.* These people can be Jews, gentile, or whoever—anyone who has the righteousness from God that comes by means of faith, not by means of works.	Galatians 3:9
6	*On the other hand, people who derive from works of the law are under a curse.* If you want to misinterpret the Mosaic law as a means of salvation, then have fun trying to do everything it says. According to that wrong interpretation, you'll be cursed if you fail to follow the law perfectly.	Galatians 3:10
7	*Because Habakkuk said the one who is righteous by means of faith will live,* it's very clear that nobody will be declared to be righteous in God's eyes by means of the law.	Galatians 3:11

10. Gk: ὅτι δὲ [*the conjunction δὲ continues the argument with a second reason*] ἐν νόμῳ οὐδεὶς δικαιοῦται παρὰ τῷ θεῷ δῆλον (δῆλον; a predicate adjective linked to the "nobody"). This reads: "Also, this is because it's clear that nobody is declared to be righteous in God's eyes by means of the law."

Paul continues in the same vein:

> The law is not based on faith; on the contrary, it says, "The person who does these things will live by them." (Gal 3:12, quoting Lev 18:5)

"Law" and "faith" are two different paradigms for obtaining righteousness from God. Like oil and water, they do not mix and they do not come from the same source—because they have very different motivations. The NIV reads, "the law is not based on faith," but perhaps a better rendering is "the law does not come *from the same place* as faith."[11]

Paul then unloads an accurate quote from Leviticus that is ripe for misunderstanding. In Lev 18:5, God said: "Keep my decrees and laws, *for the person who obeys them will live by them.* I am the LORD." This verse has generated a lot of confusion. When Moses wrote it in Leviticus, he meant that obedience to the law would bring *a blessed life.* He wasn't referring to eternal life, but a *blessed quality of life* that comes from God when a believer obeys from the heart.[12] Moses' audience already had a relationship with God ("I am the Lord your God," Lev 18:2). This means the quotation has nothing to do with *how to initiate* the relationship—it's about *growing* in the already existing relationship with God.[13]

But, without context, it seems like Paul is once more quoting a text that teaches salvation by means of works.[14] It seems like Paul is saying: "The

---

11. Gk: ὁ δὲ νόμος οὐκ ἔστιν ἐκ πίστεως. This means: "Now [δὲ *continues the argument*], the law does not come from the same place as [*the preposition* ἐκ *expresses source*] faith." The NIV understands the preposition as expressing the *basis* or *grounds* of a "law mindset" = it isn't based on faith. This is certainly possible, but I believe *source* better captures the contrast Paul has been going for throughout this section.

12. "What is envisaged is a happy life in which a man enjoys God's bounty of health, children, friends, and prosperity. Keeping the law is the path to divine blessing, to a happy and fulfilled life in the present (Lev. 26:3–13; Deut. 28:1–14)" (Wenham, *Leviticus*, loc. 3364–65).

13. "The phrase 'the man who obeys them will live by them' should thus be viewed as promising a meaningful, secure life for those who are faithful to God and who exhibit their faithfulness by obedience to the Law. Hence, the verse pertains more to sanctification than justification, as the repeated phrase 'I am the LORD your God' makes plain (18:2, 20). This phrase indicates that the Israelites already have a relationship with God; they are not called to obey in order to enter or initiate this relationship" (Rooker, *Leviticus*, 241).

14. It says: ὁ ποιήσας αὐτὰ ζήσεται ἐν αὐτοῖς, which reads, "the one who does these things will live by means of them." Paul seems to amend the LXX quotation to fit, but the true sense remains. The crux is what "live" means.

law doesn't come from the same place as faith. It's a totally different thing—even the law itself says you'll only live (i.e., have eternal life) *by means of keeping God's laws and decrees."* But, remember, because the Mosaic law was never the means of salvation, for Abraham or anyone else, then Paul can't really mean this.

So, what is Paul saying?

Paul once more rightly quotes the *text* but suggests the wrong *meaning*.[15] The "law" he mentions here is the wrong understanding of the Mosaic law, not the law as it really is. Again, he has adopted the false teachers' perspective for the sake of the argument—to show how very different "the way of the law" is from "the way of faith."

"Do you really want to go the way of legalism?" he asks. "Then, if you want eternal life, make sure you do *everything* in the law—just like it says. Have at it!"

Paul's argument now looks like this:

1	*Justification from God comes by means of faith.* God gives Christians his Spirit and works miracles by means of believing the gospel, and not by means of works of the law.	Galatians 3:5
2	*It was the same with Abraham.* In the same way, Abraham also believed God, who then credited him with righteousness.	Galatians 3:6
3	*Who, then, is a child of Abraham?* Everyone whose righteousness derives from faith is a child of Abraham.	Galatians 3:7
4	*Gentiles were always part of the gospel plan.* God promised to justify the gentiles by faith and swore that a special descendant from Abraham would bless the nations with the gospel.	Galatians 3:8
5	*People who derive from faith and trust in Jesus share the same blessing of righteousness that God gave Abraham.* These people can be Jews, gentile, or whoever—anyone who has the righteousness from God that comes by means of faith, not by means of works.	Galatians 3:9
6	*On the other hand, people who derive from works of the law are under a curse.* If you want to misinterpret the Mosaic law as a means of salvation, then have fun trying to do everything it says. According to that wrong interpretation, you'll be cursed if you fail to follow the law perfectly.	Galatians 3:10
7	*Because Habakkuk said the one who is righteous by means of faith will live,* it's very clear that nobody will be declared to be righteous in God's eyes by means of the law.	Galatians 3:11

---

15. See Harris, *Leviticus,* 597–99.

On Bad Checks, "Mirror Reading," and the Mosaic Law

| 8 | *We know that the "law" (that is, your wrong understanding of the Mosaic law) doesn't come from the same place as faith—it has very different motivations.* In fact, according to your own wrong understanding of Lev 18:5, if you want to have eternal life, you gotta do everything the law says. Good luck with that . . . | Galatians 3:12 |

> Christ redeemed us from the curse of the law by becoming a curse for us, for it is written: "Cursed is everyone who is hung on a pole." (Gal 3:13, quoting Deut 21:23)

I think we're making a mistake if we think "curse of the law" is the Mosaic law itself. The law isn't a curse. It isn't a bad thing. It isn't a burden, because it has nothing to do with salvation. The Mosaic law is simply a vehicle for holy living, while God's people remained in a holding pattern waiting for Christ. We've always obeyed from the heart *because* he's already rescued us—not the other way around. "Give me understanding, so that I may keep your laws and obey it *with all my heart* . . . I reach out for your commands, *which I love*, that I may meditate on your decrees" (Ps 119:34, 48). The man who wrote this didn't think he was "under a curse."

So, to return to our verse (Gal 3:13), from what "curse" did Christ redeem us?

Because Paul has been contrasting (a) those who derive from faith who are blessed with faithful Abraham (Gal 3:9) with (b) those who derive from works of the law who are under a curse (Gal 3:10), then (c) it seems best to see this "curse" from which Jesus has liberated us as being the wrong-headed, legalistic understanding of salvation. In the context of Paul's letter, this perversion of God's message is the curse from which Jesus has rescued us—he has shown us the *true* way, the *real* way of salvation.

To be sure, many people (like Simeon and Anna; see Luke 2) never fell victim to a works-righteousness version of "salvation." But, many more people *did* forget. They forgot that Moses wrote about love being the foundation for relationship with God—"circumcise your hearts!" (Deut 10:12–13, 16; 30:6). They forgot what the scripture says about King Josiah: "Neither before nor after Josiah was there a king like him who turned to the LORD as he did—*with all his heart* and with all his soul and with all his strength" (2 Kgs 23:25; cf. Deut 6:5; Mark 12:33). They forgot what the psalmist wrote: "I desire to do your will, my God; *your law is within my heart*" (Ps 40:8). He wants to do God's will *because* he loves God from the heart. Obedience comes from love.

Faith Working Through Love

Once we understand that Paul is saying, "Christ freed you from the curse of legalism—that is, 'the law' as you wrongly understand it!" then we must deal with his citation of Deut 21:23 ("for it is written: 'Cursed is everyone who is hung on a pole'"). Again, he adopts his opponent's wrong view for the sake of argument.

How so?

Deuteronomy 21:23 is about the death penalty for capital crimes. The offender's body must be displayed on a pole for all to see but removed before sundown. This public display is a sign of God's curse.

What does this have to do with Jesus? Well, he was displayed on a pole, as it were—on a cross. He suffered for our capital crime of rebellion against God.

But what does *that* have to do with Christ liberating us from the curse of the law? After all, Christ did not die to rescue us from slavery to the Mosaic law. We know this because the psalmist wrote things like: "My soul is consumed with longing for your laws at all times" (Ps 119:20). The solution is to see Paul as once more accurately quoting a *text*, but creatively applying its *meaning*. His thinking goes like this:

1. Christ freed you from the curse of legalism—from the wrong understanding of the Mosaic law that you're pushing.

2. That's why Deut 21:23 says that a person who commits a capital crime and is publicly displayed on a pole is under God's curse—because Christ died and was "cursed by God" to free you from your legalism.

3. You see, your legalism is actually a capital offense. You think you're right with God because of your works, but you're really just as bad as everyone else. You're still a criminal with no legal cover.

4. But Jesus has now freed you from this curse by being "cursed by God" on your behalf.

So, Paul isn't making a negative assessment of the Mosaic law. The "curse" here isn't even about the Mosaic law—it's about legalism.

1	*Justification from God comes by means of faith.* God gives Christians his Spirit and works miracles by means of believing the gospel, and not by means of works of the law.	Galatians 3:5
2	*It was the same with Abraham.* In the same way, Abraham also believed God, who then credited him with righteousness.	Galatians 3:6

3	*Who, then, is a child of Abraham? Everyone whose righteousness derives from faith is a child of Abraham.*	Galatians 3:7
4	*Gentiles were always part of the gospel plan. God promised to justify the gentiles by faith and swore that a special descendant from Abraham would bless the nations with the gospel.*	Galatians 3:8
5	*People who derive from faith and trust in Jesus share the same blessing of righteousness that God gave Abraham. These people can be Jews, gentile, or whoever—anyone who has the righteousness from God that comes by means of faith, not by means of works.*	Galatians 3:9
6	*On the other hand, people who derive from works of the law are under a curse. If you want to misinterpret the Mosaic law as a means of salvation, then have fun trying to do everything it says. According to that wrong interpretation, you'll be cursed if you fail to follow the law perfectly.*	Galatians 3:10
7	*Because Habakkuk said the one who is righteous by means of faith will live, it's very clear that nobody will be declared to be righteous in God's eyes by means of the law.*	Galatians 3:11
8	*We know that the "law" (that is, your wrong understanding of the Mosaic law) doesn't come from the same place as faith—it has very different motivations. In fact, according to your own wrong understanding of Lev 18:5, if you want to have eternal life, you gotta do everything the law says. Good luck with that ...*	Galatians 3:12
9	*Christ redeemed you from the "curse" of legalism—from your wrong understanding of salvation as something you must earn. Deuteronomy 21:23 says that someone who is executed for a capital crime and publicly displayed on a pole is cursed by God. Well, Jesus has now liberated you from the "curse" of works righteousness by becoming cursed by God on your behalf.*	Galatians 3:13

He redeemed us in order that the blessing given to Abraham might come to the Gentiles through Christ Jesus, so that by faith we might receive the promise of the Spirit. (Gal 3:14)

Christ liberated us from this curse of legalism for two reasons: (a) so that the blessing God granted to Abraham would come to pass for the nations through Christ Jesus, and (b) so that we'd receive the promise about the Spirit by means of this faith.[16]

---

16. Gk: ἵνα εἰς τὰ ἔθνη ἡ εὐλογία τοῦ Ἀβραὰμ γένηται ἐν Χριστῷ Ἰησοῦ, ἵνα τὴν ἐπαγγελίαν τοῦ πνεύματος λάβωμεν διὰ τῆς πίστεως. The two purpose (ἵνα) clauses explain why "Christ redeemed us from the curse of the law" (Gal 3:13).

Paul employs two purpose clauses: (a) "He liberated us so that ..." (ἵνα ... γένηται),

Christ brings the blessing to the nations. But he can't do it if we're still toiling away on our resumes, trying to score a job interview with God. As long as we're trusting in our resumes (in our knowledge, skills, and abilities), then we don't want the blessing. We're not interested.

But once Jesus frees and liberates us from that mindset—once we shred our resumes and trust in the righteousness he's offering to give us as a gift—*then* we can receive the promise about the Holy Spirit. How do we receive it? By means of faith. Not by means of our resume. Not by means of our professional references. Not by means of a selectively edited, bullet-point list of reasons why we're so awesome. Instead, we receive his righteousness by means of faith and trust in God and his promise—just like Abraham did.

Before God can rescue us, he must liberate us from slavery to our resumes, to our so-called achievements, to the idea we can earn favor with God. "I don't ignore the grace of God, because if we become righteous through the Law, then Christ died for no purpose" (Gal 2:21 CEB).

---

and (b) "so that we'd receive the promise about the Spirit..." (ἵνα ... λάβωμεν) to explain why Christ redeemed us from the curse of the law (i.e., legalism). Christ is the personal agent (ἐν Χριστῷ Ἰησοῦ) who brings to the nations the same blessing God granted to Abraham, and faith is the *instrumental means by which* (διὰ τῆς πίστεως) we receive the promise about the Spirit. The article before "faith" (τῆς πίστεως) may well be anaphoric (i.e., "by means of this Abraham-like faith I've been talking about"), referring back to the particular kind or quality of faith he's already discussed (Gal 2:16, 3:7, 8, 9, 11).

On Lady Tremaine and God's Promise
(vv. 3:15–22)

THE STEPDAUGHTER WAS ESSENTIALLY a slave in her own home. But what could she do? Her father had died, and the cold and cruel stepmother wasted no time in forwarding the prospects of her own two homely daughters. And so, bit by bit, the poor stepdaughter became no better than a servant—forced to sweep, clean, cook, and tend to the very home in which she had known such joy and carefree light when she was a little girl.

I'm speaking, of course, about *Cinderella*. There is a moment early in the film when word comes from on high that there was to be a royal ball in honor of the prince. The boy hadn't yet married and so the king and the grand duke had decided enough was enough—"it's high time he married and settled down!"

The stepmother, Lady Tremaine, saw her chance. What an opportunity for her daughters! If she could marry one of them off to the prince, her life's work would be nearly complete. Cinderella, lurking in the corner, sidled over bravely and declared she could go to the ball, too! Her stepsisters mocked her. How ridiculous! Never!

But Lady Tremaine, never one to miss an opportunity to twist the knife into the odd back, said she could go. "I see no reason why you can't go . . . if you get all your work done."

Cinderella is ecstatic and rushes away to dig out an old dress from a closet. The stepdaughters descend upon their mother, aghast. How could she agree to such a thing! Outrageous! Didn't she realize what she'd just said? Lady Tremaine smiled like an evil cat and purred, "Of course. I said, 'if.'"

There is a moment of silence. Then, they all begin cackling. Cinderella won't go to the ball—not if they can help it! They'll make sure she *doesn't* get her work done.[1]

Lady Tremaine and her schemes are a helpful way to picture Paul's point in our passage (Gal 3:15–22). God made a promise to Abraham—a promise based on faith and trust, not merit. Jesus is the ultimate "child of Abraham," the one who makes all these promises come true. So, who partakes in these promises? It's the ones who believe in the true "son of Abraham," Jesus.

The alternative is to see God as a bit like Lady Tremaine, putting a theoretical "if you do this, then I give you that" out there *all while knowing* we can't pull it off. This is basically what the Jewish agitators are proposing (see Gal 3:1–6). It's a warped twisting of the old covenant, and it doesn't lead anywhere. Cinderella wouldn't have made it to the ball without a divine intervention from the Fairy Godmother, because she was trapped in a cycle she couldn't break. So too, we can never complete a "follow these rules and I'll give you salvation" program—it's an escape room from hell from which we won't ever find our way out.

Paul says there is a different way—a better way. The way it was supposed to be from the beginning. A way Abraham understood. Paul wants us to understand that, so he begins with an analogy about Abraham.

> Brothers and sisters, let me take an example from everyday life. Just as no one can set aside or add to a human covenant that has been duly established, so it is in this case. (Gal 3:15)

Sometimes it's helpful to put things in everyday terms. Suppose you have a contract or some other legal arrangement.[2] We all know that, once the signatures are on the dotted line, then the deed is done. It's sealed. You can't add to or delete anything. It is what it is. Well, Paul says, it's the same in this case with God and his arrangements with us.

"How so?" you ask. Paul answers . . .

> The promises were spoken to Abraham and to his seed. Scripture does not say "and to seeds," meaning many people, but "and to your seed," meaning one person, who is Christ. (Gal 3:16, quoting Gen 12:7; 13:15; 24:7)

---

1. Geronimi et al., *Cinderella*.
2. The Greek word here is the same one we often translate as "covenant," and some translators assume Paul is referring to a will. It doesn't matter—Paul just wants you to imagine a legal contract in your mind.

On Lady Tremaine and God's Promise

God made promises—an irrevocable contract—with Abraham and his descendant. But Paul points out something pretty curious. The promise was to Abraham and his descendant—singular. God did not make promises to all Abraham's offspring, but just to Abraham and to *one descendant in particular*, who is Christ.[3] This is critical:

1. God *did not* make his promises to Abraham and all the ethnic Jewish people.
2. Instead, he made his promises to Abraham and to one special descendant—Jesus.

What's the point?

Paul is saying that, if God made unbreakable promises to Abraham and his special descendant Jesus—promises based on faith and trust (remember that "Abram believed the LORD, and he credited it to him as righteousness," Gen 15:6)—then God certainly hasn't *changed* the terms of the promise later on. "It was not through the law that Abraham and his offspring [*singular—Jesus*] received the promise that he would be heir of the world, but through the righteousness that comes by faith" (Rom 4:13).[4] So, the Jewish agitators who are peddling the "work to earn your salvation" message are wrong. They *have* to be wrong. If they're right, then God changed the terms of the agreement.

Darth Vader once said, "I am altering the deal! Pray I don't alter it any further."[5] Well, God doesn't alter deals. Unlike Vader, he's trustworthy.

> What I mean is this: The law, introduced 430 years later, does not set aside the covenant previously established by God and thus do away with the promise. (Gal 3:17)

---

3. Gk: τῷ δὲ Ἀβραὰμ ἐρρέθησαν αἱ ἐπαγγελίαι καὶ τῷ σπέρματι αὐτοῦ. οὐ λέγει· καὶ τοῖς σπέρμασιν, ὡς ἐπὶ πολλῶν ἀλλ' ὡς ἐφ' ἑνός καὶ τῷ σπέρματί σου, ὅς ἐστιν Χριστός. "Now [*a conjunction of transition*]—the promises were said to Abraham and his descendant. He [*the antecedent likely refers to God (not Scripture; cf. NASB, KJV, CSB), because God spoke the promises to Abraham*] did not say 'and to the descendants' (as if to many people), but instead to one person ('and to your descendant'), who is Christ."

4. Gk: Οὐ γὰρ διὰ νόμου ἡ ἐπαγγελία τῷ Ἀβραὰμ ἢ τῷ σπέρματι αὐτοῦ, τὸ κληρονόμον αὐτὸν εἶναι κόσμου, ἀλλὰ διὰ δικαιοσύνης πίστεως. "This is because [*explanatory conjunction*] the promise [*subject nominative*] to Abraham and his descendant that he would inherit the creation was not by means of law, but by means of righteousness that comes from [*genitive of source*] faith."

5. Kershner, *Star Wars: Episode V*.

Notice that Paul *had* referred to "promises" (plural) which God gave Abraham (Gal 3:16). But *now*, at Gal 3:17, he collapses these into *one single promise*. All those individual promises to Abraham (Gen 12:2–3) are really part of one larger, all-encompassing promise that makes the others happen. Paul continues to refer to *one single promise* at Gal 3:18, and this will become important at Gal 3:19.

> For if the inheritance depends on the law, then it no longer depends on the promise; but God in his grace gave it to Abraham through a promise. (Gal 3:18)

The Mosaic law didn't change the terms of the deal. If we have faith like Abraham, then we're children according to the promise. Things didn't change at Mount Sinai. Instead, it's the wrong ideas about relationship with God that have warped the common understanding of the Mosaic law by Jesus' day, and Paul's, too. This inheritance about which Paul speaks is the promise to Abraham that he would "inherit all creation" (Rom 4:13). We'll have to wait to see Paul explain *how* this will happen. In the book of Romans, Paul said this promise about the inheritance came not by means of law-keeping, but by means of righteousness that comes from faith (Rom 4:13). He says the same thing here, at Gal 3:18:[6]

1. If this inheritance derives from the law, then it no longer derives from the promise God made. It depends on our own effort.

2. But—*and this is the key*—God graciously gave that inheritance to Abraham by means of promise!

3. So, any hint of "I get that inheritance from God by trying real hard and earning righteousness!" is just plain wrong. Always has been. Always will be.

God doesn't change the terms of the deal. Righteousness from God (and, thus, a share in the great inheritance promised to Abraham and to Christ) comes by means of faith and trust in God. It was that way with Abraham. It was that way with Moses—or else God would have altered the deal. And it's still that way now. It's *the Jewish agitators* who are off the rails,

---

6. Gk: εἰ γὰρ ἐκ νόμου ἡ κληρονομία, οὐκέτι ἐξ ἐπαγγελίας· τῷ δὲ Ἀβραὰμ δι' ἐπαγγελίας κεχάρισται ὁ θεός. "Because, if the inheritance derives from law, then it no longer derives from promise. But God graciously gave the inheritance to Abraham by means of promise."

Paul says, not him! Salvation *does not* and *cannot* come by way of doing what the law says (cf. Gal 2:21).

Why, then, was the law given at all? (Gal 3:19)

That's a fair question. If the Mosaic law was never a vehicle for salvation, then what was its purpose?

> It was added because of transgressions until the Seed to whom the promise referred had come. (Gal 3:19)

God made a constellation of promises to Abraham and to his special descendant (Gal 3:16; cf. Gen 12:2–3). These promises are all really about that special descendant—"the Seed to whom the promise referred." Paul attributes this whole bundle of promises to one representative "seed"—Jesus (see the same at Rom 4:13).[7] The promises are actually one promise, and they're embodied in a flesh and blood person who would arrive one day.

In the meantime . . . God's people waited.

The Mosaic law was a tool to hem God's people in until Christ came. It told us how to live, how to act, how to maintain loving relationship with God and with each other. It told us how to be God's people, for a particular time in a particular place, until Christ would arrive on the scene.[8] Picture God's people from the exodus to Pentecost as being in a plane, circling the airport, waiting on clearance to land. They know they'll land, but they aren't yet there.

So, God told us how to live until he "landed the plane." We break the law, we feel guilt, we confess our sin and perform the ritual to atone for that sin. We go on. It's in this way that the Mosaic law "hems us in" and keeps us on the right track until the Messiah arrives at the First Advent.[9]

---

7. For the typological implications of Paul's declaration that Abraham and his offspring would receive the promise (singular) that he would be heir of the world, see esp. Moo, *Romans*, 273–74; Murray, *Romans*, 141–42; and Brunner, *Romans*, 36–40.

8. James D. G. Dunn writes, "The law had a special relationship with Israel, particularly to protect and discipline Israel in the period from Moses to Christ. But that was a temporary role . . . Israel's inability to recognize the temporary nature of this role of the law is reflected in its continued assumption of privileged relation with God, as indicated not least by its having been given the law of God" (*Theology of Paul*, 160).

9. F. F. Bruce writes: "The law, which was given later, was a parenthetical dispensation introduced by God for a limited purpose; its validity continued only until the promise to Abraham was fulfilled in Christ, and even while it was valid it did not modify the terms of the promise (cf. 3: 17–25)" (*Galatians*, 412).

> The law was given through angels and entrusted to a mediator. A mediator, however, implies more than one party; but God is one. (Gal 3:19–20)

The Mosaic law was entrusted to a mediator—Moses. If there is a mediator, then there are at least three parties—(a) God, (b) the mediator, and (c) the people. This is a bit of a crowd. A mediator doesn't act for just one single party—he has obligations to *both* parties.[10] He shuttles between both, placating first one, then the other. Relaying a message one way, then back again, then back *again*. This is imperfect. It's cumbersome. The arrangement with Abraham and his special descendant was different because there was *only one party*. God *himself* made the covenant and *obligated himself* to carry it out.

Paul constantly emphasizes the law's temporary and transitory function, and that's what he's doing here. God's promises to Abraham didn't come via a mediator. He spoke to Abraham, Isaac, and Jacob *himself*. He made the promises *himself*. There was no go-between. But, when it comes to the law, there *was* a mediator. There *was* a go-between.

The law was a different thing—sort of a regulatory guardrail. It was a code to (a) regulate everyday life in Israel, (b) maintain relationship with God, (c) show us our sinfulness, and (d) teach us that Christ would one day cleanse us inside and out.

It did not alter the promises God first made to Abraham and his special descendant, which he later fleshed out in (a) his further promises about a future king descended from David and (b) a new and better relationship framework based on better promises. Instead, the law *regulated the believer's everyday kingdom life* while the plane (as it were) circled the airport waiting for Messiah to land on Christmas morning.

---

10. Gk: Τί οὖν ὁ νόμος; τῶν παραβάσεων χάριν προσετέθη, ἄχρις οὗ ἔλθῃ τὸ σπέρμα ᾧ ἐπήγγελται, διαταγεὶς δι' ἀγγέλων ἐν χειρὶ μεσίτου. ὁ δὲ μεσίτης ἑνὸς οὐκ ἔστιν, ὁ δὲ θεὸς εἷς ἐστιν. "Why, then, the law? It was given [*passive—given by God*] because of the lawbreaking, until the descendent [*Christ—the penultimate 'seed' of Abraham*] to whom the promise referred had arrived. It was organized and put in order [*see LSJ, s.v. 'διατάσσω,' 414*] by angels [*direct agency*] by means of a mediator. Now, the mediator does not act for just one party [*genitive of social relationship*]. But, God is one party."

The most difficult portion of Gal 3:20 is ὁ δὲ μεσίτης ἑνὸς οὐκ ἔστιν, ὁ δὲ θεὸς εἷς ἐστιν, which can be woodenly translated: "Now, the mediator is not one, but God is one" (cf. KJV, ASV). What is this "one" thing getting at? The first "one" is a genitive of social relationship and means the mediator is not *for* one party (i.e., he does not just act on behalf of one party—but both parties). But, God is one party—that's what made the promise to Abraham so much different and better. See Lightfoot, *Galatians*, 146–47.

> Is the law, therefore, opposed to the promises of God? Absolutely not! For if a law had been given that could impart life, then righteousness would certainly have come by the law. (Gal 3:21)

Well, then, was the law *hostile* to God's promises? Was it *opposed* to God's promises? Nope. The law had a different purpose, and this is why it had no power to impart life. None. Some theologians speak of the *theoretical possibility* of earning righteousness by merit. They say things like, "You could earn salvation by following the law perfectly, but nobody is perfect, so we can't get there, and that's why we need Jesus." That's not true. Paul says the law *has no power* to impart life.[11] It can't do it. That wasn't its job. It's like trying to use a cell phone as a hammer—it won't end well because that isn't what it's for. You're misunderstanding its purpose.

So, what was the law's purpose? Paul explains:

> But Scripture has locked up everything under the control of sin, so that what was promised, being given through faith in Jesus Christ, might be given to those who believe. (Gal 3:21–22)[12]

Scripture, God's vehicle for memorializing his revelation, *locked up* or *imprisoned* everything under sin's power. That is, under Satan's power. Paul is not saying that the Bible is like an evil dungeon master, but that the scripture *containing the Mosaic law* acts as a mirror that shows us who we really are.[13] It hems us in, so to speak, by giving us no alternative but to conclude that we're captives who need to be rescued. It had no power to grant life. Its value for old covenant believers (in Paul's context) is that it forced them to always remember that they needed a Rescuer who would *permanently* fix them and their world. The Mosaic law was a first-aid kit—a band-aid—on the way to see the doctor. It regulated believers' lives while they waited for the Messiah.

---

11. This is very clear. Gk: εἰ γὰρ ἐδόθη νόμος ὁ δυνάμενος ζῳοποιῆσαι, ὄντως ἐκ νόμου ἂν ἦν^ε ἡ δικαιοσύνη. "Because, if a law had been given [*passive = given by God*] that had the power [*attributive participle, linked to 'law'*] to grant life, then certainly righteousness would have come by means of the law."

12. Gk: ἀλλὰ συνέκλεισεν ἡ γραφὴ τὰ πάντα ὑπὸ ἁμαρτίαν, ἵνα ἡ ἐπαγγελία ἐκ πίστεως Ἰησοῦ Χριστοῦ δοθῇ τοῖς πιστεύουσιν. "But instead, the scripture imprisoned everything under the power of sin [*preposition = authority*], so that [*purpose clause*] the promise would be given by means of faith in Jesus Christ [*objective genitive*] to the ones [*dative of indirect object*] who believe." For the verb I render as "imprison," see Otto Michel, s.v. "Συγκλείω," §5, in *TDNT*; and LSJ, "Συγκλείω," s.v. The "giving" (δοθῇ) is linked to the promise (ἡ ἐπαγγελία) and completes the purpose clause (ἵνα . . . δοθῇ).

13. Calvin, *Institutes* 2.7.7.

What does this have to do with the promise to Abraham and his special descendant? Here it is: (a) scripture (i.e., the Mosaic law in scripture) locked everything up under the power of sin by showing them a mirror of their hearts, and (b) it did this for the purpose of generating faith in Jesus Christ, who is the means by which the promise becomes ours. The more we see our poor reflection in the law's mirror, the more we realize that God's promise can only be ours by means of faith in Jesus Christ to all who believe. "It was to make them understand their real inner life, their alienation from himself, and their need of his grace."[14]

That was the law's purpose. It wasn't a vehicle for salvation. It was a tool to make us look forward to the Messiah so Abraham's offspring—the true offspring (see Luke 3:8)—would recognize him when he arrived.

---

14. Hovey, *Galatians*, 48.

Who Are God's True Children?

(vv. 3:23—4:7)

It's here that the apostle Paul pens the only positive thing he has to say in this letter about the role of the Mosaic law in the life of a believer.

> Before the coming of this faith, we were held in custody under the law, locked up until the faith that was to come would be revealed. (Gal 3:23)

Before "this faith" in Jesus arrived on the scene (cf. Gal 3:22), the Mosaic law watched over believers like a protective guardian. It defensively hemmed them in until "the faith that was to come" (i.e., the revelation of Christ) was revealed.[1] Some English translations render this in a negative fashion (e.g., the ESV reads "held captive under the law, imprisoned . . ."), but the context suggests otherwise (see NLT, CEB). At Gal 3:22, Paul described the Mosaic law as *condemnatory* ("the scripture imprisoned everything under the power of sin"), but here he describes it as a kind of *benevolent supervision*.[2] There is no conflict:

---

1. Gk: Πρὸ τοῦ δὲ ἐλθεῖν τὴν πίστιν ὑπὸ νόμον ἐφρουρούμεθα συγκλειόμενοι εἰς τὴν μέλλουσαν πίστιν ἀποκαλυφθῆναι. "Now, before this [*anaphoric article*] faith [*accusative subject of infinitive*] in Jesus came about [*adverbial infinitive—antecedent time*] we were watched over [*LSJ, s.v. 'φρουρέω,' 1957; L&N 37.119*] under the law's authority—protectively hemmed in [*LSJ, s.v. 'συγκλείω,' 1665*] until the faith that was coming [*double accusative, object of preposition*] was revealed."

2. Galatians 3:22 refers to the Scripture as being condemnatory, but in Gal 3:23 Paul depicts the Mosaic law as supervisory (Longenecker, *Galatians*, 145).

1	*The law as a mirror.* The law showed believers their sin as if in a mirror, thus driving them to seek the promise given by means of faith in Jesus Christ to the ones who believe, and so . . .	Galatians 3:21–22
2	*The law as a guardian.* Having been driven to long for Christ by means of faith in the promise, the law watched over them and protectively hemmed them in until the faith that was to come (i.e., the full revelation of Christ) would be revealed. But now a new and better arrangement is here (Heb 8:6–7, 13).	Galatians 3:23

So, the law didn't "lock us away" for a millennium while we pined for Jesus to set us free—the Psalmist certainly didn't feel that way ("the precepts of the LORD are right, giving joy to the heart," Ps 19:8)!

> So the law was our guardian until Christ came that we might be justified by faith. Now that this faith has come, we are no longer under a guardian. (Gal 3:24–25)[3]

This means, then,[4] that the law *used* to be our guardian, but its time has now passed. The word for "guardian" here was often used to describe a servant who led a boy to and from school—a watcher and guide. That was the Mosaic law's purpose—not a vehicle for salvation, but a set of guardrails to keep our old covenant brothers and sisters headed the right way "until Christ came." It "kept us under discipline, lest we should slip from his hands."[5] This guardian's purpose[6] was to drive us to seek Christ more and more—to seek God's declaration of righteousness by means of faith in Jesus.

Paul's argument now goes like this:

---

3. Gk: ὥστε ὁ νόμος παιδαγωγὸς ἡμῶν γέγονεν εἰς Χριστόν, ἵνα ἐκ πίστεως δικαιωθῶμεν·ἐλθούσης δὲ τῆς πίστεως οὐκέτι ὑπὸ παιδαγωγόν ἐσμεν. "This means [*inferential conjunction*] the law was a protective guardian [*predicate nominative*] until Christ arrived, so that [*purpose clause*] we would be declared righteous by means of faith. But, now that [*temporal, adverbial participle*] this faith [*i.e., Jesus—anaphoric article*] has come, we are no longer under the protective guardian's authority."

4. The inferential conjunction ὥστε bears this meaning, which the NIV renders somewhat weakly as "so . . ."

5. Bengel, *Gnomen*, 4:30.

6. The Greek is a purpose clause (ἵνα ἐκ πίστεως δικαιωθῶμεν), explaining why the guardian was what it was.

1	*The law as a mirror.* The law showed believers their sin as if in a mirror, thus driving them to seek the promise given by means of faith in Jesus Christ to the ones who believe, and so . . .	Galatians 3:21–22
2	*The law as a guardian.* Having been driven to long for Christ by means of faith in the promise, the law watched over them and protectively hemmed them in until the faith that was to come (i.e., the full revelation of Christ) would be revealed. But now a new and better arrangement is here (Heb 8:6–7, 13).	Galatians 3:23
3	*The guardian's time has expired.* This means, then, that the Mosaic law's guardianship was only in effect until Christ arrived, for the purpose of preparing us to accept the promise he embodied (cf. Isa 42:6–7) and so be declared righteous by means of faith in him. Now that Christ has arrived, we're no longer under the protective guardian's authority.	Galatians 3:24–25

Throughout Galatians chapter 3, Paul has been building an argument step by step:

1. Salvation and righteousness from God have always been by means of faith—the same kind of faith that Abraham had (Gal 3:1–9).

2. And so, legalistic law-keeping has never been the way to salvation. In fact, Jesus has come to liberate us from the curse of legalism (the "curse of the law") in order that God's blessing to Abraham would come to unbelievers by means of Jesus, so that by faith we'd receive the promise of the Holy Spirit (Gal 3:10–14).

3. The Mosaic law was never a vehicle for salvation. If it were, then God's promise to Abraham and his special descendant (a promise based on faith) would have been changed—it would have been a bait and switch. But God doesn't alter deals. The law has no power to impart life. Instead, the law was given because of sins—until the promised special descendant from Abraham arrived on the scene. The law shows believers our true selves as if in a mirror, so that we'd be driven to trust *even more* in God's promise by means of faith (Gal 3:15–22).

4. The Mosaic law was a watcher, a protective guardian who hemmed us in until the revelation of Christ. Now that this faith in Christ has come, we're no longer under the protective guardian's authority (Gal 3:23–25).

Now, what does this all mean for the new covenant? For today? For our new situation now that Christ has indeed arrived? If the Mosaic law (a) is not a means of salvation, (b) has no power to impart divine life, (c) does not alter the terms of the promise by means of righteousness which God swore to Abraham and his special descendant (Jesus), then (d) where does this leave Jews and gentiles in this new arrangement?

Paul explains:

> So in Christ Jesus you are all children of God through faith, for all of you who were baptized into Christ have clothed yourselves with Christ. (Gal 3:26–27)[7]

If you are in union with Christ Jesus—bonded to him, joined together by means of faith—then you are a child of God. Not just you, but *you and everyone else* who has done the same. As we saw earlier, Paul loves this metaphorical picture of "union," and he deploys it in many ways. Now, he asks us to picture a baptism, an *immersion* under water, a *submersion* that joins us to Christ. It's as if, by faith, we're fused to Christ by means of this baptism that plunges us beneath the waves and joins us to him. Now, as we emerge from these metaphorical waters, we're clothed with Christ himself—"for he has clothed me with garments of salvation and arrayed me in a robe of his righteousness" (Isa 61:10).

He is us and we are him. We've been made new. Paul will elaborate at length about this same picture in Rom 6.

If you're a believer, then you're metaphysically fused with Christ—made one with him on an invisible level. Your Bible translation probably has the phrase "in Christ" a lot in Paul's letters, because it's one of his favorite expressions. We're "baptized *into* Christ," "buried *with* Him through baptism *into* death," "crucified *with* Him," and "alive to God *in* Christ Jesus" (Rom 6:1–11). All this language is expressing that, when we trust in Jesus, we're *made one* with him in an unseen way. Perhaps the closest thing I can compare it to is a marriage; there's a oneness that happens in marriage that's unseen, hidden, but very real. What Paul is saying is that God made these

---

7. Gk: Πάντες γὰρ υἱοὶ θεοῦ ἐστε διὰ τῆς πίστεως ἐν Χριστῷ Ἰησοῦ ὅσοι γὰρ εἰς Χριστὸν ἐβαπτίσθητε, Χριστὸν ἐνεδύσασθε. "This means [*explanatory conjunction referring back to the point at Gal 3:7–9, 14, after digression from vv. 15–25*] you are all God's children [*genitive of social relationship*] by means of this faith [*anaphoric—faith of Abraham, in Christ*] in Christ Jesus [*preposition = association*]. Because [*explanatory conjunction*] whoever has been submerged [*i.e., flooded, drowned, drenched, soaked, immersed—see LSJ, s.v. 'βαπτίζω,' 305*] into Christ [*metaphorical spatial*] has been clothed [*indirect middle, passive sense when paired with ἐβαπτίσθητε*] with Christ."

Who Are God's True Children?

promises to Abraham and his crowning descendent, Jesus—along with everyone else who has been made one with him (see Gal 3:29).

1	*The law as a mirror.* The law showed believers their sin as if in a mirror, thus driving them to seek the promise given by means of faith in Jesus Christ to the ones who believe, and so . . .	Galatians 3:21–22
2	*The law as a guardian.* Having been driven to long for Christ by means of faith in the promise, the law watched over them and protectively hemmed them in until the faith that was to come (i.e., the full revelation of Christ) would be revealed. But now a new and better arrangement is here (Heb 8:6–7, 13).	Galatians 3:23
3	*The guardian's time has expired.* This means, then, that the Mosaic law's guardianship was only in effect until Christ arrived, for the purpose of preparing us to accept the promise he embodied (cf. Isa 42:6–7) and so be declared righteous by means of faith in him. Now that Christ has arrived, we're no longer under the protective guardian's authority.	Galatians 3:24–25
4	And so, *we are all God's children by means of this faith* (i.e., Abraham's faith; cf. Gal 3:7–9) in Christ Jesus. If you have been submerged into Christ (as it were), then you've been clothed with him, too.	Galatians 3:26–27

> There is neither Jew nor Gentile, neither slave nor free, nor is there male and female, for you are all one in Christ Jesus. (Gal 3:28)[8]

In Christ's new covenant family, this world's ethnic, socio-cultural, and gender barriers are breached and torn down. This doesn't mean those distinctions cease to exist in real life. It just means the corrupted value markers these distinctions represent in our fallen world have no cachet in God's kingdom family.

1. If you're a Jew who believes Jewish people are inherently superior, then you're wrong. This was a common prejudicial assumption by some in Jesus' day—but no more.[9] Babylon's culture is upended in Christ's kingdom family.

---

8. Gk: οὐκ ἔνι Ἰουδαῖος οὐδὲ Ἕλλην, οὐκ ἔνι δοῦλος οὐδὲ ἐλεύθερος, οὐκ ἔνι ἄρσεν καὶ θῆλυ· πάντες γὰρ ὑμεῖς εἷς ἐστε ἐν Χριστῷ Ἰησοῦ. "There is no 'Jew' and 'Gentile,' no 'slave' and 'free,' no 'male' and 'female'—because [*explanatory conjunction*] you are all one in relationship [*preposition = association*] with Christ Jesus."

9. If you're interested in more about this attitude and how it shaped the actions of the religious leaders in Jesus' day and the time period from the book of Acts, see Edersheim,

2. If you're a slave who believes you're somehow less than a free brother or sister, Paul wants you to know that's all wrong. Those class markers are obliterated—God doesn't care about them at all.

3. If you're a woman who is told patriarchal[10] norms are the way things are supposed to be, then Paul says this is all wrong. Those cultural prejudices are gone—men and women are equal in God's family.[11]

The "oneness" refers to familial relationship—"you are all one in relationship with Christ Jesus."[12] Just as the one triune God is a *single constellation* or a *single society* of divine persons, so God's children are "one" in the sense that we are a *single family* in covenant relationship. The Jewish agitators would require the Galatians to become *their* (wrong) kind of old covenant Christian as a precondition for entering the family—a "Jews versus everyone else" kind of attitude.

Paul says, "No!" For good measure, he tosses the socio-cultural and gender value markers into the mix and says they're also fake preconditions. The only thing that makes you a child of God is faith in Jesus—"the work of God is this: to believe in the one he has sent" (John 6:29). And, once a child of God, the racial, economic, and gender distinctions which this world abuses so much are relativized into proper proportion.

A caste system is one of rigid stratification, where society is divided along social, racial, or class barriers.[13] One thinks of the old British class structure, or perhaps even the lot of Black citizens in Jim Crow–era America.[14] But, *Christianity is not a caste system*. We are all one in relationship with Christ Jesus. Our collective diversity isn't abolished but relativized and integrated into the one mosaic that is Christ's family. "In other words, it is a oneness, because such differences cease to be a barrier and cause of pride or

---

Sketches of Jewish Social Life, chapter 2. There are more up to date and scholarly books available, but this one is available for free to anyone with an internet connection, is short, and is accurate.

10. I mean "patriarchy" in this sense: "The predominance of men in positions of power and influence in society, with cultural values and norms favouring men" (*OED*, s.v. "patriarchy," sense 3).

11. Paul's statement has obvious social implications for how Christian men and women ought to relate to one another in marriage, in the new covenant family, and in a Babylon society. However, Paul does not elaborate on that here, so neither will I.

12. πάντες γὰρ ὑμεῖς εἷς ἐστε ἐν Χριστῷ Ἰησοῦ.

13. *Merriam-Webster*, s.v. "caste." See also *OED*, s.v. "caste," sense 4.b, accessed September 2023.

14. See Wilkerson, *Caste*.

Who Are God's True Children?

regret or embarrassment, and become rather a means to display the diverse richness of God's creation and grace, both in the acceptance of the 'all' and in the gifting of each."[15]

In short, Paul shows us a radically reshaped social world. "The unavoidable inference from an assertion like this is, that Christianity did alter the condition of women and slaves."[16]

1	*The law as a mirror.* The law showed believers their sin as if in a mirror, thus driving them to seek the promise given by means of faith in Jesus Christ to the ones who believe, and so . . .	Galatians 3:21–22
2	*The law as a guardian.* Having been driven to long for Christ by means of faith in the promise, the law watched over them and protectively hemmed them in until the faith that was to come (i.e., the full revelation of Christ) would be revealed. But now a new and better arrangement is here (Heb 8:6–7, 13).	Galatians 3:23
3	*The guardian's time has expired.* This means, then, that the Mosaic law's guardianship was only in effect until Christ arrived, for the purpose of preparing us to accept the promise he embodied (cf. Isa 42:6–7) and so be declared righteous by means of faith in him. Now that Christ has arrived, we're no longer under the protective guardian's authority.	Galatians 3:24–25
4	And so, *we are all God's children* by means of this faith (i.e., Abraham's faith) in Christ Jesus. If you have been submerged into Christ (as it were), then you've been clothed with him, too.	Galatians 3:26–27
5	*Christianity is no caste system.* Ethnic, social, and gender distinctions form no barriers and have no comparative qualitative value within Christ's family.	Galatians 3:28

If you belong to Christ, then you are Abraham's seed, and heirs according to the promise. (Gal 3:29)[17]

Who is the true child of Abraham? It is the one who belongs to Christ—the penultimate son of Abraham (Matt 1:1). Those who say Jewish people are the "real" children of Abraham are mistaken. This status has never been

---

15. Dunn, *Galatians*, 208.
16. Alford, *New Testament*, 2:343.
17. Gk: εἰ δὲ ὑμεῖς Χριστοῦ, ἄρα τοῦ Ἀβραὰμ σπέρμα ἐστέ, κατ' ἐπαγγελίαν κληρονόμοι. "In fact [*conjunction of emphasis*], if you all belong to Christ [*genitive of social relationship*], then you are all Abraham's [*genitive of social relationship*] descendant [*singular*]—heirs in accordance with God's promise [*cf. Gal 3:16*]."

a genetic identity marker, but an ideological one—the *true believer* is the real son or daughter of Abraham and an heir according to the promise.

Paul was not breaking new ground but emphasizing the broader vision that Scripture had always contained. God told Jacob "a nation and a community of nations will come from you" (Gen 35:11). There is the well-known promise from Isaiah in which God promises to not forsake non-Jewish followers: "Let no foreigner who is bound to the LORD say, 'The LORD will surely exclude me from his people'" (Isa 56:3). He swears to personally escort these gentile believers "to my holy mountain, and give them joy in my house of prayer" and to accept their offerings—"for my house will be called a house of prayer for all nations" (Isa 56:7).

The Israelite choir sang about God's reign over all the earth and envisioned a future in which "the nobles of the nations assemble *as the people of the God of Abraham*, for the kings of the earth belong to God; he is greatly exalted" (Ps 47:9). These gentiles will be reckoned as God's people. They'll be grafted in, as it were, as naturalized citizens.[18] King Solomon interpreted that constellation of promises to Abraham and his special descendant as being about Christ, whose blessings would transcend ethnic Jewish boundaries: "all nations will be blessed through him, and they will call him blessed" (Ps 72:17; cf. Gen 12:3, Gal 3:16). Solomon wrote that the nations of the earth—even those from as far as Sheba, Tarshish, and the desert wastelands—will one day pledge allegiance to God's king (Ps 72:7–9). But why? It's because of his care, his love, his compassion:

> For he will deliver the needy who cry out,
> the afflicted who have no one to help.

18. Garrett, *Problem of the Old Testament*, 173–74."The innumerable princes and peoples are to become one people; and they will no longer be outsiders but within the covenant: this is implied in their being called the people of the God of Abraham. It is the abundant fulfilment of the promise of Genesis 12:3; it anticipates what Paul expounds of the inclusion of the Gentiles as Abraham's sons (Rom. 4:11; Gal. 3:7–9)" (Kidner, *Psalms 1–72*, 196).

John Calvin notes: "He again declares that the way in which God obtained dominion over the Gentiles was, that those who before were aliens united in the adoption of the same faith with the Jews; and thus different nations, from a state of miserable dispersion, were gathered together into one body. When the doctrine of the Gospel was manifested and shone forth, it did not remove the Jews from the covenant which God had long before made with them. On the contrary, it has rather joined us to them. As then the calling of the Gentiles was nothing else than the means by which they were grafted and incorporated into the family of Abraham, the prophet justly states, that strangers or aliens from every direction were gathered together to the chosen people, that by such an increase the kingdom of God might be extended through all quarters of the globe" (*Psalms*, 2.214).

Who Are God's True Children?

> He will take pity on the weak and the needy
> and save the needy from death.
> He will rescue them from oppression and violence,
> for precious is their blood in his sight. (Ps 72:12-14)

This is not just pity and rescue for ethnic Israelites, but *for the nations*, too—"the promise is for you and your children and for all who are far off—for all whom the Lord our God will call" (Acts 2:39). In short, this king promises that "blessed are the poor in spirit"—whoever they are—"for theirs is the kingdom of heaven" (Matt 5:3).

God made several promises to Abraham (see Gen 22:17-18), and all of them are fulfilled through Christ. Remember that Paul wrote, "Scripture does not say 'and to seeds,' meaning many people, but *'and to your seed,' meaning one person, who is Christ*" (Gal 3:16). Paul is saying that (a) while God did make all those promises to Abraham—even the one about "the whole land of Canaan" (his "and to your seed" quotation here is likely from the Greek version of Gen 17:8, which is specifically about the land promise)—he also (b) made these promises to Christ as the representative son of Abraham (Matt 1:1).

There are two great wellsprings of promise—Abraham and Christ. You join each of them by means of faith. In fact, if you have one you have the other. If you join to Christ by means of faith, then you are a true child of Abraham. If God has declared you righteous by means of your faith and trust in his promises which culminate in Christ (i.e., you follow Abraham's example), then you are Christ's sibling in God's family.

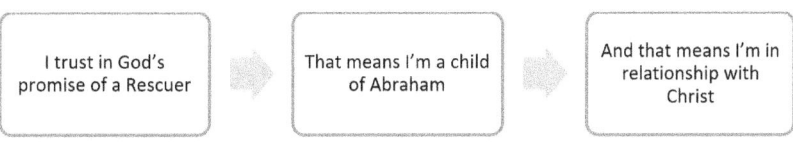

This suggests that Abraham and his physical descendants are a foreshadowing of Jesus and his spiritual brethren.[19] If so, then we can

---

19. See esp. Schreiner, *Galatians*, at Gal 3:16a-d. Jason DeRouchie writes, "If the blessing promise includes a reconstituting of the 'seed' with a global identity in Christ, then one should be cautious to separate the land promise from this same transformation. Indeed, within the argument of Galatians 3, the eschatological fulfillment of the land promise appears to stand behind Paul's argument" ("Counting Stars with Abraham and the Prophets," 480). I believe a framework called "progressive covenantalism" makes good sense of the bible's storyline. This is a *via media* between dispensationalism and covenant theology. See Gentry and Wellum, *Kingdom Through Covenant*, ch. 16-17.

understand all the precious promises to Abraham as shadows of a greater fulfillment—maybe something like this:

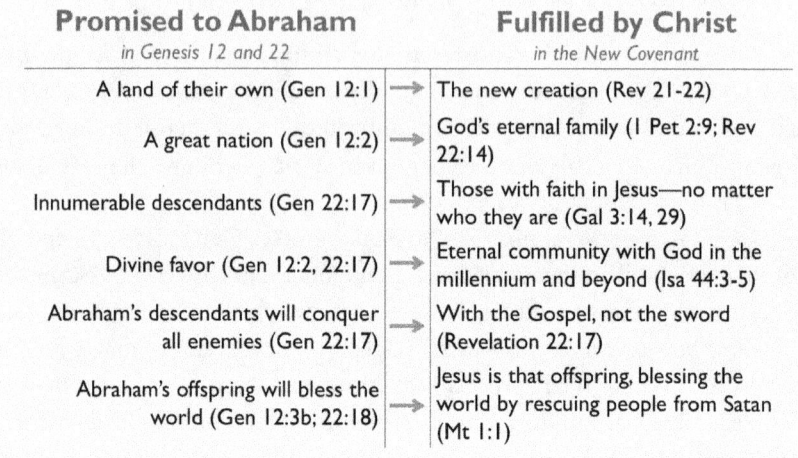

Promised to Abraham in Genesis 12 and 22	Fulfilled by Christ in the New Covenant
A land of their own (Gen 12:1) →	The new creation (Rev 21-22)
A great nation (Gen 12:2) →	God's eternal family (1 Pet 2:9; Rev 22:14)
Innumerable descendants (Gen 22:17) →	Those with faith in Jesus—no matter who they are (Gal 3:14, 29)
Divine favor (Gen 12:2, 22:17) →	Eternal community with God in the millennium and beyond (Isa 44:3-5)
Abraham's descendants will conquer all enemies (Gen 22:17) →	With the Gospel, not the sword (Revelation 22:17)
Abraham's offspring will bless the world (Gen 12:3b; 22:18) →	Jesus is that offspring, blessing the world by rescuing people from Satan (Mt 1:1)

Paul is saying that anyone who belongs to Christ is a child of Abraham and therefore an heir to all these promises. "This means you are all God's children by means of this faith in Christ Jesus" (Gal 3:26). There is no Jew versus gentile distinction, now or forever. Elsewhere, Paul said a mystery that has since been revealed is that "Gentiles are heirs with Israel, members of one body, and sharers together in the promise of Christ Jesus" (Eph 3:6). Jesus has made these two groups into one, creating "one new humanity out of the two" (Eph 3:14, 19). Gentiles are "no longer foreigners and strangers, but fellow citizens with God's people and also members of his household" (Eph 3:19).

There is a straight line starting from (a) when God chose his people by promise with Abraham, (b) connecting right to his promise to David of a perfect king, and from there (c) on to God's pledge of perfect peace through a new and better covenant arrangement. Along this track, the Mosaic law is just a guardrail keeping us on the right trail. It isn't a *different* trail at all. It was a fence that regulated everyday life while God's people waited for his story to move on.

Why is Paul saying this? Because he wants his audience to know how wrong the Jewish agitators are. They don't understand what the Mosaic law is about. It was a guardian, a guide, a guardrail to keep God's people true until the Messiah arrived.

Now comes an extended analogy.

Who Are God's True Children?

> What I am saying is that as long as an heir is underage, he is no different from a slave, although he owns the whole estate. The heir is subject to guardians and trustees until the time set by his father. (Gal 4:1-2)[20]

Paul says that the underage heir to an inheritance really has *nothing* until he inherits. It's all "in prospect" as a promise for a future date. In theory he "owns the whole estate," but it isn't yet his. Sure, *one day* it will be all his—but that day ain't here yet. Until then, he's no different than a slave, in that he's under the orders and charge of a guardian who watches over him until the time comes to inherit from his father.

> So also, when we were underage, we were in slavery under the elemental spiritual forces of the world. (Gal 4:3)[21]

In the same way that an underage heir is watched over by a master, so too were Christians once in slavery under the power of what the NIV calls "the elemental spiritual forces of the world."

What he says here is hard to understand. It's difficult enough that I'll spill a few ounces of ink spelling it out. What does the phrase behind the NIV's translation "elemental spiritual forces of the world" mean? The word means "the basic components of something."[22] This could refer to anything—the physical world, physics, Star Wars, a decent espresso. It could also refer to the transcendent powers that control this world. So, for example:

1. Paul warns the church at Colosse to not be fooled by hollow and deceptive philosophy, "which depends on human tradition and the *elemental spiritual forces*" (Col 2:8). This seems to mean the components

---

20. Gk: Λέγω δέ [transition], ἐφ' ὅσον χρόνον [temporal phrase] ὁ κληρονόμος [subjective nominative] νήπιός [predicate nominative] ἐστιν, οὐδὲν διαφέρει δούλου [genitive of comparison] κύριος πάντων ὤν [concessive particle], ἀλλ' [contrast] ὑπὸ [authority] ἐπιτρόπους ἐστὶν καὶ οἰκονόμους ἄχρι τῆς προθεσμίας [temporal] τοῦ πατρός [subjective genitive]. "This what I'm saying—as long as the heir is a child, he is no different than a slave, even though he is lord over everything. Instead, he is under the authority of a protective guardian and administrator until the Father's appointed time."

21. Gk: οὕτως [adverb of manner—referring to being a ward under a guardian's care] καὶ ἡμεῖς [ascensive], ὅτε ἦμεν νήπιοι, ὑπὸ τὰ στοιχεῖα τοῦ κόσμου [BDAG, s.v. "στοιχεῖον," sense 1c, 946; LSJ, s.v. "στοιχεῖον," 1647; Friberg, s.v. "στοιχεῖον," 357] ἤμεθα δεδουλωμένοι. "In the same way, then, while we were children, we were enslaved under the power of the world's teachings about salvation."

22. See BDAG, s.v. "στοιχεῖον," 946; LSJ, s.v. "στοιχεῖον," 1647; Friberg, s.v. "στοιχεῖον," 357.

Faith Working Through Love

that make up the false teaching from which they ought to run away. Or it could refer to the demonic forces which rule this present evil age.

2. The person who wrote the letter to the Hebrews said that by now they ought to be able to teach others about the faith, but instead "you need someone to teach you the *elementary truths* of God's word all over again" (Heb 5:12). Here, the word means the ABCs of the gospel—the rudimentary first principles they should have mastered long ago.

3. Peter said that one day, when the day of the Lord arrives, "the heavens will disappear with a roar; *the elements* will be destroyed by fire" (2 Pet 3:10). This means the components of the natural world will melt away to make way for the new creation.

But, what does Paul mean here? Because Paul hasn't spoken about evil spiritual forces at all in this section, it probably means the "basic components" of some kind of teaching or doctrine to which believers *used to be* enslaved. He's been talking about the Mosaic law[23]—warning against a false understanding of it. His audience is the Christians in the various churches in Galatia—some are Jewish and others are gentile. He seems to be talking to both ethnic groups as one body (see Gal 4:8). So, it's probably best to see the NIV's "elemental spiritual forces of the world" as referring to the false teaching, axioms, and principles about salvation and inner peace we trusted in *before* we accepted Christ as our true rescuer.[24]

My translation is: "In the same way, then, while we were children, we were enslaved under the power of the world's teachings about salvation." For the Jewish people, that false teaching was that wrong view of the Mosaic law—the idea that God gave it as a vehicle for salvation. For gentiles, it was whatever "spirit of the age" they followed. There are many teachings like this floating about today. Be true to yourself! Live your truth! Don't let anybody tell you who you really are inside! You do you! The times change, but the song remains the same.

---

23. "Certainly what Paul has primarily in view here is the law, and that as an instrument of spiritual bondage" (Fung, *Galatian*, loc. 2263).

24. "As we see it, the passage has reference to definite principles or axioms, according to which men lived before Christ, without finding redemption in them.... And since the apostle speaks of being held in bondage under these rudiments, we shall probably have to think of the prescriptions and ordinances to which religious man outside of Christ surrendered himself, and by means of which he tried to achieve redemption" (Ridderbos, *Epistle to Galatia*, 153–54). See also Hendriksen, *Galatians*, 157; and Hovey, *Galatians*, 52.

Who Are God's True Children?

So, Paul basically says (referring here to Jewish Christians like himself who have since seen the light), "so also, when we were underage, we were in slavery to this wrongheaded 'follow the Law to earn salvation' idea." One commentator wrote, "For, even though the law itself was of divine origin, the use that men made of it was wrong. Those who lived under the law in this unwarranted way lived in the same condition of bondage as that under which the Gentiles, for all their exertion, also pined."[25]

But now, Christ has come and set the record straight. He's the light which brings revelation to the gentiles and glory to Israel (Luke 2:30–31)—sweeping aside all false teaching and wrong ideas and drawing a line in the sand. He's made these two groups into one, "for through him we both [i.e., both groups] have access to the Father by one Spirit" (Eph 2:18).

1	*An underage heir no better than a slave.* He "owns everything," but controls nothing. He's under the orders of a guardian until the time set by his father to inherit. In the sense that he has no independence and autonomy, he's just like a slave.	Galatians 4:1–2
2	*Unbelievers are in slavery to false ideas about how to achieve inner peace.* Just as an heir is no better than a slave because he's overseen by a guardian who's always watching, so too are unbelievers in bondage to the world's most basic (false) teachings about how to find peace.	Galatians 4:3

> But when the set time had fully come, God sent his Son, born of a woman, born under the law, to redeem those under the law, that we might receive adoption to sonship. (Gal 4:4–5)[26]

The time came—the *set* time. The world runs according to God's clock (Eccl 3:1–8). Jesus arrived on Christmas morning. He was born under the authority of the Mosaic law to rescue us from the law's curse. The word that the NIV renders as "redeem" here means "liberation from captivity," as if from a kidnapper.

---

25. Ridderbos, *Epistle to Galatia*, 154.

26. Gk: ὅτε δὲ ἦλθεν τὸ πλήρωμα τοῦ χρόνου [*partitive genitive*], ἐξαπέστειλεν [*BDAG, s.v. "ἐξαποστέλλω," sense 3, 345; LSJ, s.v., "ἐξαποστέλλω," 586*] ὁ θεὸς τὸν υἱὸν αὐτοῦ, γενόμενον ἐκ [*preposition = derivation*] γυναικός, γενόμενον ὑπὸ [*preposition = authority*] νόμον ἵνα τοὺς ὑπὸ [*preposition = authority*] νόμον ἐξαγοράσῃ [*BDAG, s.v., 343; purpose clause*] ἵνα [*result clause*] τὴν υἱοθεσίαν [*anaphoric article, referring to Gal 3:26–29, cf. Gal 4:6; adverbial accusative*] ἀπολάβωμεν. "But, when the set time arrived, God dispatched His Son—born from a woman, born under the law's power—in order to liberate us from the law's power, so that we'd receive adoption as God's children."

Faith Working Through Love

But in what way is the Mosaic law something from which Christ must liberate us? Earlier, Paul said Christ had "redeemed us from the curse of the law" (Gal 3:13), and we saw he meant "from legalism." Paul is making the same point here, but using "law" in two different senses in the same sentence:

- First, Jesus was born "under the law's power" in that he came to be perfect for us, in our place. He subjected himself to the Mosaic law's standard to, as it were, "reset" reality as the new and better representative for all who choose him. He "honored the divine law by his personal obedience,"[27] and so "through the obedience of the one man the many will be made righteous" (Rom 5:19). He was "obedient unto death" for us (Phil 2:8).

- Second, because Jesus came to be obedient to God's law for us, he therefore *redeems* or *liberates* us from the law's power—i.e., from the legalism into which we twist the Mosaic law.

The Mosaic law, properly understood, *was not* an oppressive taskmaster. But the Jewish agitators have *made it into* an oppressive burden because they interpret it wrongly. *Specifically*, the Jewish agitators have turned it into a curse because they interpret and use the Mosaic law in a legalistic fashion. *Generally*, everyone tries to bring their "resume" to God as a credential for securing divine approval—in that sense, it's the same old legalism.

1. God did not design the Mosaic law to be a vehicle that brings salvation (the law has no power to impart life—Gal 3:21).
2. Therefore, God's people made a terrible error by interpreting and using it in that fashion.
3. So, when Paul speaks negatively about the law, he's referring to *the wrong interpretation and use* of it in popular culture—not to the Mosaic law as God intended it to be.
4. Therefore, we should interpret Paul's comments here about Christ liberating us from the law's power *in that light*—he's referring to legalism.

Christ came to set us free—all of us, Jew and gentile—from the curse of legalism, or (if you will) "resume-ism" that makes us want to get into God's family by means of merit. Jesus came here for the purpose of[28] liber-

---

27. Schaff, *Creeds of Christendom*, 3:743, "1833 New Hampshire Confession," art. 4.
28. The Greek forms a purpose clause here: ἵνα τοὺς ὑπὸ νόμον ἐξαγοράσῃ.

Who Are God's True Children?

ating us from the law's power (that is, from the legalism we're turned the Mosaic law into).

Why do this? So that[29] we'd receive adoption as God's children. Again, adoption has nothing to do with who your parents are. It has to do with faith in Jesus, who has set us free from the curse of legalism into which the Mosaic law had been twisted.

1	*An underage heir no better than a slave.* He "owns everything," but controls nothing. He's under the orders of a guardian until the time set by his father to inherit. In the sense that he has no independence and autonomy, he's just like a slave.	Galatians 4:1–2
2	*Unbelievers are in slavery to false ideas about how to achieve inner peace.* Just as an heir is no better than a slave because he's overseen by a guardian who's always watching, so too are unbelievers in bondage to the world's most basic (false) teachings about how to find peace.	Galatians 4:3
3	*At the set time, Christ came to rescue us from these false ideas.* In Paul's context, that was the false interpretation of the Mosaic law. In a general context, this is all attempts to achieve inner peace by means other than faith in Christ Jesus. Adoption follows rescue.	Galatians 4:4–5

We know Paul's point is still "salvation by means of faith versus by means of works" because he returns to it here:

> Because you are his sons, God sent the Spirit of his Son into our hearts, the Spirit who calls out, "Abba, Father." So you are no longer a slave, but God's child; and since you are his child, God has made you also an heir. (Gal 4:6–7)[30]

Why does God send the Spirit of his Son (an alternative translation would be "Spirit from his Son") into our hearts? Because we're his children. How do we become his children? By means of faith in Jesus, who came here to liberate us from the power of legalism ("the law" from Gal 4:4–5). But

---

29. This is a result clause in Greek: ἵνα τὴν υἱοθεσίαν ἀπολάβωμεν.

30. Gk: "Ὅτι δέ ἐστε [*plural*] υἱοί, ἐξαπέστειλεν [*culminative aorist*] ὁ θεὸς τὸ πνεῦμα [*accusative direct object*] τοῦ υἱοῦ [*genitive of space*] αὐτοῦ εἰς τὰς καρδίας ἡμῶν κρᾶζον [*attributive*]· αββα ὁ πατήρ [*apposition*]. ὥστε [*inferential conjunction*] οὐκέτι εἶ [*switch to singular for rhetorical emphasis*] δοῦλος ἀλλ' υἱός· εἰ δὲ υἱός, καὶ [*conclusion*] κληρονόμος διὰ [*personal agency*] θεοῦ. "Now, because you all *are* sons and daughters, God has sent the Spirit from His Son into our hearts, crying out: 'Abba!'—that is, 'Father!' This means you (yes, you!) are no longer a slave but a child. And, if you're a child, then God has made you an heir."

now, Paul writes, "because you all *are* sons and daughters, God has sent the Spirit from His Son into our hearts, crying out: 'Abba!'—that is, 'Father!'"

What does this mean? It means, Paul explains, "that you (yes, you!) are no longer a slave but a child. And, if you're a child, then God has made you an heir." He switches from plural to singular—from "because you all *are* sons and daughters" to "you are no longer a slave." He does this for emphasis—as if he's pointing right at *you* to stress the point. *You* are no longer a slave, but a child. And, if *you* are a child of God, then *you* are also an heir. Used the *right* way, the law is a guardian and God's people are heirs in waiting. Used the *wrong* way, the law is a "curse" (Gal 3:13) that makes its people "slaves" (Gal 4:7).

The Jewish agitators are peddling such a different message! They say, "Do this, do that, follow these traditions, and you'll be saved!" That's why Paul called it "a different gospel" (Gal 1:6).

Here is the progression of Paul's thought from Gal 4:1–7:

1	*An underage heir no better than a slave.* He "owns everything," but controls nothing. He's under the orders of a guardian until the time set by his father to inherit. In the sense that he has no independence and autonomy, he's just like a slave.	Galatians 4:1–2
2	*Unbelievers are in slavery to false ideas about how to achieve inner peace.* Just as an heir is no better than a slave because he's overseen by a guardian who's always watching, so too are unbelievers in bondage to the world's most basic (false) teachings about how to find peace.	Galatians 4:3
3	*At the set time, Christ came to rescue us from these false ideas.* In Paul's context, this was the false interpretation of the Mosaic law. In a general context, this refers to all attempts to achieve inner peace by means other than faith in Christ Jesus. Adoption follows rescue.	Galatians 4:4–5
4	*Because God has adopted you, he sent the Spirit from his Son to give you assurance.* So, you are a child of God and heir to the promise.	Galatians 4:6–7

On Going Back to Prison
(vv. 4:8–20)

IN 1956 HUMPHREY BOGART starred in one of his quirkier movies, a comedy titled *We're No Angels*. The year is 1895, it's Christmas morning, and Bogart and two others are convicts on Devil's Island, the notorious French penal colony. They escape that awful place and make their way to a coastal city in French Guiana and plot their next move.

Through a series of bizarre circumstances, Bogart and company find themselves tied up in the affairs of a storekeeper and his family. High jinks and hilarity ensue, complete with Christmas dinner, a pretty girl, a sinister relative, and a pet snake named Adolph. At the end of the movie their boat awaits, they have civilian clothes, they have luggage, and look like respectable gentlemen (except for Adolph). All they must do is get on the boat.

And yet, in the gathering dusk, the three convicts make a crazy decision—they decide to go back to prison! Bogart ponders the suggestion for a beat, gestures with his hat, and nods his head. "Well, if it doesn't work out, we'll do it all over again next year," he says.[1]

This isn't meant to be taken seriously. It's a comedy. But we are meant to get the absurdity of the decision—who in his right mind would go back to prison? Crazy, right?

And yet, this is exactly what the Christians in Galatia are doing. Jesus has set them free, but they're choosing to go back to prison, to slavery, to bondage. The danger is that they don't realize it. Paul explains . . .

> Formerly, when you did not know God, you were slaves to those who by nature are not gods. But now that you know God—or rather are known by God—how is it that you are turning back to

1. Curtiz, *We're No Angels*.

Faith Working Through Love

those weak and miserable forces? Do you wish to be enslaved by them all over again? (Gal 4:8–9)[2]

Paul likes to compare salvation to liberation—which is what "redemption" basically means. Jesus "saves" us, yes, but that word seems to have lost a bit of its sparkle because it's so familiar. Terms like "rescue" or "liberate" or "set free" help explain. The "ransom" language (see Mark 10:45; 1 Tim 2:6) gets across something similar—we *were* slaves to Satan, *but now* Jesus has set us free.

The Christians in Galatia, Paul says, used to be slaves to things that weren't God. Everyone has an ultimate concern, a final authority to which they pay homage—a "center" to our souls that fuels our sense of meaning, purpose, and dignity. That is our "god," and in that sense nobody is truly an atheist.[3] Whether it's a false formal religion, your job, your ego—or whatever—we all worship *something*. If that "something" isn't the one true God of the Scriptures (one God in three persons, now and forever), then it is slavery to something that by nature is not truly god.[4]

But now, all that has changed. Now they know God, or—Paul hastens to clarify, perhaps with a flash of irritation—they're *known by* God. So, how on earth could they then turn back to what they've left behind? This clarification ("known by God" instead of "you know God") stresses God's divine gift. We do choose God, but underneath all that we only choose him because the Spirit has first lifted the dark veil from our eyes so the gospel can shine in (2 Cor 4:3–6).

---

2. Gk: Ἀλλὰ [*transition, but it's sort of absorbed into the concessive and untranslated*] τότε μὲν [*concessive particle, paired with* νῦν *in v. 9*] οὐκ εἰδότες θεὸν ἐδουλεύσατε τοῖς [*article fronted for emphasis*] φύσει μὴ οὖσιν θεοῖς· 9 νῦν δὲ γνόντες θεόν, μᾶλλον [*adverb of degree; see BDAG, s.v.* "μᾶλλον" *sense 2*] δὲ γνωσθέντες ὑπὸ θεοῦ, πῶς ἐπιστρέφετε πάλιν ἐπὶ τὰ ἀσθενῆ καὶ πτωχὰ [*accusative of apposition*] στοιχεῖα [*direct object*] οἷς [*antecedent is* στοιχεῖα] πάλιν ἄνωθεν δουλεύειν [*complementary w/ verb*] θέλετε; "Beforehand, although you did not know God and were slaves to things that by nature are not gods, now *you do* know God [or, better still, have been known by God]. How, then, can you be turning back again to the world's feeble and shabby beliefs about salvation—beliefs to which you want to be enslaved all over again!?"

3. Carl F. H. Henry wrote: "Whatever may be the unregenerate man's philosophical credo, he can neither live as a human being nor understand himself without adhering to some ultimate loyalty and concern; in this sense no one can existentially be an atheist. Everyone has his private god or gods and everyman is a religious man, though most men are religiously devoted to false gods and do not trust the living God" (*God, Revelation and Authority*, 2:137).

4. Fung, *Galatians*, loc. 2365.

On Going Back to Prison

This makes their potential betrayal even more inexcusable. God has done *this*, so you repay him by doing *that*? You're walking back into slavery! How could they do this? How could they voluntarily turn back "to those weak and miserable forces" (NIV)? Paul is referring back to what the NIV translated as the "elemental spiritual forces of the world" to which unbelievers are enslaved (Gal 4:3). We saw there that Paul meant something like the "false teachings about salvation." That's also what he means here—they're turning back to "legalism as a principle of life."[5] Paul basically asks, "How, then, can you be turning back again to the world's feeble and shabby beliefs about salvation—beliefs to which you want to be enslaved all over again!?"

There's nothing wrong with the Mosaic law if it's understood and used properly, but the false teachers are playing a different game—pitching a "religion" of works righteousness. A long time ago, Martin Luther wrote:

> The law ought rightly to serve the promises and to stand with the promises and grace. If it fights against them, it is no more the holy law of God, but a false and devilish doctrine, and does nothing but drive people to despair, and it therefore must be rejected. Paul is speaking about the law in respect to proud and presumptuous hypocrites who want to be justified by it; he is not speaking about the law understood spiritually....[6]

Whether those heading back to slavery are (a) gentiles embracing a false version of Christianity based on works righteousness, or (b) Jewish believers who are reverting to the cultural legalism that Jesus and Paul criticized, the result is the same—this is a bad road that won't ever bring peace with God.[7] "Therefore, there is no difference between a non-Christian and a heretic. There are distinctions of place, rite, religion, deed, and worship;

---

5. Bruce, *Galatians*, 381. A. T. Robertson writes that the Christians in Galatia are "still in their utter impotence from the Pharisaic legalism and the philosophical and religious legalism and the philosophical and religious quests of the heathen.... These were eagerly pursued by many, but they were shadows when caught. It is pitiful today to see some men and women leave Christ for will o' the wisps of false philosophy" (*Word Pictures*, on Gal 4:9).

6. Luther, *Galatians*, 215–16.

7. "Want of power to justify is that to which the word points here" (Alford, *New Testament*, 2:346). Martin Luther writes, "... whoever has fallen from the doctrine of justification is ignorant of God and is an idolater. Therefore, it is all the same whether they afterwards returned to the law or to the worship of idols. When this doctrine is taken away, nothing remains but error and idolatry, however much it seems outwardly to be the truth, the true service of God, or true holiness" (*Galatians*, 213). See also Brown, *Galatians*, 208.

but there is the same idea in them all: 'If I do this or that, God will be merciful to me; if I do not do these things, he will be angry,'"[8] because they all miss the boat by trusting to resume-ism—to earning favor with God.

> You are observing special days and months and seasons and years! I fear for you, that somehow I have wasted my efforts on you. (Gal 4:10–11)

If you stop following Abraham's example (to believe and trust God, and be counted as righteous in response), then you're choosing slavery. The Galatian Christians are observing Jewish holidays, special occasions, and the like.[9] It's not that they *simply prefer* to observe old covenant rituals as aids to faith—Messianic Christians today do something similar.[10] The problem is that they're following the perverted ideas of the false teachers—they think they need to observe these special days (etc.) *in order to gain salvation*.[11]

These are the "weak and miserable forces" (NIV), the "weak and worthless world system" (CEB), the "weak and useless spiritual principles of this world" (NLT), the "world's feeble and shabby beliefs about salvation" (my translation) after which they're chasing. John Stott explains, "In other

---

8. Luther, *Galatians*, 213.

9. These are likely Jewish rituals, not pagan ones (Schreiner, *Galatians*, 279; Fung, *Galatians*, loc. 2380; Brown, *Galatians*, 209).

10. "It seems plain, from the fourteenth and fifteenth chapters of the Epistle to the Romans, that though the apostle considered the observing of these institutions on the part even of believing Jews as unnecessary, he did not consider it as unlawful, so long as they viewed them not as a means of justification, but merely as institutions originally of Divine appointment, and in their estimation unrepealed" (Brown, *Galatians*, 209).

11. "Many Jewish Christians continued to observe the sacred occasions as a matter of course. Paul himself appears to have regarded some of them at least as convenient punctuation-marks in his apostolic schedule (cf. 1 Cor. 16: 8; Acts 20: 16). But for Gentile Christians to adopt them de novo as matters of legal obligation was quite another matter" (Bruce, *Galatians*, 386).

Luther wrote, "These ceremonies the Galatians were constrained by the false apostles to keep as necessary to righteousness. Therefore he saith that they, losing the grace and liberty which they had in Christ, were turned back to the serving of weak and beggarly elements. For they were persuaded by the false apostles, that these laws must needs be kept, and by keeping of them they should obtain righteousness; but if they kept them not, they should be damned" (*Galatians*, 393).

Schreiner is incorrect to suggest that Paul "apparently thinks that devotion to the Mosaic law is just another form of paganism!" (*Galatians*, 278). Paul is not talking about devotion to the *real* Mosaic system. He's attacking the *false version* of the Mosaic law that these false teachers (and much of Jewish culture) is advocating.

On Going Back to Prison

words, your religion has degenerated into an external formalism. It is no longer the free and joyful communion of children with their Father; it has become a dreary routine of rules and regulations."[12]

This is why Paul throws up his hands and suggests he's wasted his time on them. They're so confused that they seem hopeless—did they *ever* understand who Jesus is and what salvation is about? Maybe not!

> I plead with you, brothers and sisters, become like me, for I became like you. You did me no wrong. As you know, it was because of an illness that I first preached the gospel to you, and even though my illness was a trial to you, you did not treat me with contempt or scorn. Instead, you welcomed me as if I were an angel of God, as if I were Christ Jesus himself. (Gal 4:12–14)

After the shock of this suggestion ("did I waste my time on y'all?" Gal 4:11)—Paul had time to ponder this line before he wrote it, so he likely did it on purpose—he switches to a softer tone. He seems to say, "Look guys—put yourself in my place and see where I'm coming from!" He loves them. They never did anything to hurt him. Paul has their best interests at heart. The false teachers are trying to throw them into confusion (Gal 1:7), but don't they remember Paul's heart toward them? They used to trust him—what happened?

Paul "became like you" in that the Mosaic law never had a hold over his non-Jewish readers. So, Paul argues, they ought to "become like me" by imitating that example—the Mosaic law (both the false version on offer *and* the true version which is flawed, is passing away, and is now obsolete [cf. Heb 8:8, 13]) *must become* a non-issue to them! They must be free from legalism—just like him.[13] "All Christians should be able to say something like this, especially to unbelievers, namely that we are so satisfied with Jesus Christ, with His freedom, joy and salvation, that we want other people to become like us."[14]

> Where, then, is your blessing of me now? I can testify that, if you could have done so, you would have torn out your eyes and given them to me. Have I now become your enemy by telling you the truth? (Gal 4:15–16)

---

12. Stott, *Galatians*, 108.

13. "He now beseeches them to become as he is, to be free from legal bondage and to know the liberty that is in Christ" (Fung, *Galatians*, loc. 2415–16).

14. Stott, *Galatians*, 112.

Faith Working Through Love

Have they changed their minds about Paul—become suspicious, distrustful, cynical—because they don't like what he's telling them? "You trust these guys over me?" Paul asks. "Really?" Paul strains to not be defensive in a shrill and desperate way—he knows this would play into the false teacher's hands.

> Those people are zealous to win you over, but for no good. What they want is to alienate you from us, so that you may have zeal for them. (Gal 4:17)[15]

The false teachers don't have good motives. They want followers. They want clicks. They want likes. Paul stands in the way, and so he must go. Their goal is to drive a wedge between Paul and the Christians in Galatia, so that the Christ-followers will turn their affections toward them.[16] They want to exclude Paul.

> It is fine to be zealous, provided the purpose is good, and to be so always, not just when I am with you. (Gal 4:18)

The Christians in Galatia are zealous. They want to do right. They want to be right. But their zeal is leading them off a cliff. They've transferred their zeal from the truth to a lie, and disaster awaits.

> My dear children, for whom I am again in the pains of childbirth until Christ is formed in you, how I wish I could be with you now and change my tone, because I am perplexed about you! (Gal 4:19–20)

Paul sounds anguished. At wit's end. Frustrated in a compassionate sort of way. He's like a mother in childbirth, waiting for a baby to enter the world. Will these "believers" in Galatia turn out to be real Christians, after all? Paul wishes he were there so he could understand. He's perplexed, confused. He wishes he could speak in kinder tones—if only he could chat with them in person. What Paul wouldn't have given for Zoom!

In the movie *We're No Angels*, the escaped convicts decide to go back to prison because the outside world is so dark. "You always know where you

---

15. Gk: ζηλοῦσιν [BDAG, s.v. "ζηλοῦσιν" sense 1b] ὑμᾶς [direct object] οὐ καλῶς, ἀλλ' [contrast] ἐκκλεῖσαι [anarthrous, complementary] ὑμᾶς θέλουσιν, ἵνα [purpose clause] αὐτοὺς ζηλοῦτε. "They're fixated on you all, and not in a good way. Instead, they want to alienate you all from us, so that you'll turn toward them."

16. "The ultimate aim of the agitators was for the Galatians to seek them (cf. NASB), not Paul, as their exclusive teachers, receiving their directions from them and obeying the law which they observed" (Fung, *Galatians*, loc. 2481–82).

are in prison," one of them says, wistfully. Things are simpler. Easier. The real world is so devious, so complicated, so twisted. It's better in prison. So, they go back. The movie fades to black as halos appear over each of their heads—even Adolph's.[17] It's a clever riff on the title. Perhaps they really are angels, after all . . .

In contrast, the situation in Galatia isn't a joke. Things aren't easier back in the prison of works righteousness. They're worse. It's a treadmill from hell that leads nowhere. We shake our heads as Bogart and company decide to go back to prison, even as we realize it's a silly comedy. How much more unbelievable is it if we forsake Abraham's example of simple faith and trust in God's promise for a false gospel?

In the depths of his confusion, Paul tries out an analogy—maybe that will express his point better. Maybe then they'll understand.

17. Curtiz, *We're No Angels*.

The Two Ladies and Their Two Jerusalems

(vv. 4:21—5:12)

Henry Knox personifies the perennial American virtues of dependability and ingenuity.[1] He was George Washington's chief artillery commander during much of the Revolutionary War. Knox was nobody's version of a dashing soldier. A 1784 portrait shows a chubby, round-faced man with at least two chins. His shoulders slope downward as if he's slouching for the portrait—one can just imagine the belly that must be there, despite being over six feet tall.

Knox had no formal military training. He was a bookseller who liked to read and devoured tomes on military history. He taught himself about artillery from books. Washington promoted him to the post over the head of an older, much more experienced professional soldier. He must have seen something in the guy.

One of Knox's greatest feats was to seize fifty-five artillery pieces from captured Fort Ticonderoga, at the southern end of Lake Champlain, and transport them to Cambridge, Massachusetts, to participate in the siege of Boston. This is a distance of approximately 220 miles on modern roads, and Knox's achievement was "one of the most impressive examples of perseverance and ingenuity in the war."[2]

Artillery pieces in that day were extraordinarily heavy—Knox's fifty-five guns weighted over sixty tons. He and his team successfully hauled these captured weapons across waterways, over hills, and down into valleys and lost not a one.

---

1. The account that follows is drawn largely from Ferling, *Almost a Miracle*, 101–4.
2. Middlekauff, *Glorious Cause*, 314.

The Two Ladies and Their Two Jerusalems

Knox later served in Washington's first administration as Secretary of War. This is an extraordinary, self-made man—a guy who *taught himself* his own profession and helped win the Revolutionary War. He was a guy who "made it happen," and his successful capture and transport of sixty tons of artillery pieces to the outskirts of Boston one cold winter is exhibit number one.

In that brief description, I took a historical figure and made him *represent* something bigger, something beyond himself. Does Henry Knox really embody dependability and ingenuity to the *nth* degree? Perhaps nobody really can, but that one incident surely illustrates the point.

Paul does something similar. He grabs a historical incident and says, "This is a great illustration for something deeper—something important."[3] He hopes this will make an impression on the Christians in Galatia, because it's important they get this. He explains:

> Tell me, you who want to be under the law, are you not aware of what the law says? (Gal 4:21)

Now, in a tone of exasperation—like that of a frustrated person to a particularly dense friend—Paul asks if they're really aware of what it means to put oneself under a system of works righteousness. This echoes what he mentioned earlier, in Gal 3:7–14. "You really want to go that way?" he asks. "I'm not sure you understand what you're doing!"

Anytime you *add something* to Jesus' "repent and believe" (Mark 1:15), you destroy the gospel. False teachers are claiming the equation is "Jesus + obey the Mosaic law = salvation." This is why some of these "foolish Galatians" (Gal 3:1) want to "be under the law." They've been fooled to believe in that false equation.

"Do you not listen to the law?" Paul asks.[4] If they actually "had ears to hear," then the Mosaic law would lead them to Christ! Instead, they are blinded. He explains:

> For it is written that Abraham had two sons, one by the slave woman and the other by the free woman. His son by the slave woman was born according to the flesh, but his son by the free woman was born as the result of a divine promise. (Gal 4:22–23)

---

3. F. F. Bruce explains, "He has in mind that form of allegory which is commonly called typology: a narrative from OT history is interpreted in terms of the new covenant" (*Galatians*, 408).

4. This is literally what he asks in Greek; the NIV tries to smooth it out.

Faith Working Through Love

"This is what I mean," Paul says,[5] and then lays it out. He grabs an incident from the book of Genesis (ch. 16) to make his point. He uses allegory, which basically means one thing is really a symbol for some hidden *other* thing.[6] This means the point he's about to make doesn't come *right from* Genesis, but he uses the incident from Gen 16 as an illustration for something else. It's a capstone to the same long argument he's been making since Gal 3. Martin Luther writes, "[A]s a painting is an ornament to decorate a house already built, so is an allegory the light of a matter that is already otherwise proved and confirmed."[7]

You'll have to read Gen 16 to understand what Paul's about to say—why don't you do it right now?

Paul focuses on two of Abraham's children—Ishmael and Isaac. Ishmael was born to "the slave woman" Hagar, whose master was Abraham's wife Sarah. The other boy was born to "the free woman" Sarah, and they named the boy Isaac.

Ishmael was born because Abraham and Sarah tried to fix things their own way. God had promised them more offspring than could ever be counted—that Abraham would be the fountainhead for all God's people. Well, the years passed, and no child came. *We gotta do something*, they figured. *Gotta take matters into our own hands.* So, Sarah declared, "The LORD has kept me from having children. Go, sleep with my slave; perhaps I can build a family through her" (Gen 16:2). Abraham was only too happy to oblige and slept with Hagar. Thus Ishmael was conceived.

Isaac, on the other hand, was born according to God's promise. Sarah conceived a child in her old age, and they had a new baby boy of their own. If they'd just waited for God to make good on his promise of an heir, Abraham's affair with Hagar to produce Ishmael wouldn't have been necessary.

This contrast—going your own way versus going God's way, the "slave" way versus the "free" way—is what Paul highlights throughout the example. Hagar represents "going your own way," when Abraham and Sarah decided to solve the problem "according to the flesh." Sarah represents "going God's way," and so she is a "free woman."

---

5. The conjunction is explanatory and need not be a formal "for," like the NIV renders it.

6. "The use of symbols in a story, picture, etc., to convey a hidden or ulterior meaning, typically a moral or political one; symbolic representation" (*OED*, s.v. "allegory," sense 1, accessed April 14, 2023).

7. Luther, *Galatians*, 228.

The Two Ladies and Their Two Jerusalems

This "according to the flesh" (Ishmael) versus "as a result of a divine promise" (Isaac) suggests two very different paths.[8]

- The first is the natural way of things without God. Paul's phrase "according to the flesh" describes the *manner* of Ishmael's conception[9]—it was due to Abraham and Sarah's own planning and strategy. They tried to force the issue and didn't wait on God.
- The second is by means of God's divine promise.[10] This doesn't mean that Isaac's conception was a miracle—only that he arrived in God's own time, according to his plan.

Hagar		Sarah
The "slave woman"	*Character*	The "free woman"
A son "born according to the flesh"	*Child*	A son born by means of a divine promise
Ignoring God's way	*The Lesson*	Trusting God's way

Paul continues . . .

> These things are being taken figuratively: The women represent two covenants. One covenant is from Mount Sinai and bears children who are to be slaves: This is Hagar. Now Hagar stands for Mount Sinai in Arabia and corresponds to the present city of Jerusalem, because she is in slavery with her children. But the Jerusalem that is above is free, and she is our mother. (Gal 4:24–26)

These two women and the two very different paths they represent stand for *two covenants*. These are the old and new covenants,[11] symbolized by two cities, two women, and two very different "children."

---

8. Hendriksen, *Galatians*, 180–81. In a similar vein, Martin Luther wrote, "Therefore, the physical children are not the children of God; only the children of the promise are God's children. By this argument Paul effectively counters the proud Jews who boasted that they were Abraham's descendants. (Christ does the same in Matthew 23 and John 8)." (*Galatians*, 227–28).

9. The preposition in this phrase likely describes *manner*. Gk: ἀλλ' ὁ μὲν ἐκ τῆς παιδίσκης κατὰ σάρκα γεγέννηται.

10. The preposition here conveys *means*. Gk: ὁ δὲ ἐκ τῆς ἐλευθέρας δι' ἐπαγγελίας.

11. Longenecker, *Galatians*, 211. It could well be the old covenant and the Abrahamic covenant, but the latter is the wellspring from which the new covenant springs. I prefer old and new covenants, but I don't see how it really matters, one way or the other. It's not worth arguing about.

Old covenant	= Sinai and the present Jerusalem (i.e., Hagar)	= she bears *slave* children
New covenant	= Jerusalem above (i.e., Sarah)	= she bears *free* children

Mount Sinai and "present city of Jerusalem" is the false teaching about the Mosaic law against which Paul has written so forcefully here. It's the heretical, works-righteousness system that so many Jewish people have adopted. It's what got Jesus killed. Paul's language is a bit shocking—he compares the old covenant to slavery! Did Jesus think that way? Did the man who wrote Ps 119 think that way ("Your statutes are my delight; they are my counselors," Ps 119:24)?

They didn't.

So, in what way are the "children" from the present Jerusalem "in slavery"? Paul must again be referring to the *wrong interpretation of the old covenant* that he's been arguing against all along. That's the best explanation.[12] The Mosaic law isn't oppressive or evil ("Direct me in the path of your commands, *for there I find delight*," Ps 119:35). It is not a tool for slavery—"I will walk about *in freedom*, for I have sought out your precepts," Ps 119:45. Nor is it a vehicle for salvation—it has nothing to do with that.

This suggests it can only be compared to slavery if it's twisted into something it's not meant to be. The Mosaic law *can become* a form of "slavery" if you twist it into a means of salvation. "For if keeping the law could make us right with God, then there was no need for Christ to die!" (Gal 2:21 NLT).

The "Jerusalem that is above" is the *true way* of salvation—the way that Abraham and the prophets understood. The way that understood that relationship with God was about all-consuming love (Deut 6:4). Not a mystical love without borders or definitions, but a love for God in which "these commandments that I give you today are to be on your hearts" (Deut 6:6). A love for God that made David sing, "I desire to do your will, my God; your law is within my heart" (Ps 40:8). The same love that makes blessed those "whose delight is in the law of the LORD" (Ps 1:2). Paul understood

---

12. Fung explains that Hagar and the present Jerusalem "stands by metonymy for Judaism, with its trust in physical descent from Abraham and reliance on legal observance as the way of salvation" (*Galatians*, loc. 2571–72).

John Calvin notes, "What, then, is the gendering to bondage, which forms the subject of the present dispute? It denotes those who make a wicked abuse of the law, by finding in it nothing but what tends to slavery. Not so the pious fathers, who lived under the Old Testament; for their slavish birth by the law did not hinder them from having Jerusalem for their mother in spirit" (*Galatians*, 138).

this—he tells us that, no matter how badly he fails to live up to his responsibilities as a Christian, "in my inner being I delight in God's law" (Rom 7:22).

The "Jerusalem that is above" is that better, heavenly country which all the saints of old longed to see—"therefore God is not ashamed to be called their God, for he has prepared a city for them" (Heb 11:16). "This is the *free* Jerusalem. Those who belong to its community are not born for bondage, but from freedom, and are educated in it. Not the law, nor the thing they themselves must do, but grace, that which they have received in Christ, determines their life."[13] This is a far different path than the corrupted old covenant system to which "the present city of Jerusalem" points.

So, Paul suggests, you have a choice of two "mothers," each corresponding to a particular path:[14]

| Go your own way | = Hagar as "mother" | = "the present city of Jerusalem" | = slavery |
| Go God's way | = Sarah as "mother" | = "the Jerusalem that is above" | = freedom |

Paul now quotes a passage from Isaiah to strengthen his point:

> For it is written:
> "Be glad, barren woman,
> you who never bore a child;
> shout for joy and cry aloud,
> you who were never in labor;
> because more are the children of the desolate woman
> than of her who has a husband."
> (Gal 4:27; quoting from Isa 54:1–3)

In Isaiah's book, this follows right on the heels of the great prophecy about the Lord's suffering servant (Isa 52:13—53:12). In that passage, God promised that his servant would justify many people and would see his "offspring," who are the true believers whom he'll rescue. After that assurance, Isaiah then says the bit that Paul quotes here in our text—the "barren woman" who has been longing to bear "children" will have her wish, but

---

13. Ridderbos, *Epistle to Galatia*, 178.

14. One wonders how much old covenant background these newer gentile believers had—did they really grasp the allegory? It is possible that Paul is responding to bad characterizations of old covenant parallels from the false teachers, so they perhaps had more background than we realize (Longenecker, *Galatians*, 212). Likewise, F. F. Bruce follows C. K. Barrett in suggesting Paul is responding to mischaracterizations by false teachers (*Galatians*, 409).

not in the normal fashion. She won't bear the children or ever suffer labor pains, nonetheless this "desolate woman" will have multitudes of them.

This is poetry, metaphor—it hints about something deeper. God often refers to his community as a woman (Isa 61:10; Isa 62:4–5; Jer 3:14; Eph 5:25–27)—sometimes an unfaithful woman (see Ezek 16, Hos 1–3). So, this woman to whom God speaks is likely Israel—his covenant family. She is "barren" because the glittering promise from Mount Sinai ("you will be my treasured possession . . . a kingdom of priests and a holy nation," Exod 19:5–6) seems to be nothing but a pipe dream when compared to the crucible of reality—a fantasy.

Children are a sign of God's blessing—but where are *her* "children"? Well, God promises that she'll have them. God's community will one day be complete, made whole, elevated to that splendor she'd never really achieved. Isaiah looks forward to the new covenant, when Jesus will make all those promises to Abraham come true.

Why does Paul quote this passage? He connects the "good mother" with Sarah, who waited upon God even through apparent barrenness. Sarah will have more children than the "other woman," Hagar.[15] The Galatian Christians are children of the free woman, symbolized by the new Jerusalem ("she is our mother," Gal 4:26)—they're Israel's "children." Anyone who shares Abraham's faith is a child of Abraham and an heir in God's family (Rom 4:16–17; Gal 3:26–29). Every new believer is a precious "child" given to that barren woman, Israel, who once thought she'd blown it and would never have offspring.[16]

> Now you, brothers and sisters, like Isaac, are children of promise.
> At that time the son born according to the flesh persecuted the son born by the power of the Spirit. It is the same now. (Gal 4:28–29)

Christians who trust Jesus and the simple Good News he preached belong to Sarah and are "children of promise." What happened between Isaac and Ishmael? Ishmael harassed his younger stepbrother (Gen 21:9).

---

15. Paul's analogy breaks down when you try to connect too many dots (Hagar was not married), but his point stands. It's an imperfect allegory to make a point, and we should take the point and not quibble over tidiness.

16. "Since, therefore, 'the Jerusalem that is above' is an eschatological term expressing a reality that will exist in the future, Paul's use of it here for the experience of the Galatian believers implies that, as Paul understood matters, the Galatian believers had come into the eschatological situation of already participating in that future reality, in that the promise made to Abraham was fulfilled in Christ (3:16; 5:1)" (Longenecker, *Galatians*, 216).

The Two Ladies and Their Two Jerusalems

"It is the same now," in that the other "children" (those who belong to the slave woman—the Old Jerusalem) harass the true children who are free.

These "slave children" are the false teachers and all who believe in the equation "Jesus + something else = salvation." Some Bible teachers believe they are the Jews and the old covenant, but this is wrong—the old covenant (properly interpreted) isn't evil and doesn't produce slavery. Instead, Paul has been arguing against the "works righteousness" crowd, and he continues that here.

> But what does Scripture say? "Get rid of the slave woman and her son, for the slave woman's son will never share in the inheritance with the free woman's son." (Gal 4:30)

When Ishmael harassed Isaac, Sarah told her husband to send Hagar away. "She has no part in any of this!" What's the connection to the situation in Galatia? Well, just as Sarah (the "mother" of freedom in this analogy) sent away Hagar (the "mother" of slavery), so too should the Christians in Galatia "get rid of" these false teachers and everyone else who believes in that fraudulent salvation equation. They have no share in Abraham's inheritance. They aren't children of the free woman—they belong to someone else entirely. Send them packing, and don't fall for their tricks!

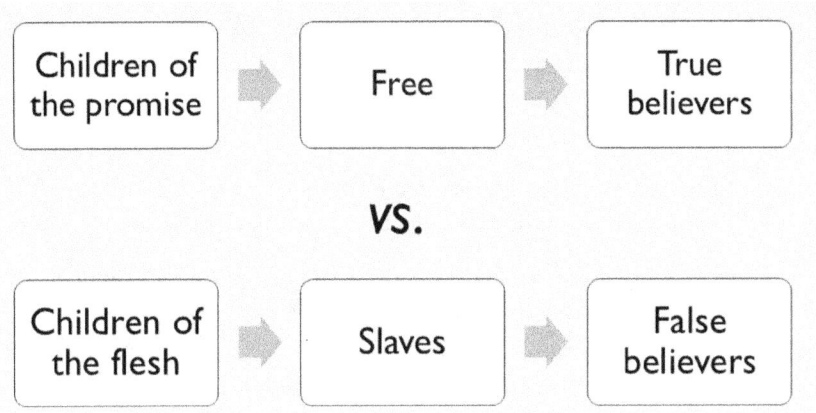

> Therefore, brothers and sisters, we are not children of the slave woman, but of the free woman. (Gal 4:31)

And there it is.

> It is for freedom that Christ has set us free. Stand firm, then, and do not let yourselves be burdened again by a yoke of slavery. (Gal 5:1)

By accepting Christ, the Galatian Christians escaped from slavery. They *were* in bondage to the "elemental spiritual forces" of works righteousness (Gal 4:3, 8–10), but that's all in the past. Paul spoke of Sarah and "freedom." Well, it was for freedom that Christ has set us free. So, don't go back to prison!

> Mark my words! I, Paul, tell you that if you let yourselves be circumcised, Christ will be of no value to you at all. Again I declare to every man who lets himself be circumcised that he is obligated to obey the whole law. (Gal 5:2–3)

If they decide to go down the "Jesus + Mosaic law = salvation" road, then they're spitting in Christ's face. We can't be perfect, and so that's why Christ came. But if, *knowing that,* you still want to try to obey the Mosaic law as if it were a way of salvation, then Christ is worthless to you. If you want to go that way, then you'd better be willing to be perfect and obey the entire law.

Good luck with that.

Again, Paul is arguing against the *common misunderstanding of the Mosaic law* that the false teachers are peddling—the same confusion with which Jesus dealt. The Mosaic law was never intended as a vehicle for salvation—it was simply a code for holy living while God's people waited for the Messiah. Centuries of tradition had crusted over top of the old covenant and turned it into a burdensome thing—a yoke of bondage.[17]

> You who are trying to be justified by the law have been alienated from Christ; you have fallen away from grace. (Gal 5:4)

The word that the NIV renders as "have been *alienated* from Christ" means to be "parted from" or to "abolish."[18] This is a moment of cosmic significance. If you choose that false equation of "Jesus + something else = salvation," then you've chosen a false message. That means you've been *parted* from Christ, *separated* from him. The union that once was is now severed, abolished.

---

17. "For Gentiles to revert to the prescriptions of the Jewish law as a necessary form of Christian lifestyle is, in effect, to make Christianity legalistic rather than Christocentric, and so not to have Christ's guidance in one's life" (Longenecker, *Galatians*, 226).

18. See LSJ, s.v. "καταργέω," sense 2, 908; L&N, s.v. "καταργέω," 13.100; and Abbott-Smith, s.v. "καταργέω," 238.

The Two Ladies and Their Two Jerusalems

The people don't do the severing—God does it. The text (and the Greek words behind it) don't read, "You've *alienated yourselves* from Christ." It reads, "You've *been alienated/parted* from Christ." Why has this happened? Why has God cut them loose from Christ? Because they "have fallen from grace."[19] They *keep on trying* to be declared righteous or be justified by means of the law,[20] and that isn't ever going to work.

Some Christians today might interrupt and ask, "Is Paul saying they've lost their salvation?" The answer is that Paul is not addressing that question here, and we shouldn't pretend he did—even in the interests of theological tidiness.[21] He's issuing a frustrated warning. In real life we know we must balance one statement with another. Paul isn't addressing salvation, he's just issuing a harsh warning. If you choose that wrong route, you've fallen from grace and God will sever you from relationship with Jesus—because that's the choice you made. This is very dangerous. Stop it now and come to your senses! He says all this to make them reflect, to think about what they're doing.

> For through the Spirit we eagerly await by faith the righteousness for which we hope. For in Christ Jesus neither circumcision nor uncircumcision has any value. The only thing that counts is faith expressing itself through love. (Gal 5:5–6)[22]

This passage should probably begin with "but" (see the New Living Translation here) because it's expressing a contrast—you can either choose works righteousness and thus fall from grace, or you can eagerly await final righteousness through the Spirit. Y'all can do that, *but we* will do this (etc.).

Jesus is all that matters. Not circumcision. Not tithing. Not your job. Not your family pedigree. Not your education. Not how smart you are. In

---

19. This particular phrase is epexegetical, meaning it explains a statement just made. "You have been severed from Christ, you all who want to be justified by the law—you have fallen from grace!" (κατηργήθητε ἀπὸ Χριστοῦ, οἵτινες ἐν νόμῳ δικαιοῦσθε τῆς χάριτος ἐξεπέσατε).

20. Gk: οἵτινες ἐν νόμῳ δικαιοῦσθε. The verb is passive ("be declared righteous") and is an iterative present ("keeps on trying"). The preposition expresses *means*.

21. "We should not try to diminish the force of these words, in the interest, perhaps, of this or that theological presupposition" (Hendriksen, *Galatians*, 196).

22. Gk: ἡμεῖς γὰρ πνεύματι [*dative of means*] ἐκ πίστεως ἐλπίδα [*accusative direct object, with* δικαιοσύνης] δικαιοσύνης [*objective genitive, object of verb* ἀπεκδεχόμεθα] ἀπεκδεχόμεθα. ἐν γὰρ [*explanatory*] Χριστῷ Ἰησοῦ οὔτε περιτομή τι ἰσχύει οὔτε ἀκροβυστία ἀλλὰ [*strong adversative conjunction*] πίστις δι' [*means*] ἀγάπης ἐνεργουμένη. "But we, through the Spirit, are eagerly waiting for the righteousness for which we hope. We do this by means of faith. Because in union with Christ Jesus neither circumcision nor uncircumcision means anything. What matters is faith expressing itself through love."

Faith Working Through Love

union with Christ, all of that is now useless (see Eccl 1–2)—all that really matters is faith *proven* by love (see 1 Cor 13). "If I had the gift of prophecy, and if I understood all of God's secret plans and possessed all knowledge, and if I had such faith that I could move mountains, but didn't love others, I would be nothing" (1 Cor 13:2 NLT).

The Spirit is who enables us to eagerly wait for the righteousness for which we hope. This isn't a "Gee, I sure hope I make it to the finish line . . ." kind of uncertainty about your status before God. No, it's the declaratory "Well done, good and faithful servant! . . . Come and share your master's happiness!" (Matt 25:21) from Jesus that good servants long to hear when this mortal life is over.

We trust in God and his promise of pardon and restoration. That's what "pardon" means—a formal remission of the legal consequences of a crime.[23] We trust that "in the gospel the righteousness of God is revealed" (Rom 1:17). Not a righteousness that's based on "trying to be justified by the law" (Gal 5:4), but "a righteousness that is *by faith* from first to last" (Rom 1:17).

That's why "in Christ Jesus neither circumcision nor uncircumcision *has any value*. The *only thing that counts* is faith expressing itself through love" (Gal 5:5–6). Nothing we do can trigger God's gift of righteousness. Instead, what counts is faith/trust in Jesus and his message. This true faith then *works* or *expresses itself* by means of love for God and neighbor.

- Just as a rabid Seattle Seahawks fan's faith in her team will naturally *work* or *express itself* in love by means of flags, bumper stickers, and other swag . . .

- So too will our faith in God's legal pardon and adoption into his family *work* or *express itself* by means of loving obedience to his commands (Deut 10:12–13).

Rather than the ethos of the Christian life being (a) the Mosaic law as a tutor, protective guardian, or watcher who keeps us on the right path until Christ comes, by reminding us of our moral failures and providing grace and atonement for sin, (b) the new covenant ethos is about faith expressing itself through love, because of what Christ *has now* done—"therefore love is the fulfillment of the law" (Rom 13:10). This is why Paul said that love is the only thing that counts.

---

23. See *OED*, s.v. "pardon," sense 5.a, accessed September 2023.

The Two Ladies and Their Two Jerusalems

> You were running a good race. Who cut in on you to keep you from obeying the truth? That kind of persuasion does not come from the one who calls you. (Gal 5:7–8)

What happened to you all? You used to understand. You used to get it. You used to know the truth. Where did you go wrong? This teaching didn't come from Jesus—it came from someone else.

> "A little yeast works through the whole batch of dough." I am confident in the Lord that you will take no other view. (Gal 5:9–10)

Paul quotes a line from one of his letters to the church in Corinth (1 Cor 5:6). Just a little yeast will make the entire loaf of bread rise. In the same way, just a little bit of falsehood will ruin the entire Christian message. But, he says, I'm confident that you'll correct your course, come to your senses, and tell those troublemakers to hit the road.

> The one who is throwing you into confusion, whoever that may be, will have to pay the penalty. (Gal 5:10)

Paul reminds us that troublemakers will pay, in the end. "The LORD examines the righteous, but the wicked, those who love violence, he hates with a passion" (Ps 11:5).

> Brothers and sisters, if I am still preaching circumcision, why am I still being persecuted? In that case the offense of the cross has been abolished. (Gal 5:11)

Verse 11 is difficult. The best explanation seems to be that these false teachers are spreading lies about Paul, suggesting he *really* preaches "Jesus + Mosaic law = salvation" elsewhere, but has abridged his message to them for sinister reasons.[24] This doesn't make any sense, Paul says, because he's hated and persecuted everywhere *by these same people!* If he preached the false message, the Jewish agitators would have much less of a problem. Christianity's great offense is that it requires people to admit, "I've been wrong about everything, and nothing I do myself can ever fix my relationship with God!"

There's a reason why Jesus' death makes people so angry—because it means we're criminals and that Jesus was executed in our place. Our salvation hinges on us admitting this to God and choosing to love him rather than ourselves. It asks us to admit that we're no good, but that Jesus was

---

24. See Longenecker, *Galatians*, 232–33.

voluntarily indicted and executed in our place, for our crimes, as our substitute. That's what the Christian story says as soon as someone looks at the cross and asks, "Why did *that* have to happen?" It makes us humble ourselves and exalt him. That offends us, and so the cross makes people angry. We don't naturally want this, and that's why, in order for anyone to respond to the truth, God must first remove that dark veil so the gospel light can shine in (2 Cor 4).

> As for those agitators, I wish they would go the whole way and emasculate themselves. (Gal 5:12)

These people are so obsessed with circumcision, why don't they just cut their penises off? "What could be more fitting?" Paul chortles. Prove the depth of your commitment to God—off with the penis! Nobody can suggest Paul lacked a sense of humor.

In the next part of the letter to the Christians in Galatia, he explains how to properly use this "freedom" from legalism.

On Freedom and Paul's "Third Way"
(vv. 5:13–26)

FREEDOM RINGS OUT AGAIN. It's a big thing with Paul. After the return from exile, God's people gradually overcorrected from externalism into legalism by the time of Jesus and the apostles—an ossified, frigid works righteousness. This target is Paul's rhetorical foe through the letter. Almost always in this letter when Paul refers to *slavery*, *the law*, or *freedom*, he's referring to the perverted form of "the faith" that had developed by his day—a system so crusted over with the barnacles of tradition that it wasn't the old covenant religion anymore. "You have let go of the commands of God and are holding on to human traditions" (Mark 7:8). It's this backdrop that helps us understand what the apostle says now:

> You, my brothers and sisters, were called to be free. But do not use your freedom to indulge the flesh; rather, serve one another humbly in love. (Gal 5:13)

So, when Paul reminds the Christians in Galatia that "you were called to be free," he means something like "free from the legalism and false religion the Jewish establishment is peddling." Not free from relationship with God. Not free from partaking in the faith that Abraham had—but free from *the false system* that had developed atop the old covenant and crusted over it. But if they're free from that—and from the old covenant framework entirely—then what was their matrix of authority? What was the new law? How did God regulate his people?

Christian have always struggled with how authority ought to work. Some say "the church" decides—this is the outsourcing option. Others say the Bible alone is the answer—this is individualism and (if church history is any indication) a potential road to apostasy.[1] Others say we ought to primarily rely on the Holy Spirit—but this is the potential road to subjective mysticism. The true pattern of authority is the Holy Spirit speaking in and through the Scriptures.[2] The scriptures are but one link in an integrated revelatory chain that goes like this:

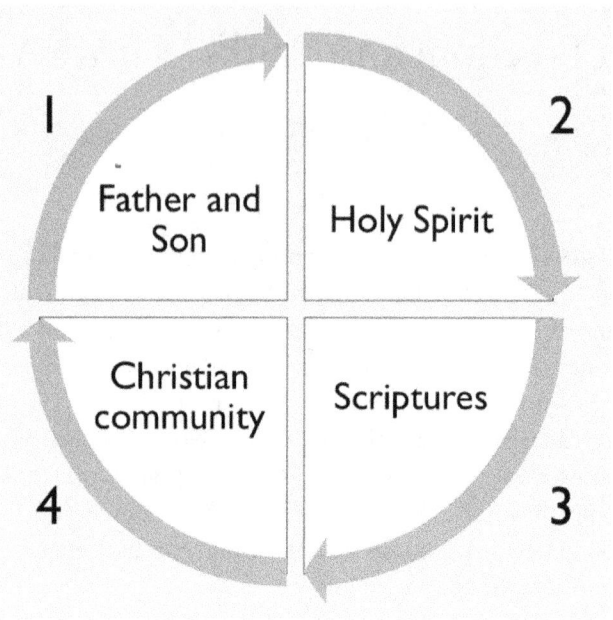

Father and Son speak to the Christian community through the Holy Spirit by means of the Scriptures, and we respond in prayer and loving obedience. There have always been some in the Christian community who abuse God's love and grace. Perhaps they wouldn't put it quite so crudely, but there it is nonetheless. It's folks like this who may be creeping around the churches in Galatia, whispering that, because the old covenant is abolished, we're now free to do whatever we want. "Not so!" Paul declares. Don't use your freedom from legalism as an *excuse*, a *pretext*, as an *absurd*

---

1. Some Christians—especially those from the free church tradition—may be confused at this point. One key emphasis from the Protestant Reformation was *suprema scriptura*—that Scripture was the *supreme* or *highest* channel of authority for Christian faith and life, not the only channel, but the final one. This is most often called *sola scriptura*, but *supreme scriptura* is a better term (see esp. Garrett, *Systematic Theology*, 1:206). This doesn't mean "the Bible alone," but rather that the Scriptures are the supreme channel, the yardstick by which everything must be measured.

2. Ramm, *Pattern of Religious Authority*, 28. See also Calvin, *Institutes*, 1.7.

On Freedom and Paul's "Third Way"

justification.³ The NIrV renders this as "don't use your freedom as an excuse to live in sin," and the NEB reads, "do not turn your freedom into licence for your lower nature."

> For the entire law is fulfilled in keeping this one command: "Love your neighbor as yourself." If you bite and devour each other, watch out or you will be destroyed by each other. (Gal 5:14–15)

The key, Paul says, is to read and interpret the law *through a prism of love—through relationship*.⁴ This isn't a new thing—it was there in the old covenant all along—but *it's become a new thing* in light of Jesus' authoritative interpretation and application of that first covenant. After all, didn't Leviticus (of all places!) say that we must love our neighbor (Lev 19:18)? Isn't that what Jesus said was the sum of the old covenant law (Mark 12:28–34)? Isn't that what even a scribe figured out from his own study of the Torah (Mark 12:32–34)? That's why Paul said elsewhere that love was the fulfillment of the law (Rom 13:10).

So, what to do with this sudden freedom from crushing legalism? This freedom from the weight of all the external expectations of "right behavior" as meritorious? The freedom from the cold scrutiny of religious leaders anxious to condemn you? The solution isn't to run wild and party. It isn't to rip up the Torah and burn it in celebration. It's to retain the Torah (Paul and Jesus both quoted Leviticus, after all!), but interpret it *the real way*—through a paradigm of covenant love for God and for one another. Without love, all the new covenant community will do is destroy itself with infighting and selfish dealing (cf. Mic 2:1–5; 3:1–8). Paul illustrates this with an analogy of animals biting and eating one another. Real Christianity expresses itself in loving service to each other (cf. Acts 2:42–47).

When Paul says, "serve one another in love," he means the *manner*, the *way*, the *inner disposition that prompts* the service.⁵ We don't need a book

---

3. See LSJ, s.v. "ἀφορμή," sense 2, 292.

4. "In this entire summary, Paul's purpose is both to let the law come into its own proper validity in the life of believers; and to graft its fulfillment upon a different principle from that of human self-vindication through works—namely, the salvation brought by Christ. For the love, in which the law has its fulfillment, is the fruit of faith (verse 6)" (Ridderbos, *Epistle to Galatia*, 201).

5. The preposition in ἀλλὰ διὰ τῆς ἀγάπης δουλεύετε ἀλλήλοις could refer to personal agency ("serve one another by love") but this option is typically for active and personal agents, not attributes or virtues. It could be instrumental means ("serve one another by means of love" or "with love"). I believer *manner* is best—Paul is describing *the way* we ought to serve one another.

or a podcast to teach us *how* to love one another—all we need to do is ask ourselves how *we would wish* to be treated. Your own heart is your teacher![6] Emil Brunner wrote persuasively about how brotherly love is the necessary witness of the church's life in union with Christ.

> The Spirit who is active in the Ekklesia expresses Himself in active love of the brethren and in the creation of brotherhood, of true fellowship. Thus the Ekklesia has to bear a double witness to Christ, through the Word that tells of what He has bestowed upon it, and through the witness of its life, through its being, which points to Him as its vital source.[7]

But, how to "be free," be holy, and yet still live without legalism? The answer is a conjunction of word + Spirit. Remember, the same apostle Paul elsewhere said that the Scripture had two jobs: (1) to bring people to faith in Christ, and (2) to teach us how we ought to live as children of the King (2 Tim 3:14–17). This is the tail end of that organic "revelatory chain" we mentioned earlier. Jesus promised he would *continue* to make his Father known to Christians "in order that the love you have for me may be in them and that I myself may be in them" (John 17:26). This suggests an ever-present communication between Jesus and his people—but how? Through the Spirit (John 14:26–27; 16:12–15). How does the Spirit speak to us? Primarily through God's message, his story recorded in Scripture—it's the Spirit's sword, after all (Eph 6:17)!

> So I say, walk by the Spirit, and you will not gratify the desires of the flesh. (Gal 5:16)

Paul says we must live a certain way—that's what the "walk" metaphor means. How, then, shall we live? In union with the Holy Spirit, in *relationship* with him.[8] Instead of incessant reference to laws and traditions (e.g., "can I do *this* on the Sabbath?"), a new covenant believer lives in personal

---

6. Luther, *Galatians*, 265.
7. Brunner, *Church, Faith, and the Consummation*, 134.
8. I take the dative in πνεύματι περιπατεῖτε to be a dative of association. Most commentators opt for a dative of agency ("by the Spirit"), but in this circumstance the agent usually performs the action of the verb (in this case, the Holy Spirit, if the dative truly expresses agency), whereas in our text Paul is telling *Christians* to perform the action. Daniel Wallace dismisses dative of agency and suggests *means* (*GGBB*, 165–66), but this is quite difficult to explain in exposition. Another option is *manner*, which answers the implicit "how" of the verb. But, on balance, I believe a dative of association is the best option. Regardless of the syntactical category one chooses, the root idea is that we cannot live without the influence, leading, and direction of the Spirit.

relationship with the Spirit of God. This is warmth, not frigid rules. Again—
and this cannot be stressed enough—love for God was always the basis of a
proper old covenant relationship (see Deut 10:12–22). But after the return
from exile a creeping legalism set in among the community that gradually
ossified this love ethic into a works righteousness that rescued nobody.

Now, in the new and better covenant, Jesus ups the ante (as it were)
on love as the hinge for Christian life, doctrine, and practice—it's love that
fulfills the whole purpose of the old covenant law.[9] Jesus' relentless focus on
this love ethic is why the apostle John is so fixated on love (see 1 John 3).
It's also why Paul emphasizes freedom from a works-righteousness ethic in
favor of a life lived in loving relationship with God via the Holy Spirit—remember that revelatory chain we mentioned earlier by which Jesus promised to never leave us alone (John 17:26; see John 14:26–27; 16:12–15)?

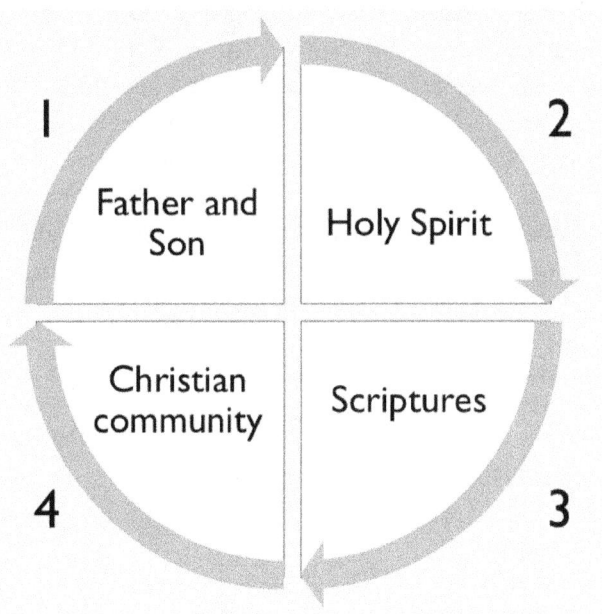

Live in union with the Spirit! This is a bit loose for people who prefer
lists, categories, and a catalog of rules. But, if taken too far, that's the road
to a new legalism, and they just broke free from all that. So, we keep the

---

9. "So it is love—love that responds to Christ's love and that expresses a new existence
in Christ (cf. 2:20)—that motivates the ethical life of a Christian, with the results of that
love ethic fulfilling the real purport of the Mosaic law" (Longenecker, *Galatians*, 243).

Torah but read it in dialogue with God's message from the Scriptures, by the power of the Spirit.

This isn't a rote promise that "if you do this, you'll never sin!" It's a general truism, like many sayings in Proverbs. Paul is just saying that, to the extent you live in real union and relationship with the Spirit (in conjunction with the Scriptures), then you will not be controlled by your own lusts. His wording in Greek is as emphatic as possible; it could be rendered something like "you will *never ever* carry out the lusts of the flesh."

> For the flesh desires what is contrary to the Spirit, and the Spirit what is contrary to the flesh. They are in conflict with each other, so that you are not to do whatever you want. But if you are led by the Spirit, you are not under the law. (Gal 5:17–18).

God is changing us from who we are into who he wants us to be. "And we all, who with unveiled faces contemplate the Lord's glory, are being transformed into his image with ever-increasing glory" (2 Cor 3:18). This means there is an ongoing, internal struggle as this renovation happens. Our "old person" doesn't want to fade to black, and our "new person" must struggle to assert itself in our hearts and minds (see Eph 4:22–24). We win this battle to the extent we're led by the Spirit—and *to that extent*, we're free from legalism, self-righteousness, and the crushing weight of meeting impossible standards. To the extent we allow the Holy Spirit to lead and energize us, we're free from the "law" of works righteousness.

Basically, Paul's audience is situated in a culture that presents two different authorities for the Christian life:

1. The Jewish agitators are offering "Jesus + obey all the Mosaic Law." This is externalism. It's legalism. It's a bad option.
2. Other folks are offering a "do whatever you want" vibe.

Both these options are unacceptable, and so Paul offers a third way[10]—a life lived according to God's will as expressed in the Scriptures, interpreted through a prism of love for God and neighbor, by the power of the Spirit. To be led by the Spirit (Gal 5:18) is to be *guided*, to be *led toward* some goal[11]— to be shepherded. In the Christian faith, that goal is Christ-likeness—to be renovated from who you were and *guided* and *led* into the image of God's dear Son (2 Cor 3:18).

---

10. Fung, *Galatians*, loc. 3057.
11. LSJ, s.v. "ἄγω," sense 2.2.

On Freedom and Paul's "Third Way"

So, we have a choice to make. Paul now compares the fruit of two paths—the flesh versus the Spirit. The "flesh" means *our bodies*, but more specifically our *lusts*, our *sinful desires*. It means the appetites and passions that characterize who we used to be (and partly still are),[12] rather than the "mind of Christ" that is the prototype and pattern for our moral renovation in process.

> The acts of the flesh are obvious: sexual immorality, impurity and debauchery; idolatry and witchcraft; hatred, discord, jealousy, fits of rage, selfish ambition, dissensions, factions and envy; drunkenness, orgies, and the like. I warn you, as I did before, that those who live like this will not inherit the kingdom of God. (Gal 5:19–21)

These contrasting lists are rightly famous. They're not exhaustive (Paul ends the list with "and the like"), but they're representative enough to get the point across. A tree is known by its fruit (Luke 6:43–45). God's people have his "seed" planted within them, and God's seed always generates recognizable fruit (1 John 3:9). Perhaps a Christian's fruit isn't all it should be, but the point is that it's recognizable. You might have a pitiful apple tree in your backyard, and even if it only produces a few sorry apples each year, you still recognize them as apples. So it is with Christians . . . and with those who serve a very different master. "This is how we know who the children of God are and who the children of the devil are: Anyone who does not do what is right is not God's child, nor is anyone who does not love their brother and sister" (1 John 3:10).

There are four general categories in this list. This doesn't mean everything "bad" in this life should be situated in these categories; it's just how this particular list shakes out:

1. *Sexual crimes.* Sexual immorality, impurity, and debauchery.

2. *Spiritual adultery.* Idolatry and witchcraft.

3. *Love of self.* Hatred, discord, jealousy, fits of rage, selfish ambition, dissensions, factions, and envy.

4. *Drunkenness.* Drunkenness is just what it sounds like, and what the NIV translates as "orgies" means the general sort of "carrying on" that happens at, say, alcohol-saturated parties.

---

12. "The flesh, as the seat of the affections and lusts, fleshly nature" (LSJ, s.v. "σάρξ," sense 2, 1585).

Because this is rotten fruit, people who practice these things—whose lives show a pattern of rotten fruit—will not gain possession of the kingdom of God.[13] Their actions make it clear to which master they really belong. Because Paul says these rotten fruits "are obvious," I'll only remark on a few of them here:

1. *Sexual immorality.* As the incarnate Messiah (the divine person with a human nature), as a Jewish man whose mission involved perfectly obeying the old covenant law in our place, as our substitute (see 2 Cor 5:21), Jesus' frame of reference to define sexual ethics was Lev 18. As the eternal Son within the one Being who is God, Jesus gave Leviticus to Moses.[14] This suggests the sexual boundaries depicted there are still in effect—all of them.

2. *Impurity.* This literally means "dirty." It's figurative here, meaning activity that morally pollutes you. How do we know what these activities are? Well, that's why you have the Scriptures! Again, Paul isn't saying we burn the old covenant and start from scratch—he's appealing to God's moral laws as standards of behavior loving children *should want to do*. We love God because he first loved us (1 John 4:19), and this love produces fruit. The opposite of that is to live a polluted, morally filthy life.

The apostle now shares the other side of the coin—the fruit of a Spirit-referenced and led life:

> But the fruit of the Spirit is love, joy, peace, forbearance, kindness, goodness, faithfulness, gentleness and self-control. Against such things there is no law. (Gal 5:22–23)

There are all virtues, or what some would call *moral qualities*.[15] They come from within. They aren't measurable. They can't be quantified or plotted on a chart. They're inner character qualities that flow from a heart

---

13. The phrase is ἃ προλέγω ὑμῖν καθὼς προεῖπον ὅτι οἱ τὰ τοιαῦτα πράσσοντες βασιλείαν θεοῦ οὐ κληρονομήσουσιν. It can be rendered, "I am warning you beforehand, just as said previously, that the ones who are practicing such things will not gain God's kingdom." The key word is πράσσοντες, which in this context means "to practice" (LSJ, s.v. "πράσσω," sense 4, 1460).

14. Leviticus 18 begins with "The LORD said to Moses . . ." (Lev 18:1). We know this is the triune God speaking, because the divine name of Yahweh is always signified by a capital "LORD" in our English Bibles.

15. *OED*, s.v. "virtue," sense I.1.a, accessed July 2023.

disposition. The word "fruit" can also be translated as *crop* or *harvest*. Paul's talking about the product of your heart, the "crop" that the gospel has yielded in your life. No believer's life is perfect. But would an impartial observer see this fruit in your life—no matter how underdeveloped it might be? Do they flow from your heart, habits, and appetites?

Love. Jesus is the paradigm for love, which is unearned and undeserved (see Hos 1–3). This means we love others especially if they don't deserve it. This is hard to do, obviously, but it's clear that a "get off my lawn!" vibe is not a fruit of the Spirit—but quite the opposite.

How many Christians are curmudgeons? Are bitter? How many of us sing "They'll Know We Are Christians" and then leave the church building and ignore everything we just sang? How many of us do *anything at all* to make love the defining virtue of our lives? Take any steps to make that a reality? How many of us have prayed, "God, make me love you more, so I'll love people more"? How many conservative Christians in America are more passionate about Donald Trump, who personifies corruption and debauchery, than about Jesus of Nazareth—who personifies love, kindness, and grace?

> In Christ there is no East or West,
> In Him no South or North,
> But one great Fellowship or Love
> Throughout the whole wide earth.[16]

Would that our goal would be make this true in our hearts and lives!

Joy. This is a spirit of *pure delight*, or *great pleasure* and *happiness*.[17] It's an inner glow that comes from experiencing the joy of union and relationship with the Father, through the Son, by the power of the Spirit. It's what the angel Gabriel said Elizabeth would experience when she gave birth to their son John (Luke 1:14). It's what the angels in heaven do when just one sinner repents (Luke 15:7). Jesus told the disciples that, when they see him alive after his impending death, "no one will take away your joy" (John 16:22).

Are you a happy person? If you're a Christian, and your outlook is more about misery and gloom than joy, then perhaps there's a problem? Of course, life is difficult, and we all go through seasons of drought. But, overall, do you have *joy, happiness,* and *delight* in your life because of your

---

16. Oxenham, "No East or West," 322.
17. See LSJ, s.v. "χᾰρά," 1976; and Abbott-Smith, s.v. "χᾰρά," 479.

salvation? Pray for God to give you joy. Pray the Psalms. Ask God for a joyful disposition. Ask him to change your mindset—to see the world through new eyes. Ask him to teach you to love life in the Spirit. Pray all that before you read the Scriptures.

> Oh the sheer joy of it!
> Living with Three,
> God of the universe,
> Lord of a tree,
> Maker of mountains,
> Lover of me!
> Oh the sheer joy of it!
> Breathing thy air;
> Morning is dawning,
> Gone every care,
> All the world's singing,
> "God's everywhere."[18]

Peace. This means an *inner tranquility*, a *trouble-free spirit* or *conviction* because "we have peace with God through our Lord Jesus Christ, through whom we have gained access by faith into this grace in which we now stand," (Rom 5:1–2). It speaks of security, of safety, of a certainty that all will be well, because you have "peace that transcends all understanding," (Phil 4:7). Jesus is our peace (Eph 2:14). The apostle Paul apparently didn't write these virtues in any particular order, but if he had then "peace" would have gone before "joy," because the first *produces* the second.

> O what a happy soul am I!
> Although I cannot see,
> I am resolved that in this world
> Contended I will be;
> How many blessings I enjoy
> That other people don't!
> To weep and sigh because I'm blind,
> I cannot, and I won't.[19]

Forbearance. This means we *put up with* things—"love covers over all wrongs" (Prov 10:12; cf. 1 Pet 4:8). The Pharisees didn't like forbearance because their idea of relationship with God was an unwitting legalism—an adoption dependent on performance. When *what we do* is the basis of

---

18. Cushman, "Sheer Joy," 209.
19. Crosby (at age eight), "Blind But Happy," 211.

On Freedom and Paul's "Third Way"

relationship, there is little tolerance for failure. Real grace isn't that way at all. An honest thirst for personal holiness is a non-negotiable fruit of real faith (1 Pet 1:15–16), but that doesn't *create* relationships. Grace does. Love does. Unearned mercy does.

That has implications for our relationships—we have *patience*. How willing are we to give in? To not insist on our own way? To listen to other voices? To be patient? To be understanding? Think of how much God has put up with from you—has he lost patience yet? It could also mean a kind of *patience* as the world falls apart around us, and in that sense it's basically the same as *peace*. We'll only want to cultivate forbearance in our lives if we truly appreciate God's patience with us—seen most clearly in Christ's voluntary death for us, in our place, as our substitute. The "cross + resurrection + ascension" trilogy is the prism for seeing and living real life.

> Whenever there is silence around me
> By day or by night—
> I am startled by a cry.
> It came down from the cross—
> The first time I heard it.
> I went out and searched—
> And I found a man in the throes of crucifixion
> And I said, "I will take you down,"
> And I tried to take the nails out of his feet.
> But he said, "Let them be
> For I cannot be taken down
> Until every man, every woman, and every child
> Come together to take me down."
> And I said, "But I cannot hear you cry.
> What can I do?"
> And he said, "Go about the world—
> Tell everyone that you meet—
> There is a man on the cross."[20]

Kindness. The word sometimes means a kind of "moral uprightness" (see Rom 3:12), but it can also mean an interpersonal kind of goodness that's *almost* a synonym for love.[21] It's difficult to draw a hard line between these virtues, because they shade over into one another. The idea here seems to be a softness of heart, a kindness, a loving disposition toward other people.

---

20. Cheney, "There Is a Man on the Cross," 143.

21. See *TLNT*, s.vv. "χρηστεύομαι, χρηστός, χρηστότης," 511; and Abbott-Smith, s.v. "χρηστότης" 484.

Faith Working Through Love

It's this same "kindness" that describes Jesus' mission to rescue us (Rom 2:4; Titus 3:4).

If we walk in union with the Spirit—in *living relationship* with him—then kindness should always threaten to overflow from our hearts and into real life. Some of us have problems with kindness. I'm not talking about being an introvert or being shy and perhaps being misinterpreted as unkind. I'm asking whether, if we could open your heart, "kindness" would be stamped inside. Do you have a desire to be kind, to be loving, to be tender-hearted? Or, are you a quarrelsome person? Do you only show kindness to select people?

God changes us to be more like Christ over the course of time. Is kindness gradually working its way into the overflow of your heart and mind? If we have God's "seed" within us, then his fruit will come. Pray and ask God to give you kindness, as you ponder how kind Christ has been to you.

> If I speak in the tongues of men or of angels, but do not have love, I am only a resounding gong or a clanging cymbal. If I have the gift of prophecy and can fathom all mysteries and all knowledge, and if I have a faith that can move mountains, but do not have love, I am nothing. If I give all I possess to the poor and give over my body to hardship that I may boast, but do not have love, I gain nothing. (1 Cor 13:1–3)

Goodness. The idea here is quite close to kindness, but perhaps shading more to sweetness and gentleness. It's not exactly the moral uprightness of an external act ("he always does good!"), but more of an inward *disposition*, a *virtue*, a *character* that's suffused with goodness, sweetness, tenderness.[22] Saint Paul said he was convinced the Christians in Rome were "full of goodness" (Rom 15:14). That didn't mean they "always did good" (though perhaps they did), but it seems to indicate something like "you're all *good* people—*sweet and gentle* people!" Paul prayed that God would grant to the Christians in Thessalonica their "every desire for goodness" (2 Thess 1:11), which again suggests an inward virtue rather than the moral quality of an outward action.

Pretend you're at a funeral and someone says, "He was a good man!" What does that mean? It doesn't mean so much that he did good things, but instead it refers to character. Not character in the sense of "his good outweighed the bad"—erase all imagery of *doing things* from your mind at this point. The focus is character, attitude, demeanor, disposition—you're saying the guy was kind, sweet, gentle, nice, tender-hearted.

---

22. *TLNT*, s.vv. "ἀγαθοποιέω, ἀγαθωσύνη," 1.

We're selfish people. We want to look out for ourselves. We weren't made that way, but we've become that way because of the fall (see Gen 3). Part of "being made in the image of God" is that we alone among God's creatures have the capacity to know God, to receive and acknowledge his love, and to love him back in return. There's an "I-Thou" connection with God ready to be wired up—one that no cat or dog will ever have. God is relational. Father, Son, and Spirit are "one" in the sense that their mutual love is the reality that (as it were) binds them together into one society of persons, one constellation, one compound being. It's the inward circularity of divine life that explains the mutual indwelling language that Jesus used (see John 14–16).

When God restores this "image" through salvation, part of what that means is that he renovates our capacity for relationship *as it was meant to be*—on both the vertical (us to God) and horizontal (us to others) planes. We can now begin the work of patching up our relationships so they better reflect the nature of the triune God whose image we mirror. That means these virtues Paul keeps pressing—kindness, goodness, gentleness—are possible . . . if we have union with Christ.

> Let me live in my house by the side of the road—
> It's here the race of men go by.
> They are good, they are bad, they are weak, they are strong
> Wise, foolish—so am I;
> Then why should I sit in the scorner's seat,
> Or hurl the cynic's ban?
> Let me live in my house by the side of the road
> And be a friend to man.[23]

Faithfulness. Paul means loyalty, trustworthiness, and reliability. To whom? To God and to covenant brothers and sisters. It's not just a "when I give my word, I mean it!" kind of vibe, but the more holistic idea of "she's such a loyal friend—I can always trust her!"

Faith is often a synonym for "trust," and that's what it means to "believe in Jesus"—it means *to trust* his representations about who he is and what he's done for us. We trust God. We're loyal. We've pledged allegiance to him. We're the same way toward our brothers and sisters in the believing community. These virtues interpenetrate one another, build upon each other. We're loved by God, so we have peace, and so we have joy, and kindness, and goodness, and patience, and faithfulness to God and to one another.

---

23. Foss, "House by the Side of the Road," 244.

And, of course, we can be faithful like this because God has first been faithful to us in Jesus.

> Thou hast given so much to me,
> Give one thing more—a grateful heart:
> Not thankful when it pleaseth me,
> As if thy blessings had spare days,
> But such a heart whose Pulse may be
> Thy praise.[24]

Gentleness. This is "a spirit of gentle friendliness."[25] It's a mild-mannered kind of disposition. The apostle isn't declaring everyone must try to be Mr. Rogers, but he is saying that a "gentle friendliness" ought to characterize our interactions with others.

Self-control. Paul means a mastery over one's emotions and desires. We get better at this as the *person we were* gradually fades into the background to be replaced by the *person we now are* in union with Christ. The question to ask is, "Am I getting better at suppressing the old me?" This isn't a matter of sheer willpower, but a character renovation the Holy Spirit works from the inside out. Self-control is one of the virtues that the apostle Peter said "will make you useful and fruitful as you get to know our Lord Jesus Christ better" (2 Pet 1:8 NIrV).

God changes us so we can honor him with our life and work. Self-control is part of the harvest the Spirit reaps from within our hearts from that change. The question, of course, is whether we pray for change, for self-control, for greater holiness. Or, whether we remain on autopilot.

> Thy way, not mine, O Lord,
> However dark it be!
> Lead me by thine own hand,
> Choose out the path for me.
> Smooth let it be or rough,
> It will still be the best;
> Winding or straight, it leads
> Right onward to thy rest.
> I dare not choose my lot;
> I would not, if I might;
> Choose thou for me, my God;
> So I shall walk aright.[26]

---

24. Herbert, "Heart to Praise Thee," 256.
25. Friberg, s.v. "πραΰτης," 326.
26. Bonar, "Thy Way, Not Mine," 219.

On Freedom and Paul's "Third Way"

This all seems like a tall order. What we must never forget is that Paul isn't talking about a transaction, a "do this for God, and he'll do this for you" arrangement. That would be legalism and works righteousness. You must always read every single command from Scripture in light of Christ and his Good News, as the fruit of trusting that message, owning it—as the natural harvest that comes from a personal encounter with Jesus of Nazareth, by the power of the Holy Spirit (2 Cor 4:3-6). These aren't the fruit of hard work, but *the fruit of the Spirit*.

Paul continues:

> Those who belong to Christ Jesus have crucified the flesh with its passions and desires. Since we live by the Spirit, let us keep in step with the Spirit. Let us not become conceited, provoking and envying each other. (Gal 5:24-26)

Hopefully you haven't *literally* crucified yourself! Paul is employing the same metaphors he uses in the letter to the church in Rome ("for we know that our old self was crucified with Him," Rom 6:6)—if you're in union with Christ, then your old person is dead and gone. Your *flesh and bones* remain, but your *spirit*, your *soul*, your *heart*, your *mind* have changed. Spiritual birth has occurred, a God-seed has been planted, and things will never be the same again.

We can walk away from the old habits. God has given us the power to walk away—to be led by the Spirit instead of our flesh. Instead of remaining unwitting slaves to our own lusts and ultimately to Satan, we've been set free. Jesus defeated Satan (Heb 2:14-15) and killed death itself for all who trust him and his message (1 Cor 15:54-57). In return, he's given the Holy Spirit to his brothers and sisters so he and the Father can teach us, communicate with us, mold us into the Son's image. We must make a conscious, everyday choice to live with incessant reference to the Spirit.

Paul uses a military metaphor here that the NIV rightly keeps[27]—we must "keep in step" with the Spirit, "march in step" (NIrV) with him. The Spirit "calls the cadence" in that we live in union—in *relationship*—with him[28] ("we live by the Spirit"), and so we can and must choose to march in

---

27. See LSJ, s.v. "στοιχέω," 1647; Abbott-Smith, s.v. "στοιχέω," 418.

28. Once again, I believe this is a dative of association (contra NIV and most English translations). The military metaphor further supports this usage over against *agency* or *means*. We are, as it were, marching in step with the Spirit, which means we have to "stay with him."

tune to his call. We can do that because we're now free from both a false legalism *and* from Satan.

The danger is that it's possible to fool ourselves, to become conceited and arrogant while maintaining an unwittingly fraudulent front of piety. We can do "good things" and even produce some fruit—tellingly, in this context the "fruit" will rarely be a virtue or a moral quality like those Paul listed. In short, we can become Pharisees. It's to that danger that Paul now turns.

On Brotherly Love and Reaping the Whirlwind

(vv. 6:1–10)

THE FRUITS OF THE Spirit aren't a theoretical thing. They're real, and never more so than in our everyday life with other people. So, Paul gets down to brass tacks here and explains how this fruit should work and show itself every day. But . . . that's when we start to lose people. It's easy to say something in church, to nod your head or intellectually agree. It's something else to do it.

Paul said we must always march in step with the Spirit (Gal 5:25), because we live in union—*in relationship*—with the Spirit. Then he warns us against being conceited, which means to be proud for no reason.[1] We like to make performance an idol. We like to compare ourselves to others. We like to silently judge other people. This produces a tepid legalism that only grows stronger if we don't work to crush it. We can get like that without even noticing. The apostle knows this—it's why he's talking about it here.

The tell is simple—legalists never glory in the fruits of the Spirit. This is because those are *virtues*, which means they're about *character, attitude, demeanor*, the *heart*. A legalist (or a legalist apprentice) will never boast about the fruits of the Spirit—she'll always boast about something *external*, something *measurable*, something at which it's easier and cheaper to *point*. Never forget that.

So, it's no accident that when Paul wants to discuss the error of arrogance, pride, and vain-glory—to explain how to avoid Gal 5:26—he turns to external things. If we could hear his voice, we would know his tone and

---

1. LSJ, s.v. "κενόδοξος," 938. The word occurs only once in the New Testament and once in the apostolic fathers. The CEB has "arrogant" and the NIrV offers up "proud."

know how to read this passage better. Is this written in a forceful and confrontational tone, or is it more a warning from a worried friend? I see the tone as "affectionate disappointment"—the frustrated urgency that characterized the first four chapters can't have faded too far into the background. I interpret the apostle's tone here as "I fear for you, that somehow I have wasted my efforts on you" (Gal 4:11).

> Brothers and sisters, if someone is caught in a sin, you who live by the Spirit should restore that person gently. (Gal 6:1)

A believer is caught in the act. He stands ashamed. He didn't plan it, but it happened, and now what to do? How should Christians react? It's easy to cloak a cruel and harsh spirit with a religious gloss. So, Paul detonates that bridge by declaring that if someone is caught in a sin—something that isn't premeditated, but perhaps overtakes the believer by surprise or by way of a sinful impulse[2]—then the folks who are truly spiritual should restore that person with a spirit of gentleness, of friendliness.

The NIV tries to help by rendering "you all who are spiritual" as "you who live by the Spirit." This is right, but perhaps it helps too much. It's an adjective. It describes the true Christian—she is *spiritual*, she *has the fruits of the Spirit* (Gal 5:22–23). In other words, Paul says, the spiritual person must show the fruits of the spirit in *real* life, toward *real* people, in a *real* situation.[3] Living in union and relationship with the Spirit isn't an abstract thing, an idea that exists on paper as a nice utopia. It's real. We can make it

---

2. See Friberg, s.v. "προλαμβάνω," 330; Abbott-Smith, s.v. "προλαμβάνω," 381; and Gerhard Delling, s.v. "προλαμβάνω," in *TDNT*. Albert Barnes captures the spirit of the matter: "hurried on by his passions or temptations to commit a fault" ("Galatians," 390). See also Schreiner, *Galatians*, 357. The idea is that there is no premeditation, no "high-handed" or defiant sin (Num 15:30–31). This is essentially the distinction between the "unintentional" and "deliberate" sins from the Mosaic law (Lev 4:1—6:7; cf. Num 15:22–29 vs. Num 15:30–31). Alvah Hovey (*Galatians*, 72) and A. T. Robertson (*Word Pictures*, on Gal 6:1) believe the proper sense is that the individual has been "caught in the act" or "surprised" during the commission of sin.

The main feature of the Greek is that the verb is passive—the guy is surprised, or detected, or discovered, or overtaken by something. Ἀδελφοί ἐὰν καὶ προλημφθῇ ἄνθρωπος ἔν τινι παραπτώματι = "Now, brothers and sisters, if someone has been overtaken in reference to a transgression . . ." This doesn't help us discern which option is best, but it really doesn't touch my main point—this is not a "defiant" or "high-handed" (KJV) sin in the sense of Num 15:30. It's not premeditated, defiant, or contemptuous of God. It's the sin of a believer who just messes up—plain and simple.

3. "A proud or contentious spirit would utterly disqualify one for the service contemplated by the apostle in this exhortation" (Hovey, *Galatians*, 72).

real. We must make it real. That starts with not being legalists toward one another when we sin.

> The apostle does not say in what manner this is to be done; but it is usually to be done doubtless by affectionate admonition, by faithful instruction, and by prayer. Discipline or punishment should not be resorted to until the other methods are tried in vain.[4]

Paul continues:

> But watch yourselves, or you also may be tempted. (Gal 6:1)

The legalist doesn't like to contemplate this scenario, because he already "knows" he's better, faster, stronger, and smarter than everyone else. "Well," Paul says, "you'd better check your ego, because you aren't any of those things."

> Carry each other's burdens, and in this way you will fulfill the law of Christ. (Gal 6:2)

Paul keeps pressing the fruits of the Spirit because this is where the rubber meets the road. This is Christianity.[5] If you *love* your covenant brothers and sisters, then you won't cast them aside when they're overtaken in a transgression. If you have *joy*, your focus will be more on God's love and grace and less on a cold disapproval of others. If you have *peace*, you can be patient with other people because your own status isn't dependent on measuring yourself favorably against others. If you have *kindness* and *goodness*, then you have a tender-hearted, sweet, and gentle disposition that is eager to forgive.

If you're *faithful*, then you'll show loyalty toward your brothers and sisters by wanting to help them. If we have *gentleness*, then we'll want to be kind friends toward others. In short, the opposite of a Pharisee. And, if we live in relationship with the Spirit, we'll pray for *self-control* so we don't do things we ought not do—which means we sympathize when our brothers and sisters fail in that goal, just as we do, too. "One of the ways in which He bears these burdens of ours is through human friendship."[6]

---

4. Barnes, "Galatians," 391.

5. In his commentary, Timothy George helpfully draws out "four important truths about practical Christian living" from Paul's command in Gal 6:2 (*Galatians*, 413), but I believe the apostle's focus is on our attitudes and actions *toward other people*. So, I won't dwell on personal implications here because Paul's focus is on practical outworking toward others.

6. Stott, *Galatians*, 157.

We each have burdens, sins, temptations, struggles. We can either be islands, or we can carry these for one another. Help each other. Pray for one another. Be understanding. Be kind and good. "Anyone who claims to be in the light but hates a brother or sister is still in the darkness" (1 John 2:9).[7]

What will we do? What does the law of Christ say?

It says to love your neighbor as you love yourself (Gal 5:14; see Lev 19:18, Mark 12:28–34)—this is what James later called the "royal law" (Jas 2:8). Again, this doesn't mean Jesus and Moses are at odds. It means this has been God's heart all along, and the majestic intensity of the Spirit's work in the lives of new covenant believers makes this possible. Not a spirit of eager condemnation, but of loving correction (see John 7:53—8:11). The old covenant law was never an end in and of itself, nor was it ever intended as a vehicle to achieve righteousness in God's eyes. Obedience was always predicated on love for God (Deut 6:4–5), and Paul is saying that now—as the story has progressed further along into the new covenant—the Mosaic law is explicitly interpreted christocentrically.[8]

> If anyone thinks they are something when they are not, they deceive themselves. (Gal 6:3)

The truth is that you're nothing. I'm nothing. We are nothing. We're only haters rescued by grace. That means we *must not be* so quick to condemn, to throw people away, to say "Aha!" If you are in a Christian community where there is a deficit of love, of patience, of understanding—no fruits of the Spirit applied to *real* people, in *real* life, in *real* situations—then you should flee.

> Again it is apparent, as in Galatians 5:26, that our conduct to others is governed by our opinion of ourselves. As we provoke and envy other people when we have self-conceit, so when we think we are "something" we decline to bear their burdens.[9]

---

7. Hovey observes, "Though the Fourth Gospel was not yet written, it is evident that Paul knew the substance of the Lord's sweet and wonderful command to his disciples" (*Galatians*, 73). Timothy George writes, "The work of restoration should be done with sensitivity and consideration and with no hint of self-righteous superiority" (*Galatians*, 411).

8. "The law, according to Paul, must be interpreted christocentrically, so that it comes to its intended completion and goal in Christ. The 'law of Christ' is equivalent to the law of love (5:13–14), so that when believers carry the burdens of others, they behave as Christ did and fulfill his law. In this sense Christ's life and death also become the paradigm, exemplification, and explanation of love" (Schreiner, *Galatians*, 360–61). See also Martyn, *Galatians*, 548.

9. Stott, *Galatians*, 159.

Life in relationship with the Spirit—in step with him (Gal 5:26)—isn't a polite mission statement, a vision poster, or some bumper sticker. Love is the animating force that binds Father, Son, and Spirit together into one society of persons, one constellation, one compound being—God literally is love (1 John 4:8). Part of being restored to the image of God (see 2 Cor 3:18) is the renovation of love as that animating force that binds us to God and to one another in the believing family. The fruits of the Holy Spirit are the *crop*, the *harvest* the gospel reaps in your life from the fountainhead that is God's love (John 3:16). A harvest isn't theoretical—it's either there or it's not. These are virtues because they come from within and so cannot be consistently faked.

A legalist will not like any of this. She'll equivocate. She'll talk about holiness (1 Pet 1:15-16). She'll talk about standards. She'll get exasperated when one mentions love, patience, kindness, goodness—as if these are Pollyanna ideals for naïve folks who hail from Mayberry. Paul takes a sledgehammer to this lie: "You are nothing, so don't think you're something. You're no better than him."

Instead, we ought to do something completely different.[10]

> Each one should test their own actions. Then they can take pride in themselves alone, without comparing themselves to someone else, for each one should carry their own load. (Gal 6:4-5)

There's a movie starring Paul Newman and Robert Redford titled *The Sting*. Both men play con artists running a swindle on a gangster played by Robert Shaw. One scene takes place on a train. Newman and Redford are preparing for the first act in this long-running con game. This particular hook involves poker. Newman's character must successfully cheat during a game to set Shaw up.

Newman sits at a table, shuffling cards like a virtuoso. He does several cute little card tricks, and then he fumbles the deck and cards go flying everywhere. Redford stares at him, horrified. Can Newman get it together? Will he fumble the thing when it counts, too? Newman scowls, gathers the cards, and says to Redford, "Just worry about your end, kid."[11]

In other words, "You worry about your part. I'll take care of mine!"

---

10. The NIV drops the adversative conjunction at the beginning of Gal 6:4, which should be rendered as something like "instead" or "but." The phrase can be translated: "Instead, each one must examine their own work" (τὸ δὲ ἔργον ἑαυτοῦ δοκιμαζέτω ἕκαστος). See the ESV, NASB, KJV, RSV.

11. Hill, *The Sting*.

Faith Working Through Love

That's what the apostle Paul is saying here. Worry about yourself. Weigh and judge your own actions. Do self-reflection rather than judgmental condemnation. Then you can have pride in your own holiness rather than tut-tutting about everyone else's alleged *lack* of that virtue. This isn't a license for self-righteousness, but a call to find grounding and foundation for peace in *your own fruit of the Spirit*, which is the harvest of God in your soul. After all, the day is coming when the Lord will assess the quality of what each believer has built upon the foundation that is the gospel—we'll be graded according to our own fruit (1 Cor 3:10–15).[12]

> Don't compare yourself with Pastor Jim or Deacon Smith or Sister Jones. God wants you to bring your own life before the open pages of his Holy Word. Are you more loving and patient than you were this time last year? How do you gauge your gentleness and self-control, your kindness and faithfulness? No one who honestly brings his or her life before God in this kind of way is going to have any interest in "comparing himself to somebody else."[13]

A legalist finds peace by comparing himself first to a standard and then to others, graded on a curve. A Christian boasts and glories in what the Spirit is doing in his life. So, each believer must "carry their own load" in the sense that we worry about our end—we focus on the Spirit's renovation project in our own lives, rather than comparing ourselves to others. The true believer need not fear hellfire—that isn't even on the table here—but we should serve the Lord with an eye toward being acknowledged as good and faithful children when Jesus returns.

> Nevertheless, the one who receives instruction in the word should share all good things with their instructor. (Gal 6:6)

This is a little aside from Paul that has no real connection to what's come before or what comes next.[14] The NIV tries to make a connection, but the word it translates "nevertheless" can also mark a quick transition and be rendered "now" or something colloquial like "by the way." This is a

---

12. Schreiner notes that the verb here ("then they can take pride in themselves . . .") is future, and so interprets vv. 4–5 as referring to the judgment of believers (*Galatians*, 361–62). He is correct, but I want to emphasize the present-day implications too.

13. George, *Galatians*, 417–18. Also Stott: "In other words, instead of scrutinizing our neighbour and comparing ourselves with him, we are to test our 'own work' for we will have to bear 'our own load'. That is, we are responsible to God for our work and must give an account of it to Him one day" (*Galatians*, 159).

14. Ridderbos, *Epistle to Galatia*, 216–17.

throwaway comment that's almost spontaneous. It's about how a teacher in the congregation deserves to be compensated. Perhaps all this talk about people worrying about *their own* selves, focusing on *their own* fruit of the Spirit, has spurred Paul to quickly remind people that their teachers in the congregations (who hopefully talk about this stuff) deserve some love![15]

> Do not be deceived: God cannot be mocked. A man reaps what he sows. (Gal 6:7)

This comment reminds us of Hosea (Hos 10:12–13). Our actions are the seed we plant. The consequences of those actions are the crop, the fruit, the harvest. When we say one thing and do another, we're hypocrites. When we say we love God, and don't love one another, and don't show the fruits of the Spirit toward brothers and sisters who are overtaken in a transgression, then we're ridiculing God. We're insulting him. We're mocking him. "To their loss they are crucifying the Son of God all over again and subjecting him to public disgrace" (Heb 6:6). Alvah Hovey remarks, "Contemptuous treatment of him is sure to bring evil on those who are guilty of it."[16]

It's so easy to fool ourselves. Christians have been doing it since the beginning of time. The Israelites in Amos's day were so cocksure that they *longed* for the day of the Lord—yet they were the evil ones (Amos 5:18)! Down south in Judah, her leaders, priests, and prophets were as corrupt as can be, yet they honestly blustered, "Is not the LORD among us? No disaster will come upon us!" (Mic 3:11). In post–Civil War America, some Christians began pushing a "biblical" polygenesis—an allegedly scriptural perspective that taught that black people were a separate species from white people.[17] We do evil and are so blind that we see everyone else's faults but our own. We think we're holy when we're actually quite evil. "Don't be deceived!" Paul warns.

> Whoever sows to please their flesh, from the flesh will reap destruction; whoever sows to please the Spirit, from the Spirit will reap eternal life. (Gal 6:8)

---

15. Martyn speculates that Paul must have left competent teachers in the Christian communities in Galatia, and that the congregations are intent on dismissing these folks due to sinister influence from the enemies of the gospel Paul criticizes throughout the letter, and so Paul reminds them of their duties to these teachers (*Galatians*, 552). Who knows! Martyn's proposal makes good sense, but we just have no idea.

16. Hovey, *Galatians*, 74.

17. Noll, *America's Book*, 482–85.

Again, life in union with Christ doesn't mean works righteousness, of which legalism is a symptom. Nor does it mean lawlessness, a "we can do whatever we want!" ethos. It means marching in union—*in relationship*—with the Holy Spirit. Relationship produces observable fruit, either for God or for a very different master (1 John 3:7–10). What fruit are we bearing? What's our "harvest"? More specifically, what seeds are we planting that generate this fruit? The answer tells us all we need to know about the crop to which we belong when Christ sends forth the harvesters at the end of the age to bring in the sheaves (Matt 13:30, 40–43).

> Let us not become weary in doing good, for at the proper time we will reap a harvest if we do not give up. Therefore, as we have opportunity, let us do good to all people, especially to those who belong to the family of believers. (Gal 6:9–10)

The beloved apostle closes this section by implying an equation that suffuses the whole letter:

1. God loves us.
2. God rescues us.
3. God gives us the Holy Spirit.
4. We love God in return, and therefore produce spiritual fruit.
5. One of these spiritual fruits is brotherly love.

Alvah Hovey observed:

> The apostle simply reiterates the teaching of his Lord. His exhortation is but the statement, in another and practical form, of the Saviour's "new commandment," which was, at the same time, as old as the spiritual nature of man . . . . The extraordinary love of the early Christians to one another was a surprise to the heathen, and was, in many cases, the principal thing which recommended the new religion to their attention, and compelled them to see in it a beneficent power.[18]

We don't know when the time of harvest will come, but we must do our bit while we wait. This means those virtues—that fruit of the Spirit—applied in real life to real people. To all people, of course, but especially to those in the household of faith. Christ's family is a global community. What kind of crop will we have to show Jesus when he returns to gather in the harvest?

18. Hovey, *Galatians*, 75.

The "New Creation" or Bust

(vv. 6:12–18)

PAUL NOW PRESSES A few reminders and offers his assessment of the Judaizers' motives. This is really a postscript, a few closing lines summing up the matter and issuing a broadside or two against his opponents. What's quite clear is Paul's genuine worry about the Christians in Galatia. The situation is so dire—believing in a false version of the "gospel"—that Paul is compelled to once more speak very plainly to press home his remarks.

> See what large letters I use as I write to you with my own hand!
> (Gal 6:11)

Paul often uses a secretary to transcribe his letters (see Rom 16:22). But here, at the end of this unpleasant but necessary communique, Paul takes the pen from his secretary's hand and writes the last bit himself. The Christians in Galatia who handled the letter would immediately see the different handwriting and hopefully be touched by the gesture.[1] In a letter that contains so many stern rebukes, a loving and personal touch like this is a nice gesture.

Paul reveals that this isn't an honest dispute between two parties who have a theological disagreement.

---

1. For a representative analysis along this line that doesn't attribute Paul's "large letters" to poor eyesight, see Longenecker, *Galatians*, 289–90. The old *Scofield Reference Bible* is representative of the tradition that sees great significance in Paul's handwriting here: "But now, having no amanuensis at hand, but urged by the spiritual danger of his dear Galatians, he writes, we cannot know with what pain and difficulty, with his own hand, in the 'large letters' his darkened vision compelled him to use" (Scofield, *Scofield Reference Bible*, 1248).

Faith Working Through Love

> Those who want to impress people by means of the flesh are trying to compel you to be circumcised. The only reason they do this is to avoid being persecuted for the cross of Christ. (Gal 6:12)

The Jewish agitators are pushing for "converts" in order to avoid persecution. Paul says this is the "only" reason they're doing what they're doing.[2] We don't know the precise situation. Many believe the Jewish agitators fear persecution from the larger Jewish community—and that may well be the issue.[3] Another possibility is that they fear local Roman authorities who may have little patience for what they perceive to be an exclusivist cult.[4] Here is a sketch of the situation to help us figure out the battle space.[5]

1. *The Roman Empire was a syncretistic society.* All sorts of religions flourished and were tolerated to some degree. All that was asked in return by Jesus' day was a sort of mega-pluralism—a respect and homage to the cult of the emperor.

2. *The Jews were generally not loved but tolerated.* Yes, they had their invisible God who couldn't be represented by images or idols, and they had a fanaticism about their God being the "only one." Yes, it was weird and exclusivist. But, for all that, Jews were a *known* quantity. They were understood, acknowledged, and tolerated within limits. They'd carved out a precarious place for themselves in the Roman world.[6]

---

2. The Greek is clear: μόνον ἵνα τῷ σταυρῷ τοῦ Χριστοῦ μὴ διώκωνται. The ἵνα + subjunctive, combined with the negation, tells us they are doing this for the purpose of escaping persecution. Paul clarifies that their sole motive (μόνον) is this objective. Dunn (and others) suggest Paul is exaggerating the "only" part for rhetorical effect (*Galatians*, 336).

3. On the theory that the agitators don't so much fear the Romans but sanctions from their own Jewish communities, see Hendriksen, *Galatians*, 242–43; Ridderbos, *Epistle to Galatia*, 242–44; and Barnes, "Galatians," 397–98. This is only a representative sample—most commentators take this view.

4. Bengel observes that either option is possible; persecution might come "from the Jews, or even from the Gentiles, who now bore more easily with the antiquity [antiquated usages] of the Jews, than with the supernatural novelty [new doctrine and rule] of the Christian faith" (*Gnomen*, 4:57).

5. For a reliable survey of this period, see esp. Grant, *Jews in the Roman World*, parts 3 and 4. See also Bruce, *New Testament*, chapters 21–22.

6. Michael Grant observed that it was "an emphatic principle of Roman rule that every community should, as far as possible, be allowed to maintain its national customs, including the worship of its own gods in its own way. Pagan cults, after all, tolerated one another; religious exclusiveness was regarded as weird. And so, paradoxically, the Roman authorities issued tolerant dispensations in favour of the intolerant Jewish God" (*Jews in the Roman World*, 60).

3. *The Christians were a different story.* At first, the Romans saw them as a Jewish cult, and so "the Way" initially had some measure of quasi-legitimacy. But the movement was rapidly being recognized as a "new thing." This "new thing" got no love from the Roman authorities, who didn't know or understand what it was about. A new, exclusivist cult that pronounced that this man Jesus was the true king? A martyr whose death was stirring unrest in various places throughout the Mediterranean basin? This was trouble.

    It makes sense that anxious Jews who were attracted to Christianity might seek shelter from potential Roman persecution by hiding under a Jewish umbrella—hence the *very Jewish flavor* of their "gospel." However, as Jewish unrest grew in Judea from the mid-50s AD onward, culminating in the revolt of 66–70, the wisdom of aligning oneself with that party would be increasingly open to question.

4. *On the other hand, the Christian movement was also the target of repeated Israelite attacks, most infamously at the very hands of the apostle Paul!* The apostle's later persecution by and incessant trouble with outraged Jews throughout the Mediterranean proves the depth of hostility that Christianity provoked in their community. This reaction operated on two levels. On the one hand were the theological conservatives, characterized by the Pharisee party among the Sanhedrin, who believed Christianity was leading good Jews into apostasy. Christians were therefore dangerous and subversive heretics who must be stopped—*now*. On the other hand, we have the more populist reactions from officials and laypeople in the provincial synagogues—the people from whom Paul encountered such opposition during his missionary travels.

    Either way, the Jews saw "the Way" as a heretical cult, and Judaism had a long tradition of bringing a sledgehammer to a fistfight when stirred to action and fueled by religious fervor. Phineas was celebrated for killing an Israelite as the man cavorted with a Moabite prostitute (Num 25:1–13). Centuries later, Mattathias struck down a fellow Israelite who offered pagan sacrifice in obedience to the Seleucid king, thereby sparking the Maccabean rebellion (1 Macc 2:15–41).

    Ironically, Paul himself was later this same group's arch-foe. Paul spoke movingly about the persecutions he suffered (Gal 5:11), and the book of Acts is all the testimony one needs to see that his main foes were the pious Jews who thought they were doing the Lord's work by taking Paul off the board. To quote Joseph Stalin, "Death solves all problems. No man, no problem!"⁷ (see John 11:49–50). Indeed, it was the enraged Jews whose hysterical reaction at seeing their nemesis in the flesh resulted in Paul's arrest (Acts 21:27–36). They then engineered more than one hare-brained plot to kill him while he remained in Roman custody—a conspiracy involving no less than certain key members of the Sanhedrin and perhaps forty fanatics who pledged to not eat or drink until Paul was slain (Acts 23:12–15; 25:1–3).

5. *In between Paul and full-blown Judaism were the Jewish-flavored Christians, represented by the hardliners in the Jerusalem congregation who were always suspicious of Paul (Acts 23:17–24) and very uneasy with Peter's forays into Gentile evangelism (Acts 11:1–18).* It was this party that pressured Peter, whom they always considered "their man," to stop fraternizing with gentiles (Gal 2:11–21). It was these same people who sent emissaries out to Antioch to pressure the new believers there to add "obedience to Moses' law" as a condition of salvation (Acts 15:1–4). It was the Jerusalem community which had earlier sent Barnabas to Antioch after hearing word that a large group of gentiles had converted and joined the church there (Acts 11:22). Barnabas was likely on orders to "scout out" the situation, not because the Jerusalem leaders were overjoyed about new converts, but because these new believers *were gentiles.*

The book of Acts depicts James as trying desperately to hold the gentile and Jewish constituencies together in the Jerusalem congregation, even securing a concession from Paul to placate the hardliners in their midst (Acts 21:22–24). Much earlier, this same congregation struggled with hostility among both the Jewish hardline and the more "worldly" widows among them (Acts 6:1). Not unlike the way regional prejudices colored the practical outworking of the gospel in the Jim Crow south, these Jewish Christians were officially "fine" but functionally *very uneasy* with full gentile participation in the Jesus community. It is people from this group who are the Jewish agitators stirring up trouble among the Galatian congregations.

6. *So, the Christians found themselves in a difficult spot by the mid-50s AD.* Despised by the Jews as an apostate cult on the one hand, while on the other they were scrutinized with increasingly furrowed brows by local Roman authorities of varying competence and quality. Pilate himself was a mid-level civil servant of modest abilities whose weakness was obvious to the wily Annas and his son-in-law Caiaphas.

---

7. Conquest, *Stalin,* 79.

The "New Creation" or Bust

The question now is—what do these Jewish agitators fear the most? Do they fear persecution from provincial Roman authorities or from increasingly fundamentalist Jewish (non-Christian) hardliners? On balance, the evidence favors the second option. The gossip is that Paul (and, by extension, his converts) lead Jews away from the Torah and convince them to forsake Jewish customs (Acts 21:21). This is *kinda* true, though not for the reasons they think. But nuance has never been sexy. In every age, those who shout the loudest have a remarkable ability to carry a larger, more passive bloc along with them. This is why a few partisans could whip a crowd into a frenzy when they spotted Paul in the temple courtyard (Acts 21:27–28).

And so the more Jewish-oriented Christians who "were not bold enough to defy the prejudices of their unconverted fellow-countrymen"[8] sought cover from the Jewish hardliners.

> The rival mission considered Paul's activity as a threat to the larger group (the Jewish people), which had to be preserved. These teachers were also acutely aware that apostates could be persecuted by the zealous (as Paul himself had done prior to his conversion; Gal 1:13–14, 23). It would have been in everyone's best interests, they would have thought, to make it clear to both non-Christian and Christian Jews that the Jesus movement was in no way a movement that promoted apostasy.
>
> By reinforcing Jewish (Christian) adherence to the Torah, and all the more by bringing Gentiles to the light of the law, the rival teachers could save themselves, the church in Judea, and the churches in the Diaspora where Jewish communities were strong, from the intramural persecution that perceived apostasy could invite.[9]

If you're a Jewish person who is attracted to Christianity (for whatever reason), what is one way to (a) escape the wrath of the Jewish fundamentalist hardliners who have hounded Paul from one end of the eastern Mediterranean to the other, and (b) still retain Jesus-ish teachings? One possibility is to combine Judaism with Jesus. First, you emphasize the fraudulent heritage of works righteousness to which the true old covenant religion had degenerated—the rally-cry[10] of Acts 15:1: "Unless you are circumcised, according to the custom taught by Moses, you cannot be saved!" This is the tradition that Paul earlier labeled "a different gospel" (Gal 1:6). Second, you

---

8. Lightfoot, *Galatians*, 302.
9. deSilva, *Introduction to the New Testament*, 436.
10. Stott, *Galatians*, 176.

just add "Jesus as Messiah" into the mix. Be a good Jew . . . and believe Jesus is the Messiah, *then keep doing both.*

This is a desperate *tertium quid*—a "third thing" that will likely please nobody. But, by hiding under the old covenant cloak, these Jewish agitators hope to "avoid being persecuted for the cross of Christ" (Gal 6:12). They fear the stigma of identifying themselves with Jesus, his message, and all this implies.[11] This means "the cross of Christ" has some hold on them, which suggests (a) they either are professing Christians already, or (b) they're intrigued enough by the Christian story to be tagged *as being* Christians—which is essentially the same thing in the eyes of suspicious Jewish communities at home and abroad. Either way, the Jewish emphasis of their teaching—the entire point at issue in Paul's letter—is to some extent a front.

Perhaps some would think it presumptuous of Paul to say this—has he become a mind reader? How does he know what their motives really are? But the fact is that Paul is the most experienced missionary in the Christian community. He has experience. He knows the ground. He knows the players. He knows the motives. He speaks with the sure confidence of a man who knows his job very, very well. It's the same kind of experience that enables a professional in any field to hear the bare facts of a situation and then pronounce an opinion that seems clairvoyant and telepathic—especially when it's proven right.

"How did you know that!" we ask. Experience, that's how.

> Not even those who are circumcised keep the law, yet they want you to be circumcised that they may boast about your circumcision in the flesh. (Gal 6:13)

Nobody can keep the law when it's framed as a meritocracy—not even the Jewish agitators. Yet, they want people to buy in on a system that had twisted the old covenant into a relationship with God based on good works. And why? So they could use them as cover for being "Jewish," to escape the taint of being Christian. What a ridiculous situation! They claim the cross of Christ, yet spend all their time denigrating it—boasting about their converts' circumcision—in order to escape suspicion by the local authorities![12] With "believers" like that, who needs enemies?

11. Dunn, *Galatians*, 336.

12. John Calvin remarks, "It is the usual practice of ambitious men meanly to fawn on those from whose favour they hope to derive advantage, and to insinuate themselves into their good graces, that, when better men have been displaced, they may enjoy the undivided power" (*Galatians*, 182).

The "New Creation" or Bust

> May I never boast except in the cross of our Lord Jesus Christ, through which the world has been crucified to me, and I to the world. (Gal 6:14)

Paul has a different focus. The world is dead to him. Babylon is dead to him. The harlot atop the beast, with all her charms and wiles and beauty, is dead to him (Rev 17). The world has been crucified to him. Of course, no mortal human is *totally* dead to the world, and Paul has told us about his own struggles to stay faithful to Jesus (Rom 7:7–12). But we get the idea. Paul has made the decision to follow Jesus and boast in "the cross," to not knuckle under and look for some cover to shield himself from the Roman authorities. He crossed that bridge a long time ago and then burned it behind him.[13]

The cross is the *means* or *instrument* that has brought about this new reality.[14] Paul is very fond of metaphysical language to describe spiritual realities (see Rom 6). In an unseen but extraordinarily real way, Christ's death on a cross, his burial, and his resurrection have significance far beyond their physical implications for his own body. When we pledge allegiance to Jesus, we somehow *participate*, are *amalgamated into*, are *united* with him and his death, burial, and resurrection—and nothing is ever the same.

Jesus is crucified	= Our "old person" is crucified
Jesus dies	= Our "old person" dies
Jesus is buried and gone	= Our "old person" is buried and gone
Jesus raises from the dead to new life	= We're "born again" and have spiritual life

This isn't typology—it's real. This is why the cross is *literally* the instrument that crucifies Paul to the world, that makes it dead and gone to him. But this "crucifixion" goes both ways—*it makes the world dead to him and him dead to the world*. The bridge has been taken out. There is no path back

---

13. "What Paul means is that every rationale for individual and corporate existence which is independent of God (as in Rom. 1:21–22), together with its system of beliefs and values and corresponding life-style, has been condemned and put to death so far as he is concerned; and that he himself has likewise been rendered inoperative so far as the attractions of such rationales, belief and value systems and life-styles are concerned" (Dunn, *Galatians*, 340–341).

14. In the phrase δι' οὗ ἐμοὶ κόσμος ἐσταύρωται κἀγὼ κόσμῳ, the preposition expresses *means*, and the relative pronoun refers back to the cross (τῷ σταυρῷ τοῦ κυρίου ἡμῶν Ἰησοῦ Χριστοῦ) and not to Jesus. The pronoun ἐμοί is a dative of reference, expressing that the world has been crucified *in reference to him* or *so far as he is concerned*. Not only that, but Paul adds that "I have been crucified with reference to the world" (κἀγὼ κόσμῳ).

for either party—for Paul or the world. Neither can return. The dye has been cast. Quite literally, Paul says, "We're both dead to each other."

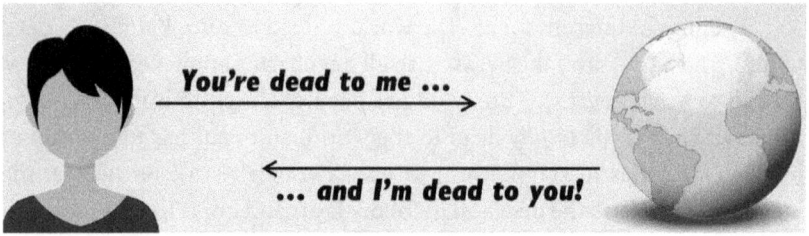

A great sea change has happened, triggered by a divine encounter with Christ by way of the Holy Spirit. Reality has changed, life has changed—his mind and heart have changed. This is why Paul can never do what his opponents do—to boast in so-called converts as a cover to escape persecution. He can only boast in the cross of Christ because it's what changed everything. For the Christian, it's not simply an event we look back on with a sweet smile. It's the engine that triggered an entirely new reality—*the true and real reality*.

Because of Jesus and the new and better relationship that comes along with the new and better covenant, Paul can sum up the whole matter with this:

> Neither circumcision nor uncircumcision means anything; what counts is the new creation. (Gal 6:15)

This is the grand summary of the whole issue in this letter.[15] Are you a Christian? Have you had an encounter with Jesus via the Holy Spirit? Has the Lord opened your heart to understand the things of God? Has the Spirit lifted aside that Satanic veil so the gospel can shine in (2 Cor 4:3-4)? Have you been born again? Do you have spiritual life? These questions are all getting at the same idea—have you been made new in relationship with Jesus Christ?

> If anyone is in Christ, the new creation has come: The old has gone, the new is here! All this is from God, who reconciled us to himself through Christ and gave us the ministry of reconciliation: that God was reconciling the world to himself in Christ, not counting people's sins against them. And he has committed to us the message

---

15. Longenecker, *Galatians*, 296. "Paul uses it to climax all of his arguments and exhortations in 1:6—5:12 with respect to the Judaizing threat."

The "New Creation" or Bust

of reconciliation. We are therefore Christ's ambassadors, as though God were making his appeal through us. We implore you on Christ's behalf: Be reconciled to God. (2 Cor 5:17–20)

In Christ, we're changed. Reconciliation triggers moral and spiritual renovation in our hearts and minds. The "ministry of reconciliation" of which Paul speaks is the good news that triggers this divine renovation. This is the Christian community's mission, its ethos, its *telos*. We're ambassadors who represent the new Jerusalem in kingdom outposts scattered here and there across rural and urban Babylon. We show and tell about Jesus so people would choose to be reconciled to God.

Against that mission, what exactly is circumcision? It's nothing. The Jewish agitators want external rites to be the main thing, but they are not—it's the new creation that is the first principle. "Political laws, human traditions, church ceremonies, and even the law of Moses are without Christ; therefore, they do not bring us righteousness before God. We may use them as things both good and necessary, in their place and time; but if we talk of the matter of justification, they do not help but harm very much."[16]

The new creation is the issue, and it's the only issue that matters. Circumcision, uncircumcision—it doesn't matter. Legalists always focus on these things because it's what they think God wants. They think relationship with God is about "doing the right things," and so they think it's *really important* to identify the right things so we can all do them. Paul says no—all that's pointless. It's downstream of the first principle, which is "are you a new creation in relationship with Jesus?"

Who are the people who follow this rule? Who are the folks who *really get* that this "new creation" business is the hinge upon which everything turns?

> Peace and mercy to all who follow this rule—to the Israel of God. (Gal 6:16)

True believers are the ones who understand all this—the ones who aren't defined by outmoded covenant markers, but by the inward love that comes from being a new creation in union with Christ. The "true" Israelites are the ones whose hearts are marked with God's covenant sign (Rom 2:28–29)—who've been "branded" (as it were) by the Holy Spirit. The true child of Abraham is the person (whether she be Jewish or whatever) who has the same faith and trust in God that Abraham had (Rom 4:16; cf. Gal

---

16. Luther, *Galatians*, 301.

3:7). In union with Jesus Christ, we are all children of God through faith (Gal 3:26). Paul explained earlier that "if you belong to Christ, then you are Abraham's seed, and heirs according to the promise" (Gal 3:29).

> And by "the Israel of God" he means without doubt the true Israel, those who are sons of God through faith in his Son, whether of Jewish or Gentile descent after the flesh.[17]

Some Christians believe Paul refers to two groups: (a) gentiles who follow the rule of "new creation or bust," and (b) the Jewish folks who do likewise. This is grammatically possible, but contextually unlikely.[18] In this letter Paul simply isn't concerned about a future for Israel—turn to Rom 9–11 if you want to see that discussion. In a context in which he's combatting legalist Judaizer posers, the very last thing the apostle would do would be to toss out onto the table a reference to ethnic Israel as a bloc.[19] No—his focus here is on real believers, no matter who they are.

The "true circumcision," Paul declared elsewhere, are "we who serve God by his Spirit, who boast in Christ Jesus, and who put no confidence in the flesh" (Phil 3:3). When Jesus rescues us, he marks us with an invisible "circumcision" (so to speak) on our heart that declares us to be his (Col 2:11). This marker is a beacon saying that we're now alive with Christ.

So, in that vein, the "true Israel" are those people (Jewish, Canadian, Azeri, Chilean, or whatever) who understand that the new creation is the only thing that matters for relationship with God, *because it's the only thing that establishes this relationship!*[20] There are not "two peoples" of God, nor

---

17. Hovey, *Galatians*, 78. Lightfoot observes, "It stands here not for the faithful converts from the circumcision alone, but for the spiritual Israel generally, the whole body of believers whether Jew or Gentile; and thus kai is epexegetic, i.e., it introduces the same thing under a new aspect" (*Galatians*, 305).

18. See esp. Hendriksen, *Galatians*, 246–47.

19. Longenecker is especially on the mark here (*Galatians*, 298).

20. In the phrase καὶ ἐπὶ τὸν Ἰσραὴλ τοῦ θεοῦ, the conjunction is ascensive and homes in on the "them" and explains who they are. It's essentially appositional. The genitive in Ἰσραὴλ τοῦ θεοῦ is subjective—God's Israel, which basically means "God's people." This suggests it could be a possessive genitive, but that usage is generally for personal property, not people in a relationship. We have a translation conundrum here, because the true force of "Israel" in this context is to emphasize the "real believers." A more colloquial rendering (and perhaps a more accurate one) would be something like "peace and mercy to them—the true believers." On my interpretation of "Israel of God," see Alford, *New Testament*, 2:360; deSilva, *Galatians*, 145; Stott, *Galatians*, 180; esp. Schreiner, *Galatians*, 380–82; Luther, *Galatians*, 303; and the NLT, RSV, NIV, REB. For a contrary view that sees two groups (gentiles and Jews), see Fung, *Galatians*, loc. 3730.

does church "supersede" or "replace" Israel. Instead, non-Jewish believers have been adopted into Israel and treated as if we were born there (see the analogy of the olive tree at Rom 11). Then, together with the believing ethnic Jewish people, all true believers are the nation of "Israel."[21] Gentiles are grafted into the nation of Israel in the same way foreigners become naturalized American citizens—they're not born as Americans, but they *become* Americans.

Jesus said this would happen. A Roman soldier once begged Jesus to heal a servant who was terribly ill. Jesus offers to go at once to heal the man. But the soldier demurs—surely Jesus can just give the order right there and right now, and the servant will be healed!

> When Jesus heard this, he was amazed and said to those following him, "Truly I tell you, I have not found anyone in Israel with such great faith. I say to you that *many will come from the east and the west, and will take their places at the feast with Abraham, Isaac and Jacob in the kingdom of heaven. But the subjects of the kingdom will be thrown outside, into the darkness*, where there will be weeping and gnashing of teeth." (Matt 8:10–12)

Who are these people who will come from the east and west and eat at this great "supper" when Jesus returns to take his throne? They aren't ethnic Israelites. They're gentiles—even Roman soldiers like this man! Even more, some of the folks who assume they've got their tickets punched because they're ethnic Jews ("the subjects of the kingdom") will be cast outside, into eternal darkness. What does this mean? It means that membership in the kingdom of heaven—a spiritual reality that will take physical form when Jesus returns (Rev 19:11—20:6)—isn't about blood, but *belief*. It's about who has the faith of Abraham. The true "Israelites" are those who have this faith—whatever their nationality is.

These are the people who follow the rule that "neither circumcision nor uncircumcision means anything; what counts is the new creation" (Gal 6:15). The ones who live this rule out have God's "peace and mercy," because they're the ones who are "the Israel of God" (Gal 6:16)—who are God's *Israel*, God's *people*.

> From now on, let no one cause me trouble, for I bear on my body the marks of Jesus. The grace of our Lord Jesus Christ be with your spirit, brothers and sisters. Amen. (Gal 6:17–18)

---

21. See Garrett, *Problem of the Old Testament*, 159–74.

Faith Working Through Love

Paul concludes with what one commentator called an "impatient grumpiness,"[22] but this seems a bit unfair. It more about exasperation, a dusting off the hands with an "I'm done with this!" sort of attitude. It's not directed at the Jewish agitators, but at the Galatians believers.[23] "Forget those people," he says. "Don't cause me anymore trouble by letting them confuse you about the gospel again. I'm done with them, and you should be, too!" Paul has suffered for Christ—literally suffered. He's been beaten, left for dead, imprisoned, and bears *real* scars and *real* marks on his body that testify to his dedication for Christ.

Again, he asks, "What is 'circumcision versus uncircumcision' when compared to the love, forgiveness, and reconciliation that God offers through his dear Son?" In a twenty-first-century American context, we might ask, "What is 'Republican versus Democrat' when compared to Christ?" If a local church puts any external rite, habit, tradition, or so-called essential *in front of* the gospel, as a prerequisite, then run away. Fast.

The late pastor John Stott wrote this about the scandal of the cross of Christ:

> Every time we look at the cross Christ seems to say to us, "I am here because of you. It is your sin I am bearing, your curse I am suffering, your debt I am paying, your death I am dying." Nothing in history or in the universe cuts us down to size like the cross. All of us have inflated views of ourselves, especially in self-righteousness, until we have visited a place called Calvary. It is there, at the foot of the cross, that we shrink to our true size.[24]

This is what Paul wanted the Galatians to see. It's what he wants us all to see. I hope we do.

---

22. Dunn, *Galatians*, 346.
23. See Fung, *Galatians*, loc. 3771.
24. Stott, *Galatians*, 179.

Bibliography

Abbott-Smith, G. *A Manual Greek Lexicon of the New Testament*. 2nd ed. New York: Charles Scribner's Sons, 1922.
Alford, Henry. *The New Testament for English Readers: A Critical and Explanatory Commentary*. Vol. 2. New ed. London: Bell and Co., 1872.
Arndt, William, et al. *A Greek-English Lexicon of the New Testament and Other Early Christian Literature*. Chicago: University of Chicago Press, 2000.
Athas, George. *Bridging the Testaments: The History and Theology of God's People in the Second Temple Period*. Grand Rapids: Zondervan, 2023.
Bainton, Roland. *Here I Stand: A Life of Martin Luther*. Nashville: Abingdon, 1950.
Barnes, Albert. "Galatians." In *Barnes' Notes*, vol. 11. Grand Rapids: Baker, 1998.
Barry, John D., et al., eds. *Lexham Bible Dictionary*. Bellingham, WA: Lexham, 2016.
Bengel, Johann Albrecht. *Gnomon of the New Testament*. Edited by M. Ernest Bengel and J. C. F. Steudel, translated by James Bryce. Vol. 4. Edinburgh: T&T Clark, 1860.
Berkouwer, C. G. *Faith and Justification*. Translated by Lewis Smedes. Grand Rapids: Eerdmans, 1954.
Bonar, Horatius. "Thy Way, Not Mine." In *Treasury of Religious Verse*, edited by Donald T. Kauffman. Westwood, NJ: Revell, 1962.
Brown, John. *An Exposition of the Epistle of Paul the Apostle to the Galatians*. Edinburgh: William Oliphant and Sons, 1853.
Bruce, F. F. *Acts*. Rev. ed. New International Commentary on the New Testament. Grand Rapids: Zondervan, 1988. Kindle.
———. *The Epistle to the Galatians*. New International Greek Testament Commentary. Grand Rapids: Eerdmans, 1982.
———. *New Testament History*. Reprint, New York: Doubleday, 1980.
———. *Paul: Apostle of the Heart Set Free*. Grand Rapids: Eerdmans, 1977.
Brunner, Emil. *Christian Doctrine of the Church, Faith, and the Consummation*. Translated by David Cairns and T. H. L. Parker. Philadelphia: Westminster, 1960.
———. *Letter to the Romans*. Philadelphia: Westminster, 1959.
———. *Our Faith*. Translated by John Rilling. New York: Charles Scribner's Sons, 1962.
Carson, D. A., and Douglas Moo. *An Introduction to the New Testament*. 2nd ed. Grand Rapids: Zondervan, 2005.

Bibliography

Calvin, John. *Commentary on the Book of Psalms*. 2 vols. Bellingham, WA: Logos Bible Software, 2010.

———. *Commentaries on the Epistles of Paul to the Galatians and Ephesians*. Bellingham, WA: Logos Bible Software, 2010.

———. *Institutes of the Christian Religion*. Translated by Henry Beveridge. Reprint, Peabody, MA: Hendriksen, 2011.

Catechism of the Catholic Church. 2nd ed. New York: Doubleday, 1995.

Chafer, Louis S. *Systematic Theology*. Vol. 3. Reprint, Grand Rapids: Kregel, 1976.

Cheney, Elizabeth. "There Is a Man on the Cross." In *Treasury of Religious Verse*, edited by Donald T. Kauffman. Westwood, NJ: Revell, 1962.

Chrysostom, John. "Commentary of St. John Chrysostom, Archbishop of Constantinople, on the Epistle of St. Paul the Apostle to the Galatians." In *Nicene and Post-Nicene Fathers*, First Series, vol. 13, edited by Philip Schaff, translated by Alexander Gross. New York: Christian Literature Company, 1889.

Cohen, Shaye J. D. *From the Maccabees to the Mishnah*. Philadelphia: Westminster, 1987.

Collins, Hercules. *An Orthodox Catechism: Being the Sum of Christian Religion, Contained in the Law and Gospel*. Edited by Michael Haykin and G. Stephen Weaver Jr. Palmdale, CA: RBAP, 2014.

Conquest, Robert. *Stalin: Breaker of Nations*. New York: Viking, 1991.

Craig, William L. *Atonement and the Death of Christ: An Exegetical, Historical, and Philosophical Exploration*. Waco, TX: Baylor, 2020.

Crosby, Fanny. "Blind But Happy." In *Treasury of Religious Verse*, edited by Donald T. Kauffman. Westwood, NJ: Revell, 1962.

Curtiz, Michael, dir. *We're No Angels*. 1955; Los Angeles, CA: Paramount Pictures.

Cushman, Ralph. "Sheer Joy." In *Treasury of Religious Verse*, edited by Donald T. Kauffman. Westwood, NJ: Revell, 1962.

DeRouchie, Jason. "Counting Stars with Abraham and the Prophets: New Covenant Ecclesiology in OT Perspective." *Journal of the Evangelical Theological Society* 58:3 (Sept. 2015) 445–85.

deSilva, David. *Galatians: Handbook on the Greek Text*. Waco, TX: Baylor University Press, 2014.

———. *Introducing the Apocrypha: Message, Context, and Significance*. 2nd ed. Grand Rapids: Baker, 2018.

———. *An Introduction to the New Testament: Contexts, Methods and Ministry Formation*. 2nd ed. Downers Grove, IL: InterVarsity, 2018.

Dunn, James D. G. *Galatians*. Black's New Testament Commentary. London: A&C Black, 1993.

———. "New Perspective View." In *Justification: Five Views*, edited by James Beilby and Paul Eddy, 196–201. Downers Grove, IL: IVP Academic, 2011.

———. *Theology of Paul the Apostle*. Grand Rapids: Eerdmans, 1998.

———. "Whence, What and Whither?" In *New Perspective on Paul*, 1–97. 2nd ed. Grand Rapids: Eerdmans, 2007.

Edersheim, Alfred. *Sketches of Jewish Social Life in the Days of Christ*. New York: Hodder & Stoughton, 1876. https://bit.ly/3Y4hmxH.

Erickson, Millard. *Christian Theology*. 3rd ed. Grand Rapids: Baker, 2013.

———. *Concise Dictionary of Christian Theology*. Rev. ed. Wheaton, IL: Crossway, 2001.

Ferling, John. *Almost a Miracle: The American Victory in the War of Independence*. New York: Oxford University Press, 2007.

Bibliography

Foss, Sam Walter. "The House by the Side of the Road." In *Treasury of Religious Verse*, edited by Donald T. Kauffman. Westwood, NJ: Revell, 1962.

Friberg, Timothy, et al. *Analytical Lexicon of the Greek New Testament*. Grand Rapids: Baker, 2000.

Fung, Ronald Y. K. *Galatians*. New International Commentary on the New Testament. Grand Rapids: Eerdmans, 1988. Kindle.

Garrett, Duane A. *The Problem of the Old Testament: Hermeneutical, Schematic and Theological Approaches*. Downers Grove, IL: IVP Academic, 2020.

Garrett, James Leo, Jr. *Systematic Theology: Biblical, Historical, and Evangelical*. Vol. 1. 4th ed. Eugene, OR: Wipf & Stock, 2014.

Gentry, Peter J. and Stephen J. Wellum. *Kingdom Through Covenant: A Biblical-Theological Understanding of the Covenants*. 2nd edition. Wheaton: Crossway, 2018.

George, Timothy. *Galatians*. New American Commentary 30. Nashville: B&H, 1994.

Geronimi, Clyde, et al., dirs. *Cinderella*. 1950; Burbank, CA: Walt Disney Studios.

Grant, Michael. *Herod the Great*. Rockville, MD: American Heritage Press, 1971.

———. *Jews in the Roman World*. London: Weidenfeld & Nicholson, 1973.

———. *Saint Paul*. Reprint, London: Orion, 2011.

Harris, R. Laird. *Leviticus*. Expositor's Bible Commentary 12. Grand Rapids: Zondervan, 1990.

Hays, J. Daniel. *From Every People and Nation: A Biblical Theology of Race*. New Studies on Biblical Theology. Downers Grove, IL: InterVarsity, 2003.

Hendriksen, William. *Galatians and Ephesians*. Grand Rapids: Baker, 1979.

Henry, Carl F. H. *God, Revelation and Authority*. Vol. 2. Waco, TX: Word, 1976.

Herbert, George. "A Heart to Praise Thee." In *Treasury of Religious Verse*, edited by Donald T. Kauffman. Westwood, NJ: Revell, 1962.

Hill, George Roy, dir. *The Sting*. 1973; Universal City, CA: Universal City Studios LLC.

Hillerbrand, Hans J., ed. *The Reformation: A Narrative History Related by Contemporary Observers and Participants*. New York: Harper & Row, 1964.

Hodge, Charles. *Systematic Theology*. Vol. 2. Reprint, Oak Harbor, WA: Logos, 1997.

Houghton, Myron. *Law and Grace*. Schaumburg, IL: Regular Baptist Press, 2011.

Hovey, Alvah. *The Epistle to the Galatians*. American Commentary. Philadelphia: American Baptist Publication Society, 1890.

Kershner, Irvin, dir. *Star Wars: Episode V—The Empire Strikes Back*. 1980; Los Angeles, CA: Twentieth Century Fox Film Corporation.

Kidner, Derek. *Psalms 1–72*. Tyndale Old Testament Commentary. Downers Grove, IL: InterVarsity, 1973.

Kittel, Gerhard, et al., eds. *Theological Dictionary of the New Testament*. Grand Rapids: Eerdmans, 1964–.

Liddell, Henry George, et al. *A Greek-English Lexicon*. Oxford: Clarendon, 1996.

Lightfoot, J. B. *Saint Paul's Epistle to the Galatians*. 10th ed. New York: MacMillan, 1890.

Lindberg, Carter. *The European Reformations*. Oxford: Blackwell, 1996.

Longenecker, Bruce. *Galatians*. Word Biblical Commentary 41. Nashville: Thomas Nelson, 1990.

Louw, Johannes P., and Eugene Albert Nida, eds. *Greek-English Lexicon of the New Testament: Based on Semantic Domains*. New York: United Bible Societies, 1996.

Lumpkins, William. *Baptist Confessions of Faith*. 2nd ed. Philadelphia: Judson, 1969.

Luther, Martin. *Galatians*. Crossway Classic Commentary series. Reprint, Wheaton, IL: Crossway, 1988.

Bibliography

Marshall, I. Howard. *New Testament Theology.* Downers Grove, IL: InterVarsity, 2004.

Martyn, J. Louis. *Galatians: A New Translation with Introduction and Commentary.* Anchor Yale Bible 33A. New Haven, CT: Yale University Press, 2008.

McClain, Alva. *Law and Grace.* Reprint, Winona Lake, IN: BMH, 1973.

McCune, Rolland. *A Systematic Theology of Biblical Christianity.* Vol. 1. Detroit: Detroit Baptist Theological Seminary, 2006.

McGrath, Alister. *Iustitia Dei: A History of the Christian Doctrine of Justification.* 4th ed. Cambridge, UK: Cambridge University Press, 2020.

Merriam-Webster Dictionary. 11th ed. https://www.merriam-webster.com/dictionary/.

Middlekauff, Robert. *The Glorious Cause: The American Revolution, 1763–1789.* Rev. ed. Oxford History of the United States. New York: Oxford University Press, 2005.

Moo, Douglas. *Epistle to the Romans.* New International Commentary on the New Testament. Grand Rapids: Eerdmans, 1996.

Motyer, J. Alec. *Isaiah.* Tyndale Old Testament Commentary. Downers Grove, IL: InterVarsity, 1999.

Murray, John. *Epistle to the Romans.* Grand Rapids: Eerdmans, 1968.

Neusner, Jacob, trans. *Mishnah: A New Translation.* New Haven, CT: Yale University Press, 1988.

Nock, A. D. *St. Paul.* Reprint, New York: Harper, 1963.

Noll, Mark A. *America's Book: The Rise and Decline of a Bible Civilization 1794–1911.* New York: Oxford University Press, 2022.

Oden, Thomas. *Life in the Spirit.* Vol. 3 of *Systematic Theology.* San Francisco: HarperCollins, 1992.

Oxenham, John. "No East or West." In *Treasury of Religious Verse*, edited by Donald T. Kauffman. Westwood, NJ: Revell, 1962.

Oxford English Dictionary. 3rd edition. https://www.oed.com/.

Ramm, Bernard. *The Pattern of Religious Authority.* Grand Rapids: Eerdmans, 1958.

Ridderbos, Herman N. *The Epistle of Paul to the Churches of Galatia.* New International Commentary on the New Testament. Grand Rapids: Zondervan, 1953.

Robbins, Tyler. "What Is the New Perspective(s) on Paul?" *Eccentric Fundamentalist* (blog), May 15, 2024. https://eccentricfundamentalist.com/2024/05/15/what-is-the-new-perspectives-on-paul/.

Robertson, A. T. *Word Pictures in the New Testament.* Nashville: Broadman, 1933.

Rooker, Mark F. *Leviticus.* New American Commentary 3A. Nashville: B&H, 2000.

Russell, Bertrand. *Why I Am Not a Christian.* Reprint, New York: Touchstone, 1967.

Ryrie, Charles. *Dispensationalism.* Reprint, Chicago: Moody, 2007.

Schaff, Philip, ed. *The Creeds of Christendom.* Vol. 3. New York: Harper & Brothers, 1882.

———. "Council of Trent." Chap. 6.9 in *Creeds of Christendom.* Vol. 2. New York: Harper & Brothers, 1890.

Schnabel, Eckhard. *Acts.* Zondervan Exegetical Commentary on the New Testament. Grand Rapids: Zondervan, 2012.

Schreiner, Thomas R. *Galatians.* Zondervan Exegetical Commentary on the New Testament. Grand Rapids: Zondervan, 2010.

Schurer, Emil. *A History of the Jewish People in the Time of Jesus Christ.* 5 vols. Reprint, Peabody, MA: Hendrickson, 2012.

Scofield, C. I., ed. *Scofield Reference Bible.* New York: Oxford University Press, 1917.

Scott, J. Julius, Jr. *Jewish Backgrounds of the New Testament.* Grand Rapids: Baker, 1995.

Bibliography

Spicq, Ceslas, and James D. Ernest. *Theological Lexicon of the New Testament*. Peabody, MA: Hendrickson, 1994.

Stott, John R. W. *The Message of Galatians*. Bible Speaks Today. Downers Grove, IL: InterVarsity, 1968.

Stuart, Moses. *A Commentary on the Epistle to the Romans*. 3rd ed. London: Thomas Tegg and Sons, 1836.

Turretin, Francis. *Institutes of Elenctic Theology*. Edited by James T. Dennison Jr., translated by George Musgrave Giger. 3 vols. Phillipsburg: P&R, 1992–99.

Wallace, Daniel. *Greek Grammar Beyond the Basics*. Grand Rapids: Zondervan, 1996.

Wellum, Stephen. *Systematic Theology: From Canon to Concept*. Nashville: B&H, 2024.

Wenham, Gordon J. *The Book of Leviticus*. New International Commentary on the Old Testament. Grand Rapids: Eerdmans, 1979. Kindle.

The Westminster Standard. "1647 Westminster Confession of Faith." https://thewestminsterstandard.org/the-westminster-confession/.

Wilkerson, Isabel. *Caste: The Origins of Our Discontents*. New York: Random House, 2023.

Wright, N. T. *Justification: God's Plan and Paul's Vision*. Downers Grove, IL: InterVarsity, 2009. Kindle.

Wright, N. T., and Michael F. Bird. *The New Testament in Its World*. Grand Rapids: Zondervan, 2019.

Subject and Name Index

Abraham, 72–73, 75–79, 81–82, 84, 86–88, 90–94, 96, 99–101, 103–6, 121–24, 126, 165, 167, 170
    children, 47–48, 75–76, 78–79, 81–82, 84, 87, 90, 103–6, 122, 126, 165–66
Abrahamic covenant, 123
Abraham's faith, 75, 101, 103
Adam, 43, 62–64
agitators, 10–11, 14, 16, 27, 32, 58, 118, 132, 158
Amos, 155
Antioch, 20–21, 31, 35–67, 160

baptism, 3, 31, 100
beliefs, 9, 37, 43, 114–16, 163, 167
believers, 4, 9, 11, 13, 25, 29, 35, 45, 59, 78, 81, 83, 97–101, 103, 108, 118, 135, 150, 152, 154, 156, 162, 166
    new, 24, 126, 160
    new covenant, 10, 31, 136, 152
    non-Jewish, 167
bondage, 71, 108–9, 111–13, 124–25, 128
boundary markers, 14, 58
brothers, 20, 27, 59, 61, 90, 117, 126–27, 131, 133, 139, 145, 147, 150–52, 155, 167
    false, 32–33

Calvin, John, 6, 9–10, 44, 53, 55, 60, 95, 104, 124, 134, 170
child, true, 47, 103, 105, 165

child of God, 66, 100, 102, 112
children, faithful, 154
children of God, 100, 123, 139, 166
Christ, Jesus, 3, 5–17, 20–24, 26–33, 35–36, 38, 42–48, 50–67, 69–72, 75–79, 81, 85–88, 90–106, 108–18, 121, 123–31, 133, 135–37, 140–47, 151–52, 154, 156, 158–59, 161–68, 170, 172
Christian story, 4, 24, 27, 73, 78, 132, 162
Christian traditions, 11–12
Christ's atoning death, 9
Christ's family, 102–3, 156
Christ's love, 137
Christ's righteousness, 9, 52, 55
circumcision, 10, 16, 31, 58, 129–30, 132, 162, 164–68
circumcision party, 49
Cohen, Shaye, 37–42, 170
commandments of God, 41, 60
condemnation, 5–7, 44, 52, 63–64, 152
Cornelius, 36–37, 43, 45, 47, 77
covenant, 14, 16–17, 24, 43, 76, 90–91, 94, 104–5, 123, 171
    better, 12, 137, 164
    new, 12–13, 16, 46, 100, 121, 123–24, 126, 152
covenant faithfulness, 14
covenant law, old, 46, 135, 137, 140, 152
covenant relationship, old, 137
creation, new, 14, 108, 157–67
credentials, 11, 26–27, 29, 31–33, 110

Subject and Name Index

cross of Christ, 158, 162, 164, 168
curse, 6, 24, 45, 53, 61, 80–82, 84–88, 110, 112, 168
   law's, 109
curse of legalism, 86–87, 99, 110–11

delegate, 6, 52–53, 62–65
descendant, 75, 77, 91, 103
dispensationalism, 12, 105, 172
Dunn, James, 14, 21, 58, 93, 103, 158, 162–63, 168, 170

Erickson, Millard, 9, 170
externalism, 36–37, 42–43, 133, 138
Ezra, 37, 46

faith, 8–10, 12, 14–17, 30–31, 50, 52, 54–57, 60–62, 65–67, 70, 75–88, 91–92, 95–106, 108, 111–12, 129–30, 133, 135–36, 142, 144–45, 165–67, 169, 171, 173
   justification by, 4, 6, 8–9, 11, 15
   real, 73, 143
faith and trust, 52, 55, 70, 76, 79, 81–82, 84, 87, 90–91, 105, 119
faithfulness, 51, 83, 140, 145, 154
false apostles, 116
false teachers, 11, 20, 26–27, 31, 34, 72, 79, 84, 115–18, 121, 125, 127–28, 131
flesh, 7–8, 93, 121, 126, 133, 136, 138–39, 147, 155, 158, 160, 162, 166
food, 45, 79
freedom, 32, 66, 117, 124–25, 127–28, 132–35, 137–47
fruit of faith, 135
fruits, spiritual, 156
fulfillment, 16, 106, 130, 135
Fung, Ronald, 20, 22–23, 27–28, 32, 49, 61, 108, 114, 116–18, 124, 138, 166, 168, 171

Galatian agitators, 12–16
Garrett, Duane, 104, 134, 167, 171
gentiles, 28, 30–31, 33, 35–37, 43–50, 54–56, 58–59, 71, 76–79, 81–82, 84, 87, 100–101, 104, 106, 108–10, 115, 128, 158, 160–61, 166–67
gift of righteousness, 21, 63–64, 78, 130

God
   love, 2, 17, 40, 140, 155–56
   triune, 16, 102, 140, 145
Good News, 21, 23, 26, 35, 51, 54, 66, 70, 126, 147, 165
gospel, 11, 15–17, 21, 23–25, 27, 29–34, 36, 46, 49–50, 52, 54, 56, 59, 75–79, 81–82, 84, 86–87, 114, 117, 154, 157, 159–60, 168, 170
grace, 3, 8–10, 13, 21–23, 42, 66–67, 96, 115–16, 128–30, 134, 141–43, 151–52, 171–72
grounds of salvation, 12–16
guardian, Mosaic law as, 97–99, 101, 103, 106–7, 109, 111–12, 130

Hagar, 122–27
heirs, 77, 91, 93, 103–4, 106–7, 109, 111–12, 122, 126, 166
Hendriksen, William, 27, 31, 59, 108, 123, 129, 158, 166, 171
Herod, 38, 171
Hillerbrand, Hans, 52–53, 55, 171
Hodge, Charles, 15, 171
Holy Spirit, 7, 47, 53, 61, 70, 72, 88, 99, 134, 136–38, 147, 153, 156, 164–65
Houghton, Myron, 13, 171
Hovey, Alvah, 21–22, 28, 31–32, 49, 60, 67, 96, 108, 150, 152, 155–56, 166, 171
hypocrisy, 36, 43, 49

impurity, 44, 46, 139–40
inheritance, 92, 107, 127
Israel, 14, 24, 37–38, 42–43, 47, 56–57, 73, 75, 77–78, 93–94, 106, 109, 126, 165–67
Israelites, 24, 37–38, 51, 54, 71, 75, 83, 155, 159, 165, 167
   ethnic, 105, 167
   faithful, 36
Israel of God, 166

Jerusalem, 10, 21, 28–33, 38–40, 45–50, 120–31
   new, 22, 126, 165
Jerusalem church, 20, 30–33

Subject and Name Index

Jerusalem Council, 4, 48
Jewish, 10, 14, 32, 36, 40, 42–43, 46, 48, 55, 58–59, 77–79, 101, 103, 108, 124, 140, 159, 161–62, 165–66
Jewish agitators, 58, 80, 82, 90–92, 102, 106, 110, 112, 131, 158, 162, 165, 168
Jews, 28, 31, 36–37, 40, 47, 49–50, 54–55, 57–59, 77, 79, 81–82, 84, 87, 100–101, 104, 106, 158–61, 166, 171
Josiah, King, 17, 85
Judaism, 10, 14, 28, 32, 41–42, 50, 58, 70, 124, 159, 161
justice, 5, 17, 22, 51, 54–55, 76–77
justification by faith, 3–4, 8–9, 11, 50–52, 55–57, 67, 73, 76, 78–79, 81–84, 86, 115–16, 169–70, 172–73

Kauffman, Donald T., 169–72
kingdom, 3, 7, 17, 22, 37, 65, 104–5, 126, 139–40, 167, 171

land, 1, 51, 93–94, 105
law, 4, 6–9, 12–16, 36–37, 40–42, 50, 55–58, 60–61, 63, 66–67, 69–72, 76–88, 91–95, 97–99, 101, 103, 108–12, 115–16, 118, 121, 124–25, 128–30, 133, 135–36, 138, 140, 152, 161–62, 165, 170–72
  curse of the, 85, 99
  purity, 59, 66
Law and Grace, 13, 171–72
law of Christ, 151–52
law of God, 13, 63, 93
law of love, 152
legalism, 4, 7, 13–16, 36–37, 39, 41, 56–57, 60–61, 85–88, 99, 110–11, 117, 132–36, 138, 147, 156
legalists, 17, 48–49, 149, 151, 153–54, 165
life, eternal, 3, 5, 29, 52, 83–85, 87, 155
Lightfoot, J.B., 21, 46, 48, 55, 59, 61, 94, 161, 166, 171
Longenecker, Richard, 20, 32–33, 49, 61, 97, 123, 125–26, 128, 131, 137, 157, 164, 166, 171
love, brotherly, 17, 136, 149, 151, 153, 155–56

love and grace, 134, 151
love for God, 124, 130, 137, 152
lusts, 138–39, 147
Luther, Martin, 14, 20, 22, 24, 52–55, 57–58, 115–16, 122–23, 136, 165–66, 169, 171

Maccabees, 37–42, 170
merit system, 4, 13, 66
Mishnah, 37–44, 71, 79, 170, 172
mosaic law, 10, 13, 56–57, 60–61, 66, 69–70, 72, 74–75, 79–87, 92–95, 97, 99–100, 106, 108–12, 115–17, 121, 124, 128, 130–31, 137–38, 150, 152
Moses, 17, 36, 57–58, 66, 80, 83, 85, 92–94, 140, 152, 161, 165

Neusner, Jacob, 40–44, 71, 79, 172
New Perspective on Paul, 14, 58, 170, 172

obedience, loving, 70–71, 130, 134
old covenant, 12–16, 28, 90, 123–24, 127–28, 133–35, 140, 162
old covenant believers, 44, 95
old covenant rituals, 31, 116
oral tradition, 41, 45

peace, 1–2, 21–22, 50, 53, 60–61, 109, 111–12, 115, 140, 142–43, 145, 151, 154, 165–66
  inner, 108–9, 111–12
Pharisees, 15, 39–42, 45, 47–48, 51, 59, 142, 148, 151
pride, 102, 149, 153–54
promises, 92–95, 101, 105–6, 115, 126

reason, 64, 67, 69, 82, 89, 131, 149, 158, 161
Reformation, 52–53, 55, 171
relationship, 2–3, 44–46, 71, 80, 83, 85, 92, 101–2, 135–38, 141–43, 145, 147, 149–51, 153, 156, 164–66
rescue, 16, 21–23, 42, 66, 73, 86, 88, 105, 109, 111–12, 114, 125
resume-ism, 4, 6–8, 110, 116
revelation, 27–31, 95, 109, 114, 171

Subject and Name Index

righteousness, 9, 50–52, 54–57, 60–61, 63–67, 69, 72, 76, 78–79, 81–82, 84, 86–88, 91–92, 95, 98–100, 116, 129–30
  earning, 92, 95
  legal, 59
  obtaining, 56, 70, 83
righteousness of Christ, 9
righteousness of God, 4, 10, 52–56, 130

salvation, 3, 7–8, 10–17, 31, 36, 42, 47, 50, 54–57, 60–62, 65–66, 68–71, 73, 75, 77–85, 87, 90, 93, 95–96, 98–100, 107–8, 110–11, 114–17, 121, 124, 127–29, 131, 135, 142, 145, 160
Sarah, 75, 122–28
Satan, 22, 63, 66, 114, 147–48
Schaff, Phillip, 3, 52, 63, 110, 172
Schreiner, Thomas, 24–25, 29, 31–32, 46, 48–50, 56, 60–61, 105, 116, 150, 152, 154, 166, 172
scribes and Pharisees, 39–42, 45, 47
scripture, 5–6, 16–17, 41, 85, 90–91, 95–97, 104–5, 114, 134, 136, 138, 140, 142, 147
self-righteousness, 4, 51, 138, 154, 168
sins, 2, 5–7, 21–23, 42, 44–45, 52–53, 55, 57–66, 70–71, 93, 95–99, 101, 103, 130, 138, 150–52
slavery, 86, 88, 107, 109, 111–16, 123–25, 127–28, 133

slaves, 32, 65–66, 89, 101–3, 107, 109, 111–14, 122–24, 147
son of Abraham, 78, 90
special descendant, Jesus as, 77–79, 81–82, 84, 87, 91, 93–94, 96, 99–100, 104
Stott, John, 22, 27, 29–30, 32, 47–49, 116–17, 151–52, 154, 161, 166, 168, 173

Tamar, 36–37
teaching, false, 31, 108–9, 124
tradition, 27–28, 36–37, 41–42, 44–46, 50, 57, 59, 71, 77, 79, 112, 128, 133, 136, 157, 161, 168
trust, 6–7, 9–10, 15–16, 27, 52, 54–55, 57, 67, 70, 76, 79, 81–82, 84, 87–88, 90–92, 99–100, 105, 114, 117, 119, 124, 130, 145, 147, 165
truth, 6, 10–11, 21, 29, 32, 49–50, 62, 69–70, 108, 115, 117–18, 131–32, 151–52
Turretin, Francis, 9, 173

unbelievers, 28, 99, 109, 111–12, 115, 117
uncircumcision, 16, 129–30, 164–65, 167–68

works of the law, 11–16, 56, 58, 60–61
works righteousness, 48, 55–56, 69–70, 87, 115, 119, 121, 128–29, 137–38, 147, 156, 161
Wright, N.T., 5, 14, 72–73, 173

Scripture Index

Genesis
3	62, 145
12:2–3	92–93
12:3	76–77, 104
12:7	90
15:6	78, 91
16	122
16:2	122
17:8	105
21:9	126
22:17–18	105
35:11	104
38:2	36
38:13–30	36

Exodus
19	12

Leviticus
4:1—6:7	7, 150
11–15	44
18	140
18:1	140
18:2	83
18:5	83, 85, 87
19:18	135, 152
26:3–13	83

Deuteronomy
6:4	124
6:4–5	80, 152
6:5	16–17, 40, 85
6:6	124
9:5	51
10:12–13	85, 130
10:12–22	137
11:13	17
21:23	85–87
26:16	80
27:26	80, 82
28:1–14	83

Nehemiah
10:28–39	37

Psalms
1:2	124
7:11	51
9:8	51
11:5	131
19:8	98
22:1	53, 55
40:8	85, 124
47:9	104
72:7–9	104
72:12–14	105
72:17	104
96:13	51

Scripture Index

Psalms (*cont.*)
119, 81	124
119:10–11	70
119:18	81
119:20	86
119:24	124
119:34	85
119:35	124
119:45	124
146:9	76

Proverbs
10:12	142

Isaiah
19:23	77
19:23–25	77
29:22	75
35:8	77
35:8–10	77
42:1	76
42:4	76
42:6	76
42:6–7	99, 101, 103
51:2	75
51:4	75–76
51:6	77
52:13—53:12	125
54:1–3	125
56:3	47, 104
56:6–8	43
56:7	47, 104
56:8	47
61:10	100, 126
62:4–5	126

Jeremiah
3:14	126

Ezekiel
16	126
34	43

Hosea
1–3	126, 141

10:12–13	155

Habakkuk
2:4	52, 54–55, 82

Matthew
1:1	78, 103, 105
1:3	36
3:7–10	75
5:3	105
8:10–12	167
13:30, 40–43	156
23	123
23:4	42, 71
23:27–28	43
25:21	130

Mark
1:15	121
2:16–17	45
7	50, 62, 71
7:8	133
10:45	114
12:28–32	16, 40
12:28–34	135, 145, 152
12:32–34	135
12:33	85
12:38–40	44

Luke
1:14	141
2	85
2:22–24	44
2:30–31	109
3:8	96
6:43–45	139
10:29	51
15:7	141
16:15	51

John
1:18	3
3:3	7
3:16–17	66
3:16	63, 153

6:29	102	15:24	48
7:53—8:11	152	16:1–2	31
8	123	16:3	31
10:16	43, 47	16:4	33
11:45–47	39	20:16	116
11:49–50	160	21	10
14:26–27	136–37	21:17–25	48
14–16	145	21:17–26	33
16:22	141	21:18	48
17:26	136–37	21:20–26	32
		21:21	161
		21:22–24	160
		21:27–28	161
		21:27–36	160
		22:17	28
		23:5	33
		23:6–10	33
		23:12–15	160
		23:17–24	160
		26:9–11	28

Acts

2	12
2:29	105
2:42–47	135
3:25	77
6:1	160
7	27, 35
8:3	28
9:1–17	29
9:18–21	29
9:22–25	29
9:26–28	30
9:27	30
9:29–30	30
10:9–23	36, 47
10:28	36, 77
11:1–18	32, 160
11:1–2	47
11:2	47
11:17	47
11:18	47
11:19	35
11:19–26	31
11:20	35
11:21	35
11:22	160
11:25	35
11:25–26	31
11:26	35
11:27–29	31
11:28	31
13:1	35–36
13:1—14:28	31
15	4, 10, 31, 46, 48, 59
15:1	161
15:1–4	160
15:5	48

Romans

1:16	55, 78
1:17	52, 54–56, 72, 130
1:21–22	163
2:4	144
2:28–29	165
3	4
3:12	143
3:20	6
3:23–25	8
4:11	104
4:13	91–93
4:16	165
4:16–17	126
5	62
5:1	3, 22
5:1–2	142
5:10	62
5:12	62
5:12–21	63
5:15	63
5:16	63
5:17	64–65
5:18	64
5:19	65, 110
6	100, 163
6:1–11	100

Romans (cont.)

6:1–14	62
6:6	66, 147
6:18	65
7	13
7:4	61
7:7–12	163
7:7–13	60
7:22	125
8:1	6
8:2	6
8:3	7
8:4	7, 51
8:5	7
8:6	7
8:7–8	8
8:9	7
9–11	166
10:1–4	61
10:2–3	4
10:4	69, 76
11	167
13:10	130, 135
15:14	144
16:22	157

1 Corinthians

3:10–15	154
5:6	131
13	130
13:1–3	144
13:2	130
15:3	27
15:54–57	147
16:8	116

2 Corinthians

3:18	138, 153
4	132
4:3–4	164
4:3–6	114, 147
5:17–20	165
5:21	140
11:32–33	29

Galatians

1:1–2	20
1:3	22
1:3–5	21
1:6	112, 161
1:6–7	11, 23
1:7	117
1:7–9	24
1:10	26
1:11–12	27
1:11—2:10	11
1:12	20
1:13–14	28, 161
1:15–17	28
1:17	29
1:17–18	27, 29
1:18	29
1:18–20	30
1:21	30
1:22–24	30
2:1–3	31
2:1–5	31
2:2	31
2:4–5	32
2:6	33
2:7–10	33
2:9	32
2:11	36, 56
2:11–21	160
2:12	46, 49
2:12–13	36, 49
2:14	49
2:15	55
2:15–16	50, 55
2:16	56, 75, 88
2:17	57, 59
2:18	59
2:18–21	58
2:19	61
2:20	61, 65
2:21	66, 69, 88, 93, 124
3	47, 99, 105, 122
3:1	69, 121
3:1–6	90
3:1–9	99
3:2	69
3:3	70
3:4–5	72

Scripture Index

3:5	75–76, 78–79, 81–82, 84, 86	4:8–10	70, 128
3:6	72, 76, 78–79, 81–82, 84, 86	4:8–9	114
		4:9	115
3:7	75–76, 78–79, 81–82, 84, 87	4:10–11	116
		4:11	11, 117, 150
		4:12–14	117
3:7–14	121	4:13	11
3:7–9	80, 100–101, 104	4:15–16	117
3:8	76–79, 81–82, 84, 87	4:16	11
		4:17	118
3:9	78–82, 84–85, 87	4:18	118
3:10	80–82, 84–85, 87	4:19–20	118
3:10–12	81	4:21	121
3:10–14	99	4:22–23	121
3:11	54, 82, 84, 87	4:24	16
3:12	83, 85, 87	4:24–26	123
3:13	85, 87, 110, 112	4:26	126
3:14	87	4:27	125
3:15	90	4:28–29	126
3:15–22	90, 99	4:30	127
3:16	90, 92–93, 103–5	4:31	127
3:16–20	77	5:1	128
3:17	91–92	5:2–3	128
3:18	92	5:4	128, 130
3:19	92–93	5:5–6	129–30
3:19–20	94	5:6	16–17
3:19–25	60	5:7–8	131
3:20	94	5:9–10	131
3:21	95, 110	5:10	131
3:21–22	95, 98–99, 101, 103	5:11	131, 159
3:22	97	5:12	132
3:23	97–99, 101, 103	5:13	133
3:23–25	99	5:14	152
3:24–25	98–99, 101, 103	5:14–15	135
3:26	106, 166	5:16	136
3:26–27	100–101, 103	5:17–18	138
3:26–29	109, 126	5:18	138
3:28	32, 101, 103	5:19–21	139
3:29	101, 103, 166	5:22–23	140, 150
4:1–2	107, 109, 111–12	5:24–26	147
4:1–7	112	5:25	149
4:3	107, 109, 111–12, 115	5:26	149, 152–53
		6:1	150–51
4:4–5	109, 111–12	6:2	151
4:6	109	6:3	152
4:6–7	111–12	6:4	153
4:7	112	6:4–5	153
4:8	108	6:6	154

Galatians (cont.)

6:7	155
6:8	155
6:9–10	156
6:11	157
6:11–12	24
6:12	158, 162
6:13	162
6:14	163
6:15	164, 167
6:16	165, 167
6:17–18	167

Ephesians

1–2	130
3:1–8	109
7:20	5
2:11–12	56
2:12	16
2:14	142
2:14–15	50
2:15	50
2:16	50
2:18	109
3:6	77, 106
3:14	19, 106
3:19	106
4:22–24	138
5:25–27	126
6:17	136

Philippians

2:8	110
3:2–21	10
3:3	166
3:4–6	28, 79
4:7	142

Colossians

1:13	7, 65
1:13–14	22
2:8	107
2:11	166

2 Thessalonians

1:11	144
3:14–17	136

1 Timothy

2:6	114

Titus

3:4	144

Hebrews

2:14–15	147
4:16	45
5:12	108
6:6	155
8:6–7	98, 101
8:6–7,13	103
8:7–13	16
8:8, 13	117
11:16	125

1 Peter

1:15–16	143, 153
4:8	142

2 Peter

1:8	146
3:10	108

1 John

2:9	152
3	137
3:4	5
3:5	5
3:7–10	156
3:9	139
3:10	139
4:8	153
4:10	40
4:19	7, 70, 140

www.ingramcontent.com/pod-product-compliance
Lightning Source LLC
Chambersburg PA
CBHW062044220426
43662CB00010B/1645